STORIES FROM THE MESSENGERS

Praise for *Stories from The Messengers*

"Symbol." "Totem." "Archetype." "Conjure." "Magic." "Hierophany." These are old words that we thought we knew, and that we thought were very dead. Turns out they are not. Turns out they are fiercely alive and silently flying around in the world, mesmerizing, haunting, abducting, or just generally scaring the crap out of people. If you don't believe me, read this book. I'd be careful, though. As Mike is all too aware, when one writes or reads about this level of reality with this sense of clarity, reality answers back. Weirdly, of course. Good luck.

—Jeffrey J. Kripal, author of *Mutants and Mystics*, Newton Rayzor Professor of Philosophy and Religious Thought, Rice University

What is an owl? The question is more complicated than one might suppose. This book, which will be the most interesting book about owls you will ever read, does an excellent job of conveying the variety of ways in which owls exist—as Jungian archetypes, in mythology, and as living mythology. More specifically, Clelland outlines how owls figure in the worlds of those who have experienced "ufo-related" events. Clelland offers some compelling clues as to how one might consider these perplexing connections. A fascinating, delightful read.

—Diana Walsh Pasulka, author of *American Cosmic,* Professor and Chair, Department of Philosophy and Religion, University of North Carolina, Wilmington

Praise for *The Messengers*

I get a strong sense that Mike Clelland was guided to write this by the UFO intelligences and I think the reader will get that. This is the first time I have seen this level of both a book and its author being inextricably linked to the phenomenon itself since Strieber and *Communion. Communion* was clearly more than just a book; I believe the phenomenon intended it to be written, published, and read on a large scale. I think Mike's book is another example of this.

—Nick Redfern, author of *Men in Black*

Mike Clelland lifts back the curtain on a secret world most of us have no idea exists, and does so with patience and exactitude of a classical scholar. Skeptics used to accuse experiencers as opportunists out for money and attention, so how do then explain away an impressively large group of people who seem interested in sharing their remarkable stories only with each other, well out of the public eye? In addition to sharing their experiences, Mike explores our long fascination with these mystical messengers of the night, offering up an entirely new corpus of evidence to explore and debate.

—Christopher Knowles, author of Our Gods Wear Spandex

In *The Messengers*, Mike Clelland presents the reader with pieces of the UFO puzzle typically ignored or sidelined within the research field, so challenging are they to popular notions of the phenomenon. Clelland's fresh perspective encourages us to engage with an ancient and mystical enigma in a profoundly personal way, beyond the dead-end avenues of Exopolitics and official Disclosure. Serious researchers of the UFO subject—and of the abduction phenomenon in particular—will be referencing this book for decades to come.

—Robbie Graham, author of *Silver Screen Saucers*

This is a vast, exhaustive, compelling, obsessive book on the connective thread of meaning which owls, as symbol and as literal fact, play in their role as intermediary between the human and the other… *The Messengers* brings something quite refreshing and enlivening to the subject. I felt awakened again, excited and enmeshed in it – particularly, for some reason, with the chapter on reverse speech (go figure). Clelland looks toward the narrative thread of human meaning found in such baffling interactions with the "alien" other, with the owl serving as both messenger and language employed in the message.

—Brian Charles Short, author of *New People of the Flat Earth*

This is one of the most important books about the UFO phenomenon since Whitley Strieber's Communion. You will never look at owls in the same way again. Highly recommended to students of Forteana and Ufology.

—Michael M. Hughes, author of *The Blackwater Lights trilogy*

STORIES FROM THE MESSENGERS

Owls, UFOs and a Deeper Reality

By

Mike Clelland

Stories from the Messengers © 2020 Mike Clelland.

All rights reserved. No part of this book may be used or reproduced in any manner whatsoever without written permission except in the case of brief quotations in critical articles or reviews.

Clelland, Mike.
Stories from the Messengers: Owls, UFOs and a Deeper Reality

256 p.
ISBN 978-1-7339808-2-1

First edition published by Richard Dolan Press, Dec. 2020

Foreword by Whitley Strieber, Copyright 2017, Walker & Collier, Inc.

Edited by Suzanne Chancellor

Cover and illustrations by Mike Clelland

Mike Clelland's website: mikeclelland.com

Contents

Acknowledgments. viii
Foreword by Whitley Strieber. x
Introduction. 1
Chapter 1: The White Owl and the Hound of Hell. 5
Chapter 2: The Awakening of Susan MacLeod. 17
Chapter 3: Owls and the Lakehouse. 29
Chapter 4: Gypsy Woman and a White Owl. 36
Chapter 5: Stacey, Owls and the Psychic. 43
Chapter 6: Kenneth Arnold and the
    Dawn of the Modern UFO Era 54
Chapter 7: The Alan Caviness Report. 62
Chapter 8: Owls and Drones 75
Chapter 9: Denise Linn and Three White Feathers 90
Chapter 10: Adrienne and Owls 102
Chapter 11: Blipping off the Map 111
Chapter 12: Owls and Healing 121
Chapter 13: Between Two Bridges 141
Chapter 14: The Owl and the White Buffalo 153
Chapter 15: Kristin in the Desert 172
Chapter 16: Owls and the Road at Night. 193
Chapter 17: Owls and Gratitude. Don's Owl Experience. 205
Chapter 18: Owls and Gratitude. Joe's Owl Experience 221
Chapter 19: Owls and Gratitude. Kelly's Owl Experience 227
Conclusion. 238
Endnotes. 243
Index. 252
About the Author. 255

Acknowledgments

I am eternally grateful to the brave people who've let me tell their stories. They've entrusted me with something sacred, their life experiences, and I take this responsibility very seriously. This book is a result of their openness, honesty and faith. Without their sincerity, this book would not have been possible.

Over the years, many wonderful people have reached out and shared their experiences, more than could be listed below. I owe a debt of gratitude to all my comrades, and so many more. From my heart, I thank you.

Several people have asked to remain anonymous, and their stories are told either using a pseudonym or by their first name. There are a few instances when unimportant details were purposely changed to further hide their identity. Also, this book is the result of extensive written correspondence, and some quoted text in these pages has been revised slightly for grammar and clarity.

I need to send a huge thank you to Suzanne Chancellor. She was my editor, and much more. Without her dedication, this would be a much lesser book. I am indebted to her attention to detail, and her friendship.

This book is an outcome of the courage to speak aloud what we are told should be denied.

Col. John Alexander, Allison, Kim Arnold, Ashlee, Seriah Azkath, Jim Banholzer, Christopher Bledsoe Sr., Walter Bosley, Brenda, Anya Briggs, Laura Bruno, Will Bueche, Mike C, Kristen Lee Cardinal, Alan Caviness, Suzanne Chancellor, Carol Cleveland, Heather Clewett-Jachowski, Rachel Cunningham, Joshua Cutchin, Lorin Cutts, Don, Richard Dolan, Cindy Dove, Adrienne Dumas, Marla Frees, Robbie Graham, Alan Green, Aaron John Gulyas, Rosemary Ellen Guiley, Gypsy Woman, Audrey Hewins, Debbie Hewins, Nancy Hewins, Richard C. Harper, Race Hobbs, George Hansen, Budd Hopkins, Bert Janssen, Shawn Kevin Jason, Jack Jawczak, Joe, Kelly Hultman Wagner, Christopher Knowles, Susan Kornaki, Melissa Kriger, Jeffrey Kripal, Kristin, Denise Linn, Meadow Linn, Maggie, Tania Marie, Jim Marrs, Rob and Trish MacGregor, Susan MacLeod,

Acknowledgments

Joseph McMoneagle, Ben McGuire, Meghan Moriarty, Pamela Necerato-Loffredo, Peter, Diana Pasulka, Nick Redfern, Mary Rodwell, Shanelle Schanz, Jacquelin Smith, Leo Sprinkle, Starborn Support, Anne and Whitley Strieber, Jacques Vallee, Andrea Lisette Villiere, Stacey J. Warner, and Maria Wheatley.

Foreword
by Whitley Strieber

This fascinating book starts off with an old friend of mine: the white owl. When I was a little boy, a white owl would often be seen at the back of our large garden staring up at the windows of my room. No matter how often my parents shooed it away, it would soon be back, standing there in broad daylight, staring.

I would sometimes see my father out at night shining a flashlight about, trying, I suppose to see if it was coming after dark as well. Eventually, they had the screens on my windows nailed shut.

At the beginning of this book, Mike Clelland recounts a story told by crop circle researcher Bert Jansen, who was astonished to observe a glowing ball of light in a field in Wiltshire, the heart of crop circle country, and then to discover, after it had disappeared behind a shed, that there was a nest of white owls there. Mike quotes Jansen as saying "when I do see a white owl, because I'm not always sure it's a white owl. Could it be that I am actually looking at something else, it only presents itself as a white owl to me."

Or is it that owls—and not just white ones—are something different? And, in fact, that nature itself—and us, too—might be something different from what we see?

In fact, it may be that the owls who are so prevalent in the close encounter phenomenon, and, in fact, are across many cultures and throughout history seen as mystical beings are—in fact—just what our ancestors, and some of us in this present human-centric and materialistic age, perceive them to be: messengers from and residents of the beyond.

But this beyond is not supernatural. Not at all. We see it as a mysterious otherness only because we have lost our ability to perceive nature as nature really is.

It is one of the joys of this ambitious and consciousness-raising book that it opens a locked door in the mind, the door to wonder that we have firmly closed in our relentless struggle against nature—even our own nature—which is our true home and mother.

In creatures, nature manifests in two ways: as physical machinery and as the shimmering consciousness that defines it. This consciousness is not a function of the brain, but rather the brain partakes of it, and that includes the human brain.

Because of our intelligence, a condition almost unique among earthly creatures, we live by the assumption that they are not conscious and we are. But the evidence all around us suggests that this is not true, and that, in fact, living beings of all kinds are endowed with consciousness. For example, it has recently been found that even insects are conscious—that is to say, self-aware.

In a paper recently published by Andrew B. Barron and Colin Klein in the Proceedings of the National Academy of Sciences, they report that the insect midbrain functions much like the midbrain in more complex animals, tying together perceptions, memories and other functions into something that must be a simple sense of self. In other words, the machinery of even this very small brain is designed to capture a fragment of consciousness, giving the creature at least a rudimentary sense of "I am."

So the presence of consciousness in living creatures would appear to be a matter of degree. But there is more than that, much more, because it may also be that human consciousness is mediated—and rigorously so—by the intellect and that, in fact, when the left or rational brain is turned off, the world that we perceive is entirely different—perhaps much more like the world creatures who are not endowed with intelligence perceive it.

Psychotropic substances, it has been found, do not add something to the brain so much as block something—specifically, the receptors that reason and logic depend on for their function. A person experiencing ayahuasca visions, for example, is perceiving the world almost entirely with the right brain.

There have been numerous studies, most notably those conducted by Dr. Rick Strassman, that suggest that not only is this true, but there is a consistency to the visionary world that the paralyzing of the left brain opens up.

Given the fact that animals have less active left brains, it could be that they see much more of the real world than we do, and, judging from the discussion in this book, that we once knew that. When Bert

Jansen encountered the ball of light that became the nest of owls, what he was seeing was reality in a much more true form—it was, as it were, a momentary perception of the world as it really is.

Such a story, of course, makes one long to also experience reality in this more true way. But, of course, if we didn't have the left brain, all we would have would be experience, never the ability to be an objective observer, which is as powerful a tool as exists for the traveler on the path of consciousness.

To be human, we have both given up something and gained something, and what nature is trying to teach us in the language of the mystical owl, for example, and the crop circle, is that there is another grammar altogether through which we can derive the meaning of what she has to say.

As Mike explored in *The Messengers*, and here more fully, the owl is probably the central symbol of the close encounter experience. The appearance of owls in the context of close encounter can be seen as nature's way of explaining the experience to us.

In my own long life in close encounter, I learned early on that the owl was the primary way nature had of explaining my experience to me. After my first remembered encounter in December of 1985, I thought that I had seen an owl flying around in the house. But there could have been no owl there. We had no chimney. The doors and windows were closed.

I recall, as the sun set the next afternoon, forcing myself to go upstairs and look at the snow-covered window sill where I supposed that the owl, since it could not have gotten into the house, must have been sitting.

There had been no new snow and there were no tracks in the old snow. In fact, the entire close encounter experience, which has become my life, had announced itself in the form of an owl. I suppose that this was also true in my childhood, but my father died with many secrets, among them what the owls in our back garden that he found so disturbing may have meant.

But nature was speaking in her own language, which is symbolic, visual and tactile, not intellectual. A long time ago, the Egyptians perfected a system of pictorial writing that expressed both nature's way of speaking and man's, but we long since abandoned the images of the natural world that gave it such dynamism in favor of the precision of entirely symbolic text.

Let's look at the owl, though, as a word in nature's language. This word can be applied to the experience of Bert Jansen where it says that being is both the ball of light and the nesting owl—the nest and the crop circle are expressions of the same mind, that of nature itself.

When we look at the owl through the medium of the close encounter experience, it turns out that something is being explained to us. Like the owl, our mysterious visitors come by night. Like the owl, they are silent and all-seeing. And like the owl, they can reach right into our little burrows and carry us off into a transformative experience. For the awful ecstasy that the predator delivers to its prey, causing it to die to this world and be freed into the next, is very much like what the visitor does to her captive, leaving him devastated, at once killed inside and renewed inside, and living in two worlds at the same time, that of physical reality and that of a new kind of reality, the living reality of the soul, not quite physical, but also no longer theoretical.

The owl, swifting through the night, can actually hear little forest creatures scuttling in their burrows. With her strong claws she can tear right into the earth and drag her prey right up out of the ground, just as the visitor can invade the house of her target and, as has happened to me and Mike and so many others, drag us right out of our assumed reality and leave us as we are indeed left, dangling between the worlds of the living and the dead.

The message of nature is clear: you have been awakened to a greater reality. You are not simply physical matter, your destiny and your body are one and the same. You are, rather, a mystery, at once the prey and student of the flying master who has troubled your sleep and left you in the frightened anguish of wonder in which you now must live.

Nature's language is not linear nor even only visual. Nature's language is nature herself, in all her mystery and terror and wonder, the language of the justice of the earth and the balance that rests deep in every heart, as much as that of the owl at her dinner as of the creature captured in the terrible ecstasy of her talons.

Mike Clelland has accomplished something deeply mind opening

Stories from the Messengers

in this transformative exploration of the meaning of the owl in our lives and in our world.

Introduction

This is a book of remarkable real life experiences. This is also a book about owls.

Owls seem to a play a shadowy role in the UFO contact experience. They also show up in relation to highly charged events like synchronicities, ancient archetypes, dreams, shamanic initiation, magic, psychedelic hallucination, spiritual transformation, and death. I explored the owl and its connection with these divergent ideas in *The Messengers*, my first book on UFOs. That book was also my own story of how owls played a role in my life. It was an exploration into the deeply personal questions that arose from my contact experiences. The process of creation was a journey of transformation, and I was a different person when the book was completed.

Within the nearly 400 pages of *The Messengers*, I repeatedly asked, "why owls?" The question is simple, the answer isn't.

The owl is a symbol. It's much more than just a bird with big eyes, it represents something in the darkness just beyond what we know in our conscious minds. It's a red flag forcing me to pay attention, a clue to look deeper.

Again, why owls? On a purely intellectual level, I don't know, yet my gut feeling gives me a glimpse into some possible answers. Here are four ideas on what owls might mean, each of which are followed up with another question:

1. Owls are alarm clocks. The simplest answer would be that they are here to wake us up. But wake us up to what?

2. Owls are an archetype. They are a symbol, an image stored deep within humanity's genetic memory bank. It's as if there are hidden meanings locked away within our grand shared consciousness, and the owl is a key. We think in symbols, and the owl is touching us on that level, and this deeper knowing goes back to the dawn of man. But what is this hidden archetypal meaning?

3. Owls are here to announce initiation. An initiation is a ritual, like a young Catholic receiving the Eucharist during their first holy communion. Owls often seem to show up just before the arrival of a UFO, as if to announce an impending ritual. Religious scholars would argue that initiation rites are metaphoric of a profound change within the initiate. But the true believer wouldn't see the initiation as a metaphor, the change would be entirely real. But an initiation into what?

4. Owls are a totem of the transformational experience. Seeing a UFO can transform someone. I've spoken to a lot of people who've seen a strange craft in the sky, and in that moment their entire definition of reality is altered. I've also spoken to people who have had owl sightings at such highly charged moments that it transformed their lives. But a transformation into what?

These four answers to the question "why owls" are elusive. Each are dancing around the same underlying mystery. Many people have told me they've had an owl experience that's somehow tied into a spiritual awakening. It's a call to wake up, pay attention and look within. The owl is telling us to confront the deepest part of ourselves. It's a summons to transform our soul.

After immersing myself so deeply in this subject, I'm at the point where I see UFOs and owls as the same thing. Both are eerily silent in flight, and both have an aura of mystery. Both can take your breath away, and both have the power to change people's lives.

The act of writing *The Messengers* was monumental. At its core, that book was just a collection of stories. The challenge was how to convey the elusive quality of what people had shared with me. I'm proud of the ideas that unfolded in that book, yet at the same time it was heartbreaking to have to edit down so many amazing stories in a way that would serve the reader. There were accounts that had such a powerful scope, but it was impossible to fit those into the manuscript.

This follow-up book is meant to be a companion, a place that allows for these important stories to be told more completely. Each chapter in this book focuses on personal experiences, and these accounts have two things in common; an owl and a UFO, and more often multiples of each. Beyond that, they all share a mood with similar qualities of emotion and mystery.

Introduction

Anne Strieber, the late wife of author Whitley Strieber, had a simple way of evaluating the truth of a UFO report. She said, "if it's not weird, I don't trust it." She called this her B.S. detector, and I've taken her words to heart. The stories in this book are not straightforward, they are weird. The details are mixed up and confusing. People are experiencing a collision of overlapping events that leave them baffled, and synchronicities spill over like an unattended sink.

From my research, as well as my personal experiences, it's a mistake to dismiss a story with this kind of disorder. Instead, the more complicated the interwoven details, the more valid it seems. This chaos is a sign to trust the event as legitimate.

I've described this frenetic pattern as the paradox syndrome. Too much, too messy and too confusing. I don't understand the why or how, but all the disparate threads must tie into some core source. The challenge is how to follow those threads without getting lost in the mayhem.

These are stories without a conclusion. If you read this book with an eye to an answer, you will end up wanting. It might be better to imagine each account as a fable shared around a campfire as mankind has done throughout the ages, lying on the forest floor under a sky of infinite stars—and listening to a story.

Author Jeff Kripal has described the difficulties of his work. Like myself, he's been in contact with a lot of people who tell of anomalous experiences, and he said something that I understand in my bones.

> This is the thing about this material, you think you've heard the last strange thing, and then it gets stranger. What the debunker thinks is that, no—if we just had enough information it would all make sense and all the strangeness would go away. But my experience with these folks is exactly the opposite. The more they tell you the weirder it gets. Part of the reason is that they don't quite trust you in the beginning and so they tell you just sort of the surface of the story. And then they tell you a little more, and a little more. And the more they tell you the stranger it gets. It does not make more sense, it makes less sense. And I think that this is important, I think that is part of the phenomena, that it's absurd, and that it's meant to confuse us. And I think that when we look for it to make sense I think we are going down the wrong path. Because it doesn't.

The tales that unfold in these pages are confusing, as if they are leading us into darkness. But perhaps there is a deeper meaning, a second story playing out below the waterline, one that presents a hidden set of clues. Put simply, this book conveys a challenge. It will be difficult to understand these stories using only your mind, yet a deeper truth might emerge if you listen with your heart.

The owl can fly into the darkness, something that would have been magical to our ancestors. This became a metaphor for traveling to other realms. They would pass into the land of the dead and the kingdom of the gods, and return with a message. Mythologies arose out of the owl's ability to see into the night. The ancient stories were of gods and monsters, each with a lesson for our forefathers. I've come to see the modern UFO accounts as a newer version of that outdated folklore. These same stories are rising up, needing to be expressed. I am convinced that the source of our mythologies remains alive, and owls are still performing their vital role. Messages are still being delivered.

This book is my attempt to share these timeless stories.

Mike Clelland, 2018

Chapter 1
The White Owl and the Hound of Hell

There is a wonderful owl story on page 144 in *The Messengers*, and it's retold here at the beginning of this chapter. This was the first of two accounts, but the second more elaborate part was only hinted at in that book. Both are shared in their entirety here.

The initial story took place in the summer of 1997 in the rolling farmland of England's Wiltshire County, a magical landscape in the heart of the world's crop circle reports. Dutch researcher Bert Janssen had been actively investigating the crop circle phenomenon for three summers in a row, but he felt he had reached a standstill in his ability to follow the mystery any further. Then something happened that changed everything. Here are Bert's own words:

> This was my third year, and I thought this is my last year, I've done it all now, I've seen it, three years of [researching] crop circles, it's enough. Then... something happens that will draw you back the next year. What happened to me, I saw for the first time in my life, in Wiltshire, an orb, a ball of light. And not just flashing by, this was amber and it was floating over a field in the near dark of the evening.

Bert watched in amazement as this floating orb cruised around above the fields. It would slow down and then accelerate, changing size as he watched. It would grow as big as a huge balloon, and then shrink back down to the size of a grapefruit.

> I watched it for minutes, floating over the field, then it moved along and disappeared behind a shed. I was sure it would reappear again, because the shed should have blocked the view for a just a few seconds, but it never reappeared. And I thought, that's really strange, why did it disappear at that shed?

He walked across the farmer's field to the shed and tried to get in, but the only door was locked. Putting his ear to the door he heard an eerie hissing noise. He was alone and it was getting dark, so he left with plans to come back in the daylight.

Returning the next day, he walked around to the back side of the little building and saw a small window without any glass. This was up high at about the same height the orb had traveled as it passed behind the shed the night before. He thought, "Can it be that the ball of light could have gone through that window into the shed?" The window opening was up on the second floor, and Bert desperately needed to know what was inside. He had to break in through the front door, and once inside, he again heard the same eerie hissing noise. He climbed a ladder that accessed a loft to get up to the level of that open window, and discovered the source of the hissing.

> ... to my great surprise and shock, *I found a nest of white owls!* I thought, this cannot be true. So the ball of light is totally connected to these white owls. So for me the white owl and the balls of light that are seen in Wiltshire, they are somehow interchangeable. That's why I am paying so much attention when I do see a white owl, because I'm not always sure it's a white owl. Could it be that I am actually looking at something else, and it only presents itself as a white owl to me? [1]

Fourteen years later, Bert would have another powerful experience involving a white owl in Wiltshire. This happened along with his wife, Heather Clewett-Jachowski. They spend each summer together in and around the mystical landscape of southern England, a place rich with ancient lore.[2]

Heather stepped into her first crop circle in the summer of 2005 and has returned to England every year since. She is a self-proclaimed Croppie, a nickname given to the folks who spend time in the rolling farmlands seeking out these formations. Beyond investigating crop circles, Heather works as a psychic medium, intuitive healer, and shaman.

Bert began his investigations of crop circles in 1994, but in recent years he's been obsessed with the alchemical symbolism of squaring the circle. He has written, "...the idea of squaring the circle being involved in the creation of the Philosopher's Stone has haunted me for years." These arcane ratios will sometimes show up hidden within the proportions and alignments of crop circle designs, and this has fascinated Bert.

This husband and wife team run organized tours where they explore the ancient sacred sites of Wiltshire. During these trips they visit megalithic stone structures like Stonehenge, as well as medieval monuments like the soaring Salisbury Cathedral. Some of these sites hold a heightened significance, having been a focal point of sacred activity across the ages. These power places convey a palpable feeling of the divine and are often the crowning moment of these trips.

In May of 2011, Heather and Bert were in England leading an 8-day organized tour. Despite their interest in crop circles, the emphasis of this trip was on hallowed stone monuments, medieval cathedrals, and the energetic ley lines that define Wiltshire. The tour was called the 2011 Dragon Path Expedition, and there were eight clients. The group had repeatedly expressed their eagerness to see a crop circle, and each time they were reminded the tour was instead focused on ancient sacred sites. Still, the topic of circles kept coming up.

Midway through the tour, Heather and Bert took some quiet time away from the group at a local restaurant. While planning out the final few days, they talked about how much the clients wanted to see a crop circle. They had created a tightly packed list of things to see each day, and neither wanted to alter their busy schedule to try and fit in something so elusive.

Based on years of experience, they understood that the circles seem to have an agenda all their own. They just appear in the fields without any advance notice, so planning anything is nearly impossible. All you can do is wait for a new formation, then hurry out to see it once it has been discovered. It was only the middle of May, still early in the crop circle season, and at that point there hadn't been any new formations reported in the local fields.

Even though they felt it would interfere with the focus of their tour, Heather and Bert were missing the crazy adrenaline rush that comes from visiting these magical formations. They knew this feeling well from their years of racing around while investigating these circles.

Inspired by their participants' inquires and enthusiasm, they both decided they would visit a crop circle only if it met a set number of conditions. They came up with five points, and all five had to be met before they would take their clients to the site of a formation:

1. The formation would have to be located next to a power place, cathedral, or Dragon Line.

2. They would need enough free time in the itinerary to visit the formation.

3. Plenty of safe parking for their cars.

4. The formation had to be on the same side of the road as the parking.

5. The farmer would need to welcome the group into the formation.

Some of these conditions might seem odd, such as the issue of parking. But with their experience they wanted to avoid the problems that can arise on the narrow farm roads. It's common for anyone unaccustomed to the backwards traffic patterns in the UK to look the wrong way before crossing a road. This is a real hazard given how fast the locals drive.

It was after dark when Heather and Bert left the restaurant. As they got in their car, they both spoke of having an odd feeling that this night might prove interesting. Their plan was to drive to a local site called The Tires, a favorite night watch spot for the Croppies. This is nothing more than a small parking lot that looks out at what is known as the East Field, one of the most famous crop circle fields in all of England, if not the world. Another nearby vantage point for viewing the East Field is from atop Knapp Hill.

Bert was driving fast along the narrow farm roads. Heather was next to him, thinking about the tour and their busy schedule. Doubtful that their team would see any crop formations, she understood that even with the best of luck the list of five conditions might prove impossible to meet.

She suddenly cried, "Watch out!" as their Volvo narrowly missed hitting two small white birds sitting in the road. Bert violently swerved between them, like a slalom skier running through gates.

They continued the drive, shaken by the sight of those two white birds, most likely doves. It was odd that they stayed frozen in the road, and both Heather and Bert referred to this as "driving through a gate." Given what was about to unfold, this metaphor seems particularly appropriate.

About a mile from The Tires, something amazing happened. A white owl glided gracefully into their headlight beams and flew right in front of their car, just a few feet off the road. They both got the sense that it was guiding them somewhere. Caught up in the thrill of following this majestic bird throughout the night, Bert accelerated to keep up with the white owl.

Suddenly, the owl mysteriously disappeared. Then, as if the car was driving itself, they took a sharp left turn and began heading up Knapp Hill. They kept driving until they saw the white owl again, now perched on a fence post looking straight at them. Bert slammed on the brakes and pulled off to the side of the road, and they both got out of the car.

There was an electric feel in the air as they slowly approached the owl. Without a sound it spread its wings and flew away from them, gliding just a few feet off the ground.

At that moment, Heather started experiencing some odd visual sensations. She saw the ground moving, zipping along below her, getting closer and then further away. It took a moment, but she eventually realized she was *seeing through the eyes of the owl*. She saw the farmland undulating, as if she were gliding over the rolling terrain. This vision lasted only a moment and seemed entirely real.

Heather tried to make sense of what she'd just experienced. She described the visual impressions to Bert, and her certainty that the owl was heading toward the East Field.

They suddenly realized they were at site called Knob Hill, and had no idea how they'd ended up there. Their original destination had been The Tires, an entirely different location. Following that white owl into the night had dragged them off course, apparently leading them to this spot for a reason. Returning to their car, they raced along the winding farm roads toward The Tires. When they arrived at the small parking lot, the owl was nowhere to be seen. Heather wondered if she had been mistaken about what the owl had shown her.

They sat together in the dark and discussed the significance of the doves and the owl, trying to make sense of what these white birds might mean. After about twenty minutes, it seemed best to called it a night. It was late, and their plan was to be up before sunrise to visit Stonehenge.

While driving back to the hotel, as if out of nowhere, their white owl guide was back. It was once again flying lead out in front of their car, and they dutifully followed their messenger through the English countryside. Bert turned the car as the owl made a swooping left onto a dirt road bordering the South Field.

They followed to a point where the owl lifted out of the headlights and flew up into the air. Parking on the side of the road at the bottom of a hill, Bert got out of the car and walked uphill, all the while watching as the owl circled overhead. This was happening while Heather was still in the passenger seat searching her backpack for a flashlight. When she looked up she saw Bert standing in the road, but she was shocked to see something else. At the crest of the hill was an enormous black doglike figure crossing the road about thirty feet beyond Bert. She watched in horror as it disappeared into the field.

Heather jumped out of the car and shouted, "Bert, are you alright? Are you okay?" She ran up the hill past her husband, scaring the owl away. Bert ran up behind her and asked, "What are you doing?"

She gasped, "Didn't you see it? It was huge!"

"See what?" Bert replied with surprise.

"That huge black, wild looking cat-dog animal that came out of the South Field and crossed the road right here! It disappeared into the grass field on the other side!"

Heather explained what she had seen; it had a large square head with pointed ears, glowing red eyes, huge feet with long, pointy claws, and a body about six feet long. It was completely black and moved like a large wild cat stalking its prey.

She said, "I thought it might hurt you, that's why I came bolting out of the car!"

Bert thought it was cute that his wife would run to protect him armed only with a little flashlight. They spent the next half hour looking for tracks, and although they were clearly leaving their own footprints in the muddy road, they didn't find anything unusual. The crop on each side of the road was undisturbed, even though a large animal should have left some evidence of its passing. They eventually returned to their hotel.

During the events of that night, Heather felt she was seeing through the eyes of the owl, and she knew exactly where it had been headed. She has experienced that same awareness several times before, once seeing through the eyes of a deer. While on a trail in a forest she suddenly had the sensation of hearing noises much more acutely. Then she could feel herself in the body of a deer, even feeling its heart beating. It wasn't as if she had become that animal, it's more that she was sharing its consciousness for a few moments.

This is exactly the kind of thing I would expect from a shaman, this mystical connection to the natural world. What seems curious is that owls and deer are both commonly reported by the UFO abductee as screen memories. Was Heather merging with an owl and deer just because they happened to be nearby, or was the connection co-opted by some archetypal power determined to saturate these events with a deeper meaning?

It was well before dawn the following morning when the entire crew arrived at the gates of Stonehenge, one of the busiest attractions in the British Isles. Although most visitors are restricted to a fenced-off path around the iconic monument, each morning pre-arranged tours are legally allowed to enter the ancient circle of stones.

Heather and Bert were trying to make sense of the strange happenings from the night before, but their clients were now their main priority. They had made arrangements more than a year in advance for this private viewing. The guard at the site checked their reservation paperwork, then escorted them into the circle. They were all alone as the sun slowly rose, and everyone was deeply moved by its illumination on the sacred stones. It was a great honor to share this peaceful moment together, well before the tourists arrived at the hallowed site.

Afterwards, the whole crew drove to nearby Salisbury to visit the magnificent Cathedral. Then they walked the narrow streets to the medieval St. Thomas Becket Church. Just as they were about to enter the 13th century building, one of the participants announced that she wanted to share something with the group. She had been up late the night before reading about legends of Albion, the ancient name for the island of Great Britain. After digging through her purse, she opened a little book, searched for the page and said, "Here it is, the legend about the Hounds Of Hell." She stood on a bench outside the church showing everyone the picture.

Heather almost fainted when she saw the image in the book. It was the same large, wild black dog thing she'd seen the night before. She was transported back to a point years before—in that moment she heard the voice of one of her shamanic teachers describing circular time.

> This is where time bends and loops backwards and forwards on itself. Physicists call this non-local. A shaman recognizes this as sacred time, and that here she can influence events across space and time. She knows there is no now versus then. There is no difference between here and there. Everything happens simultaneously everywhere. It's like a dream where you get in a taxi in Paris, and at exactly the same time you get out of that same taxi in New York...

Heather thought about the strange events from the previous night. Why did the messenger, the white owl, ensure I was in the right place at the right time to see the Hound of Hell?

Heather wrote about this collision of myth and her real experiences:

> In Welsh mythology, there are the hounds of Annwn. Annwn is the otherworld of Welsh folklore. The Annwn of medieval Welsh tradition is an otherworldly paradise, and there is this persistent myth of the cauldron of Annwn. Some say the cauldron is a source of everlasting life itself, just like Arthur's Holy Grail.
>
> The white owl is associated with the Goddess and wisdom as well as being a messenger between the worlds. The otherworld is a place, outside of our ordinary time, where the cauldron of Annwn, or the Holy Grail, is guarded by the Hound of Hell.

Could it be that the white owl is the one who brings an initiate the invitation to enter Annwn? Is it possible that the white owl is one of the gatekeepers to Annwn who can open the doorway? If the white owl opens the gateway, does the guardian of the cauldron of Annwn, the Hound of Hell, make the decision who gets into the otherworld? Was Gwenhyfar, the white owl, one of the messengers that brought the knowledge of the cauldron of Annwn or the Holy Grail, to Arthur? Did Gwenhyfar invite me to enter Annwn? And, if so, what was the decision of the Hound of Hell?[3]

Heather was consumed with her own thoughts as everybody entered St. Thomas Becket Church. She was still shaken from the Hound of Hell image in the book as she spoke to the group, pointing out the dragon symbolism in the stained glass windows and murals. Speaking on autopilot, she described the spiral imagery and its association with the dragon. Spirals have been primary Goddess symbols since the late

Paleolithic Era when they were marked on tombs. The dragon stands for life force, like prana or Chi, symbolic of the Goddess. Carl Jung saw the dragon as a symbol for our unconscious. For the Christian mystics, the earthly aspect of the Holy Spirit were symbolized by the dragon, and the heavenly aspects were symbolized by the white dove.

On the last day of the tour, the group visited the ancient sacred sites around Silbury Hill. The morning began in Avebury, a tiny village entirely surrounded by the largest stone circle in Britain. There were originally about a hundred standing stones, which in turn encloses two smaller stone circles.

Avebury sits along a measurable stream of earth energy known as the St. Michael ley line. The term ley is meant to describe a line of within the landscape that can be traced using dowsing techniques. A ley line might be just a few miles long, or encircle the entire globe. An exceptionally powerful ley might run for hundreds of miles or more. These more energetic currents are known as dragon lines, also called the dragon's breath by the ancient Chinese.

The ley of St. Michael is an example of a dragon current. This remarkable line runs laser-like across the English countryside for over 300 miles. Numerous sacred sites, both ancient and medieval, are aligned along its course. The stone circle of Avebury is situated near the center of this line.

A second current entwines the St. Michael ley line and follows roughly the same course. This counterpart line is named the Mary ley. The names refer to the many churches dedicated to St. Michael, the Virgin Mary, or Mary Magdalene; these sites are positioned all along their namesake lines. The two lines, male and female, symbolize yin and yang dragon currents which can be likened to meandering rivers of magnetic energy. Both lines cross each other in the heart of the Avebury circle.[4]

Many researchers call the standing stones around Avebury the Dragon Temple. It's also noteworthy that the dragon is the namesake and theme of Bert and Heather's entire tour.

The group then moved on to the base of nearby Silbury Hill, the tallest prehistoric man-made chalk mound in Britain. From there they walked up a long gentle hill to visit the West Kennet Long Barrow, an ancient tomb, or barrow, built around 3650 BC. There is one entrance to this five-chambered stone structure which is partially buried in earth. Everyone walked thirty-three feet along the central passageway to the deepest room in this dark sanctuary. The interior is tall enough to stand in, and thought to be a place of ancient rituals and ceremonies. It is Britain's oldest and longest long barrow, and sits at the center of a gentle hilltop. They all stepped out of the darkness to a commanding view of the beautiful rolling farmlands.

It was from here that they saw—to their amazement—a newly formed crop circle in the fields below. Bert looked through binoculars to see a money box and a sign that read, "Welcome to the corn circle. We would welcome a donation."

Everyone realized something magical had happened. A crop circle had appeared, meeting all the conditions they had listed just three days before. The formation was in a field next to a power place that the tour was visiting. From their vantage point on the hilltop they could see there was plenty of safe parking on the same side of the road as the circle. The long barrow was the last location planned for the day, so they had free time open in their busy schedule. Finally, the farmer welcomed them into the formation with his hand written sign and donation box.

The circle was about a third of a mile away, its position aligning closely with the long axis opening of the barrow. The entire crew hurried back down the hill, got in their cars and followed Bert to the newly formed circle.

The crop circle was a perfect spiral in young green barley. This formation felt precious to the visitors, so much so that nobody stepped off the tram lines. Tram lines are the straight imprints made by the farmer's tractor when the field is initially planted. No one dared to actually explore the formation, they all had the transcendental feeling that they had entered the Holy of Holies.

The Mary Dragon Line breaks away from the St. Michael line at Avebury and goes straight through the axis of the West Kennet Long Barrow, then runs down the hill across the field and right through the center of the crop circle. The formation was in the shape of a beautiful perfect spiral which is also the symbol of the dragon, the Goddess.

Heather thought, "Of course it has to be a spiral." She felt that the Circle Makers were communicating with the Dragon Path Expedition through the symbol of the spiral.

Heather wrote:

> Is it possible that information from the future can ripple backwards, information like the Hound of Hell in one of our participant's books, the spiral-shape of the formation at West Kennet, and the conditions that must be met for our tour group to go into a crop circle? If so, who or what from the future was trying to get my attention?

There are aspects to these overlapping events that left both Heather and Bert deeply impressed. The first thing Bert did when they saw the formation from atop the West Kennet Long Barrow, was to get on his cell phone and call the folks at the Crop Circle Connector. This is a local website that keeps track of the circles, and immediately posts information on any new designs. When Bert asked what they knew about the crop circle he was looking at, they replied that they hadn't yet heard of it.

The team hadn't actually discovered the crop circle—the farmer had obviously noticed it before them and had added a donation box. Given their combined years of chasing crop circles, neither Bert nor Heather can remember another example of this. Usually any donation box will only show up days after the croppies arrive. [5]

Local researcher Glenn Broughton described this circle in his blog. He visited the site a few days after its appearance, and like Bert and his team, Broughton and his friends wouldn't enter the formation.

> None of us felt that we should venture beyond the tramlines as the crop was laid so lightly. It was very unusual, not at all like the usual clearly defined areas of laid and standing crop. This was almost like half the crop was downed loosely and the other was still standing and the two merged into one another. Using the analogy of colour, most crop circles are black and white whereas this one is definitely gray. Without the aerial photos it would be hard to imagine that this would look anything other than a mess from the air. The lay appeared to form a spiral clockwise out from the central standing stems. This continued forming a large disc that has a ring surrounding it, the whole being about thirty metres in diameter. [6]

Four weeks after the appearance of the West Kennet crop circle, an extra element was mysteriously added to the design—a new circle now surrounded the previous spirals. When Bert scrutinized the details of this additional element, he was shocked to realize he was seeing the sacred geometry of squaring the circle. He reexamined the original design within and found that it too held the ratios of squaring the circle, but he had completely missed it. Bert was left to conclude that the initial set of spiral circles had been purposely encoded with the exact sacred geometry that had been his obsession, but he hadn't noticed it.

Perhaps there was a message set there in the field for him to find and decipher. It seems the circle makers were waiting for Bert to solve their puzzle, and when he failed to read their clues they added another circle to make it more obvious. It was as if they were saying, "Okay Bert, now do you see it?"

Right from the onset, the members of the Dragon Path Expedition had been asking their guides about crop circles. It was mid-way through the tour when they created that list of conditions, never expecting them all to ever be met. Neither Heather nor Bert wanted to try to fit a crop circle into their busy schedule—it was the group that had wanted it, and then manifested it. At least that is how Bert feels, that their intention created the perfect circle to match the strict conditions laid down by their hosts.

When you listen to a radio, sometimes you need to carefully adjust the dial to get a clear signal. You can hear music, but you might not know anything about where the signal is coming from. You can be assured it's out there somewhere, but you don't need to walk through the front door of the radio station to get your proof that the signal has a source.

Bert and Heather were getting a signal. It was playing out in their reality as clearly as any radio. Something was being orchestrated for their benefit, yet the what or the where of this source is impossible to know. All I can say is that it's out there, and it's happening for some reason. My deepest sense is that this reason must be important.

Chapter 2
The Awakening of Susan MacLeod

I reached out to a woman after hearing her describe a remarkable set of events. Part of this experience involved a UFO floating above her driveway, and I sensed there was a lot more to the story. She had given a short online interview, and after listening I searched for her. After a few mouse clicks, I found her on Facebook and sent a quick note along with a link to my site. Here's her rather excited reply from November 26, 2010:

> OMG OWLS! omg...ok...'heart pounding'...if you scroll thru my page you will see my posts on the OWLS...I have to write the latest one just days ago...long story...working on it now. I think the owl is in my photos...the barred owl is the one who is always at my home...I feel stalked at times! LOL...my partner carved us an OWL Totem pole at a tribute to the owls. wow...Mike you are amazing!!!!!!!!

Now that's someone who's enthusiastic about owls! I scrolled through the pages of her site, and she has a lot of beautiful owl photos, most of them taken right in her yard.

Her name is Susan MacLeod, and she's had a lifetime of strange experiences. But one event stands out over all the others, which she now refers to as her "awakening experience." It took place on August 15 2005, and what transpired on that day is complicated, and unimaginably strange.

At the time of this event she was living in a cabin in a heavily forested area of rural Ontario with her partner and three children. They had a garage separate from the house used by her partner as his woodworking shop. There was also a traditional teepee down near a small river on the property.

Her family lineage traces back to Scotland, Ireland, and also the Mi'kmaq people of Eastern Canada. She is descended of Gaelic, Celtic and Native North Americans. The folk traditions of her ancestors from both sides of the Atlantic are filled with magical traditions, and Susan feels a deep connection to these roots. Things like shamanic journeys, psychic gifts, faeries, and nature spirits are accepted in these cultures.

Having indigenous blood was the source of an emotional divide in her family. It was during Christmas dinner in the late 1980s that Susan first heard that she had a Native background. Though unspoken, there had been a long history of shameful racial intolerance in rural Canada.

Years later when she visited the northern reserves, she learned about the "blood quota" in the native population. Young Indians were teased by their own people if they had white ancestry, and this lead to many suicides. These divisions left her heartbroken, and she eventually embraced her Native heritage. Susan said, "Our medicine wheel talks of that, all the four races of our Earth, they all meet in the middle. The middle is our creator. We are all related."

The morning of August 15, 2005 began with a call for help. Susan had gone to the dentist for a normal, but painful, cleaning procedure. She had previously suffered adverse reactions to anesthesia, and she informed both the dentist and hygienist that she didn't want to have any pain medication. At that point in her life, she'd been practicing a form of self hypnosis, and this would be her alternative to any type of anesthetic. She told the hygienist not to speak to her during the procedure. So for the next two hours she concentrated, using visualization techniques to remove herself from her physical body.

Susan could still feel pain even though she was in a state of deep meditation, so she prayed for help. Suddenly, a traditional wooden mask appeared to her. It was a mask that had been given to her by a Native Elder, and in that moment she recognized it as her guide. She was then presented with a vision of being at a ceremonial Sun Dance where a man was being pierced in the chest with an eagle claw. Susan understood this man was taking the pain instead of her.

At one point the hygienist quietly asked her if she was doing okay. Susan responded yes, but the question had jarred her out of the trance state. It took some work for her to re-enter the same focused meditative realm. Instead of the Sun Dance, she now had a vision of being in a beautiful green room with a big golden retriever. The dog was repeatedly offering its paw to Susan in a gesture of compassion. Again, she felt the pain was being taken, this time by the dog.

When the procedure was over, the hygienist said she was amazed that Susan hadn't needed any anesthesia. It was then that Susan shared her visions about the green room and the dog. The hygienist looked shocked and said, "You just described my bedroom and my dog."

After regaining her composure, the hygienist went on to finish up the cleaning. She was about to use an electric brush, and just as she put the instrument in Susan's mouth, it shut off. She tried again, and just like before—it stopped working. This happened repeatedly, and she nervously asked Susan, "Are you doing this?"

This was just the beginning. That day would get even more bizarre.

Later that night, Susan left her house at around 11 p.m., walked in the dark down a path toward a small river and entered her teepee. She was there to honor and mourn the death of a close friend named Barry. She built a small fire in the center and burned some sage. She began drumming and singing, and within minutes she heard something moving around right outside the teepee. It sounded big, and she thought it might be a bear.

It was so close that she could feel it brushing against the fabric of teepee. She assumed this must be a bear because of a strong damp musky odor. Unsettled, she drummed even louder.

After making a lot of noise, she felt a need to get back to the house. She stepped out of the teepee, walked a little way up the path and saw two red lights. Seconds later, there were more lights and multiple eyes reflecting back at her. Her first thought thought was she was seeing a group of standing bears that were frighteningly close, but that didn't seem right. Susan froze in her tracks when she realized she was looking at what appeared to be five big hairy Sasquatch standing less than twenty feet away.

Two of them were well over eight feet tall, and the other three were smaller, around four or five feet tall. Time stopped as she stood before them. She thought maybe they had come for her, that it was her time to go, and with that came a feeling of complete surrender.

Her mind was racing, yet there was a stillness of acceptance. She slowly started walking backwards on the path, the light from the teepee barely visible out of the corner of her eye. Without turning around, she entered the teepee still facing the five silent figures. Once inside, the reality of what she had seen hit her hard.

Shaking with terror she put more wood on the fire, hoping to scare off what was outside. She was in shock, and all she could do was stare at the flames. After a moment, she sensed they'd moved away, and now her need to get back to the house was more urgent. She got up the nerve to leave the teepee and stepped out into the darkness. Hurrying along the path, she saw them again—the same group of Sasquatch—now further away down the river about 150 feet away. They were motionless, and stood together in the same formation. There was a sense of relief, that they'd moved off to give her some room. The three smaller ones were side-by-side in front, and the two bigger ones stood behind them. Her impression was that they were presenting themselves, like a family in a photo portrait; mom, dad and the kids. There were five of them, matching her own family of five. There was a sense of relief that they didn't want to frighten her, that they'd retreated to give her some room.

When she got to the house, her daughter met her at the door and cried, "Mom, we need help!" Everyone was rattled, her youngest stepson was crying and her oldest stepson was pleading, "You've got to do something! There are black things and they are flying all through the house!"

The three terrified kids all described seeing dark shadow beings darting around along the walls and ceilings. They were so freaked out that there was no way she could tell them she'd just seen a family of Sasquatch. She marched throughout the house with burning sage, smudging each room with smoke while trying to reassure her frantic kids that everything was okay.

It was after midnight when things had finally calmed down enough to catch her breath. Desperate to tell her partner about seeing the family of Sasquatch, she left the house and hurried uphill to the garage where he was working in his shop. She was locked out and pounded on the door, shouting to let her in. It took some time for him to get it open because he'd jammed it shut with a piece of wood.

When he finally opened the door, the first thing out of his mouth was, "What were you doing in the teepee?"

Susan didn't understand what he meant. He explained, "There were black things flying around in here. And there were black shadow beings looking in at me through the windows!"

2: The Awakening of Susan MacLeod

Again, just like the kids, he was so freaked out she simply couldn't tell him that she had just seen a family of Sasquatch.

This was the point where the enormity of what was happening really hit her. Too much had happened at once, and she got very emotional. She needed to step away from all of the chaos and collect her thoughts. She left the garage, walked down the driveway, and stood alone in a spot where there was an open clearing in the trees. Like that morning in the dentist chair, she again asked for help. Susan gazed up into the heavens and prayed to God.

She looked up at three bright stars while praying. These points of light all slowly moved together in the sky above her, defining the corners of a giant triangle shape. Initially appearing as three different colors, she watched these stars meld into one beautiful swirling orange-amber-yellow.

She called out to her partner and he came running out to the opening along the driveway. He looked up to see these three colored lights slowly moving apart, but the stars within the triangle were being blotted out by something giant right above them. They both watched as something enormous began forming itself into a semi-solid kind of matter. It was right then that she understood that all these events, the Sasquatch, the shadow beings, and now this giant craft were somehow connected.

Looking up at the hull of what appeared to be a great ship, she realized there was a non-physical aspect to what she was seeing. It was about 200 feet above them moving slowly past the trees. The giant shape floated with an eerie smoothness in absolute silence. It was a translucent luminescent blue with little lights running along the edges.

What happened to Susan that night is baffling. Each fragment of the story needs to be reexamined, because nothing is what it seems to be. Sasquatch aren't just giant apes living in the forest, shadow beings aren't just menacing ghosts in a haunted house and a giant semi-solid triangle craft isn't just a UFO from some far off planet. There is something much stranger at play.

The events of that night were all preceded by a ceremony in her teepee. She drummed and prayed to honor a friend on his journey to another realm. It's significant that she was performing a ritual at the very moment things started getting strange.

The next morning while Susan was in the shower, the house started shaking. Thinking it was an earthquake, she grabbed her housecoat and ran out onto the front deck. Her partner and a friend were both pointing up at a white Lear jet circling the house at treetop level. It flew around three times, and was close enough for them to see that the aircraft had no identifying numbers. Susan was upset, and after it flew off she called the local airport to report what had happened. They told her that without any emblem or numbers, the plane would be impossible to trace.

All the events combined were overwhelming, and she eventually sought help from a hypnotherapist. She had a hypnotic regression in 2008 in hopes of coming to some kind of closure with the memories of the August 15 experience three years prior, but more than anything she wanted to see the family of Sasquatch again. She felt a bond with them, and an emotional need to somehow reconnect. Susan has studied hypnotherapy and was very aware of the inherent pitfalls within the procedures, so she approached it with caution.

Susan told the therapist not to lead her in any way. Honoring her request, he calmly took her through the induction process and then simply said, "Now you are back in your teepee."

While in the trance state, she saw the interior of the teepee from that night. She realized she wasn't alone—there were two little gray beings in there with her. Looking at one of the faces (she felt it was female), she suddenly started sobbing. She felt an intense connection and a familiarity. She absolutely knew that there was something beautiful and good about this small being. She didn't get what she expected from the hypnosis session—instead of peace, she was even more confused.[1]

I asked Susan the one question in the forefront of my mind, if she had any odd owl experiences around the time of her awakening event with the Sasquatch and hovering triangle. She replied: "Yes, we were literally surrounded by owls that summer. Funny you ask, I remember an owl visiting the night before, right out my bedroom window that faced the area. That fall, one was perched right outside my window and would look at us! I counted seven days that it was there!"

Susan's awakening event happened in 2005 on August 15, a date celebrated by the Catholic Church as the Feast of the Assumption of the Blessed Virgin Mary. This day commemorates the death of Mary and her bodily assumption into Heaven. It's the most important of all Marian feasts and a Holy Day of Obligation.

Anya Briggs is a gifted psychic who had her own awakening experience three years later on that same day, August 15 2008. She saw a giant UFO hovering over her apartment building in New York City, yet no one else on the busy street seemed to notice what was looming above them. She heard and felt a direct telepathic communication from whatever was inside that craft. From that point on she began writing urgently about this new chapter of her life.

Here's one more story that took place on August 15, this time in 2014. A woman was relaxing with her husband, sipping a margarita while on a dock looking out over the ocean. They were enjoying a beautiful evening when she heard the sound of an owl hooting. Surprised an owl would be so close to the ocean, she scanned the trees behind her, saw nothing, then looked up. It wasn't yet dark, and she clearly saw a silvery object shining in the sky directly above them. At first she didn't tell her very rational husband, and for the next couple of minutes she watched as it made odd maneuvers across the sky. She eventually pointed up and asked, "What's that?" Then they watched the object together for about ten minutes. He's a no-nonsense engineer type, and was genuinely perplexed.[3]

Something powerful happened on the same day for each of these three women. Both Susan and Anya refer to this as their awakening experience, and both accounts involve UFOs. The woman on the dock was looking for an owl, but saw a UFO instead—a perfect example of the core premise of this book.

Susan's earlier awakenings

Why would Susan be at the center of such a bizarre flurry of paranormal weirdness? There are no easy answers to that question. Along with the strange episodes described thus far, she's had a lifetime of other powerful experiences. Each of these events seem to have played a role, giving rise to strong psychic and healing abilities.

When Susan was only four years old, she had a near-death experience. Suffering from the German Measles with an extremely high fever, she eventually faded away to the point where she no longer had any vital signs. A priest was called in, and she was given the last rights.

She remembers being told that she had a choice; she could stay there with Jesus, or return. She replied, "I worry for my mom and dad." At that point she awoke in a bathtub full of ice cubes. The doctors told her parents that if she survived she would be blind, deaf or mentally damaged.

She feels she was sent back here, "...by the grace of God to do good things for the Earth and everything upon it." Susan was forever changed after leaving this life and returning. Afterwards, she began having experiences of extra-sensory perception, and these psychic experiences have continued throughout her life.

As a young woman in the early 1980s, Susan had an extremely vivid nightmare of having the first-person experience of being attacked in a parking garage. She woke up crying, rattled by the bloody imagery she had just endured.

It was so realistic that she woke her roommate Barb and told her what she had just experienced. After Susan went back to sleep, Barb left for work. When she saw her supervisor, she told him about Susan's dream, and the gruesome details quickly made it to the police.

Later that morning when Susan arrived at her job near Vancouver, officers from the Royal Canadian Mounted Police were waiting for her. They took her to the station and put her in an interrogation room and were preparing to arrest her because she had clearly described the exact crime they were investigating. It didn't take them long to realize she had nothing to do with the attempted murder, but her visions were so accurate that they asked for her help. Susan worked with them, and her psychic skills were essential in solving the crime.

The man they eventually arrested posted bond while awaiting trial. The same cops showed up at Susan's home and gave her the news that the assailant was now out of jail and they couldn't guarantee her safety. Regretfully, they suggested she return to her home in Ontario. The decision was difficult, but she eventually took the four day train ride across Canada back to her hometown. From that point on she's worked with police departments all across Canada.

Beginning in March of 1992, Susan had a series of visionary experiences. She tells of a giant snowy owl that came to her in a life changing dream. She felt it was there to announce a journey, so she climbed on its back and rode through the sky with this beautiful white owl, its wings wrapped around her as they flew together in magic circles. Never in her life had she felt such an intense feeling of being loved.

She was then welcomed by a pair of eyes that looked at her, and speaking with a voice they said, "I am loving you." She replied, "I am loving you."

After that experience, her life was never the same.

Susan feels her healing abilities are the result of this visionary dream, and the communion with those eyes. She feels that her psychic abilities began after the near-death experience as a girl. The events of August 15 pushed her to an even deeper awakening, allowing more powerful healing capabilities to emerge.

Like so many others who've had these kinds of experiences, she works as an energy healer, intuitive and a psychic. Over the decades she's assisted thousands of people, with a special calling to help in the First Nation villages across Canada. She offers her support for people in crisis, as well as using her psychic skills to help search for missing children. She uses intuition, sound vibration, and crystals in her healing practice. She does her work solely by donations. She also sews homemade orgone accumulator blankets following the techniques described by Wilhelm Reich.

Susan MacLeod is one of the most inspiring and big hearted people I've ever had the honor of knowing. She radiates a glowing energy that is simply wonderful. And, she's had a lot of mystical owl experiences. These aren't dreams or screen memories—these are real owls.

For example, there was a night when her home was surrounded by four hooting owls, one at each corner. She saw their calls as vibrations in radiant colors. She wrote, "They hooted to each other with the color flowing like a ribbon." She describes brilliant gold, purple and green, all within a pure white light. She knew that owls were feared in many native traditions, "But these were not to be feared. They showed me the color of frequency or vibration." It was around this time that the Elders in her community began calling her Medicine Woman. [2]

Owls around her home

Susan had two widowed guests over for Thanksgiving, a man who had lost his wife, and a woman who had lost her partner. They all went for a walk in the woods before dinner. The mood was somber, and they decided to pray to the souls of their dearly departed. The woman asked for an owl to come as that had been her partner's totem animal. The man agreed and shared that shortly after his wife died, an owl appeared in a tree and watched their home for hours. They knelt together on the forest floor, held hands, and prayed.

Within minutes, a handsome barred owl appeared on a low branch nearby. All three people walked right up to the tree, and it just calmly sat there. At this point they were all crying. Despite the tears, they took some lovely pictures. Susan said, "It took a long time for us to come out of those woods because that owl sat looking at us for over half an hour!"

This ties into a follow up story a few months later. Susan was at home waiting for her daughter and boyfriend, who had left earlier that evening to pick up her partner from work. While tending a fire in the yard, she began to worry, realizing they'd been gone a long time. Suddenly, an owl flew above her head and right over the open fire.

Susan blurted out, "Oh my God, there's been an accident!"

The owl came out of the west, and flew in the direction of town. This was important to Susan—her ancestors saw the owl sitting in the west, the place of spirit and those who pass over. She knew something had happened, and she got in her car. Just as she was about to pull out of the driveway her daughter arrived home. She said there had been a fatal motorcycle accident and the road was closed.

Weeks later, the dead man's brother called Susan's home. He'd first called the closest gas station to the accident site to ask if anyone knew details of the event. Curiously, this was where Susan's stepson worked, but he wasn't there at the time. The attendant at the station then gave the man the phone number for the stepson. He called the house and Susan answered.

She told the brother what had happened. She also told him about the owl that flew above her head and her intuitive knowing that there had been an accident. The man listened to her story and then said, "My brother collected owls."

During the time leading up to this phone call, Susan had been hearing a loud owl making a boisterous "Whoo-Hoooo!" outside her home. Her partner heard it too, and told her he thought there was someone out partying in their woods. She then went on to describe the owl calls she'd been hearing to the brother, imitated the hooting sound on the phone.

Hearing this, the man began to cry. He explained his brother was notorious for making a rowdy owl call whenever he was excited, the same exclamation Susan had just made. He added that his brother loved a good party, and would always make that loud hooting whenever he was in a joyful mood.

Susan felt this unruly owl was the same one she had previously photographed with her two widowed friends on Thanksgiving. The photos clearly show a barred owl, and upon hearing this the man said that was his brother's favorite owl.

The first time I spoke with Susan was during a difficult point in my life. I was deeply confused about all the strange UFO and owl events that had been welling up around me. I told her that these experiences had been really hard, and I wasn't coping well. I tried to come up with the right word, and said it had been terribly challenging.

She said, "Yes, it's very challenging."

She went on to explain how she copes. "So many things can happen. You just need to sit in nature, sit and be, and in that silence everything becomes very clear. But you have to get past the chaos and confusion of ourselves. It's so challenging when you go through these things. Just when you think you've seen it all—wham—here comes something else. Why did this happen? We question it, and that's just our nature, when instead we should just accept this and just say thank you."

As part of the process of creating this book, I've been sending the text to the people I'm writing about. It's their story, not mine, and I need their feedback. Like everyone else in this book, I sent a document to Susan for her to review. A little while later she sent me this message: "Wow... it's wonderful! Working on a few things [in the document]... funny tonight before I came in and was sitting down to check your message again... a HUGE white OWL flew over our pond... nice."

Think about this—Susan saw an owl just before sitting down to review the story you've just read. Ask yourself what that might mean, because I'm forced to ask myself that question all the time. This is very common, that people will have an owl encounter seemingly in connection with me.

I have been immersed in this work, and the weight of these stories can be overwhelming. It's easy to drift off track and lose sight of the core message. Then someone will tell me a simple story—an owl showing up at a significant moment. This happens so often that I've come to expect it, and if it doesn't happen I'm disappointed. I am trusting that there is a deeper meaning to these experiences. They seem to represent confirmation we are on the right path. More importantly, it's a sign for me to trust more completely, and that this path is something good.

Chapter 3
Owls and the Lakehouse

A small UFO conference has been held at the end of each summer in Portland, Maine, an event called *Experiencers Speak*. Instead of the usual talk of conspiracy theories and flying saucer reports, it's focused entirely on the UFO experiencers, the people who've had direct contact.

I was one of the presenters in 2014 and spoke for one hour about my research. The talk was titled "Owls, Synchronicity and the UFO Abductee." My presentation seemed to resonate with the attendees because afterwards a lot of people took me aside and earnestly shared their personal owl experiences.

After the two-day conference, a rather large crew of speakers and attendees traveled about an hour's drive north of Portland to a quintessential New England cabin near a lake. The host and organizer of the conference, Audrey Starborn (a pseudonym), called this a soul family gathering, because pretty much everyone in attendance was an experiencer. The plan was nothing more than for everyone to hang out together for a few days. The cabin was too small to accommodate all the visitors, so the yard was packed with tents so close to each other that it was hard to walk between them.

A curious thing happened within the first few minutes of my arrival. I was on the grass near an elevated wooden deck off the back of the cabin where a bunch of the guests were hanging out together. I was standing below them when everybody suddenly cried out in a collective exclamation, as if they all said "Wow!" at the same time.

Seconds later, Audrey leaned over the edge of the deck holding a small fluffy feather. She looked down at me and said, "An owl feather just floated down and landed right between all of us!"

This occurred in full daylight, an odd time for an owl to be in flight, and no one saw any bird above them. They described watching the little feather drifting down from high above, floating in from the direction of the lake. The feather landed at the feet of a fellow named

Matt Moniz.

The day before, Matt sat with me at the conference and rattled off a long list of personal owl experiences. Some of these were close-up sightings that seemed to play out as harbingers of important changes in his life, including owls showing up right before UFO contact events. When the feather landed at Matt's feet, he said it was a totem of how he felt. He was sitting in among friends, all of whom shared the same kinds of experiences, and his gut reaction was, "This is right."

Everyone on the deck was giddy with excitement about this little feather. Audrey felt the owl spirit had announced the entrance of the owl guy. I need to add that I didn't really know if this was actually an owl feather. There was such an owl "buzz" from our time at the conference that maybe folks just assumed as much. I was caught up in the eagerness too, and I sure wanted it to be an owl feather.

I got a few close up pictures of the little feather. It was white fluffy down and about two inches long. I showed these photos to a few bird experts while researching this essay. They all said the same thing—they couldn't be sure, but they thought it was from a turkey. This was a part of Maine where wild turkeys were common.

It's funny that everyone, myself included, would be so eager to assume that little feather was from an owl. Later that night, a barred owl was heard less than ten yards from where that feather landed. Maybe our collective owl vibe had enough power to manifest a real owl.

The word turkey is slang for a fool, so maybe I was a "jive turkey" for wanting so badly to believe it was an owl feather. But as a totem, the turkey is seen as a good messenger, symbolizing abundance and blessings from Mother Earth. The North American Indian lore will often portray the turkey as an adversary to the owl. Many traditions see the owl as something sinister, a harbinger of doom, especially the plains and desert people of the South West. Yet most of the North Eastern tribes see the owl as a wise spirit guide, though its arrival might be to offer a warning.

Later in the day as sunset approached, Suzanne Chancellor took a photo of what seems to be an owl perched in a tall tree on a nearby island in the lake. She was quick to note that it was listed in her digital camera as photo number 1111. This number sequence, often seen on clocks as 11:11, seems to show up at highly charged moments for UFO abductees. It might be nothing at all, but it can also be taken as a sign of something mystical.[1]

Suzanne was with her partner Jack at the edge of the lake in a small open area when she took the photograph. This little beach was about fifty yards from the cabin along a narrow gravel road through a forest, and had a few lawn chairs and some canoes in the grass.

I arrived at the beach shortly after the owl flew off. Suzanne and Jack were both giddy as they told me how big the owl looked as it took off from the tree and flew across the lake toward a more distant island. Jack estimated that it had a five foot wingspan. I've heard this same excitement many times—owls have a sort of majesty, and people will react strongly when seeing one.

She showed me the photo on the back of her phone but there wasn't much to see, just a dark form in the tallest tree. The image was taken from a few hundred yards away and obviously showed a big bird, but like the little feather, I wasn't certain if what they saw was actually an owl. I asked Suzanne, and she feels strongly that she and Jack saw an owl. She's an experienced birder, so I trust her on this. And given the strange events that were to unfold at that site, it sure seems appropriate that an owl would want to make an appearance.

After sunset, most of the guests at the cabin sat together around a big fire in the center of the lawn near the back deck. Some of the more psychic attendees began announcing things like: They are nearby and I can feel them. It was about an hour before midnight when a handful of folks announced they wanted to "vector in" some sort of craft. This might sound strange, but this kind of thing is par for the course in a group of experiencers. Everyone in the circle around the fire took part in a series of intention rituals. This involved some simple visualization techniques, like imagining loving white light enveloping everyone. The request was for them to show themselves.

After they'd finished setting their intentions, most of the folks left the fire and made their way down to the lake. This was the night of a supermoon, the rare occurrence of a full moon at the closest point to the Earth in its elliptical orbit. The moonlight was spectacular, and the low fog on the lake glowed with an eerie beauty. It was cold, calm, and clear.

People at the lakeside began offering different manifestation rituals and encouraged the others to join in. I've got to say, it was pretty funny to be in a crew of UFO experiencers and psychics all vying to share their favorite ways to manifest ET grooviness. It was almost, but not quite, a kind of new-age one-upmanship.

The group was actively trying to call in ET spaceships. Some of the folks used the term CE-5, which stands for Close Encounter of the Fifth Kind, to describe what they were doing. These techniques have been used by Dr. Steven Greer since the early 90s as a way to foster communication between humans on the ground and extraterrestrial intelligence in the sky. In its simplest form, it's pretty much just setting a strong intention as a group. Over the decades, Dr. Greer has made plenty of claims that are hard to substantiate. Because of this, he is considered a questionable figure by many within the UFO research community. That said, I feel that focused intention can be a powerful thing, and I'm certain it gets results.

Some of the more psychic folks, mostly women, were pointing up to one specific area in the sky below the full moon on the opposite side of the lake. They said things like, "I sense they are right there." Others were quick to agree, that they were feeling the same thing. They all seemed entirely genuine, but their pleading had an urgency that made me feel quite uncomfortable. I am not sure why I felt that way—it was like the energy was too keyed up. I eventually left the beach and walked alone up the dark road, arriving back at the cabin at about 12:40 a.m. I had been away from the beach for no more than two minutes when I heard a loud collective exclamation from the gathering down at the lake. I ran back down and everyone told of a bright light "powering up" in the exact spot where the psychic ladies had been pointing. The whole group was giddy with excitement.

Everyone I spoke with described the bright flash in similar ways. A "pure white light" that brightened and dimmed again within about a second. Some said it was like the beacon from a lighthouse that slowly turns to face the viewer, flashing and then turning away. One person compared it to a flashbulb in an old camera. It was stationary, and for that moment it was far brighter than any star in the sky.

I stood with this group on the edge of the lake for perhaps twenty minutes after the big flash, hoping that something else would happen. It was about 1 a.m. when Audrey's sister Debbie announced that it was time to wrap things up, and we all headed back up to the lakehouse. I was impressed by the patience of this group. They'd been standing around that little beach in the cold for close to two hours, and their diligence was rewarded in the end.

Also at the lake house that night was disclosure lobbyist Stephen Bassett, one of the presenters from the conference. Although a dedicated advocate for UFO issues, he's one of the least "love and light" of anyone within the research community. Stephen was standing in the moonlight on that small beach along with everyone else. He seemed a little out of his element that night, with all the grooviness and feminine energy. He ended up walking back to the cabin just the minutes before the flash of light. So like myself, Stephen didn't see it either.

The following morning folks at the cabin were asking why it took so long before the little dot in the sky lit up. Stephen Bassett spoke up, "I think they were waiting for me to leave." They might have been waiting for *me* to leave.

The first thing I did when I got up the following morning was make my way to the coffee. I was told there would be a big thermos set up on the back deck, and I hadn't yet found a cup when I noticed a woman named Carol standing wide-eyed on the deck, frantic to talk with me. Even though it was still early, she'd already been up for a while, waiting to tell me about an owl event from the night before. Shaken with emotion, she described what had happened to her and her close friend Pamela.

The two women had attended the conference and were sharing a tent at the gathering that followed. They had walked back down to the lake sometime after one in the morning, well after the big group had seen the flash of light. The moon was full and the lake was calm and foggy, a beautiful setting to sit and talk. Pam sat on a flat rock at the water's edge and Carol sat on the grass next to her. Both of them have had a lifetime of strange experiences, including UFO events. They were alone on the beach to continue the plea for some sort of sighting. They sat and talked a little, but were mostly silent.

After what seemed like less than an hour, they checked the time only to realize it was now after four in the morning! Both their phones read 4:08 a.m.

Pamela exclaimed, "What the hell? No way have we been down here that long!" They were freaked out because it should've only been 2:30 a.m. at the latest. Somehow an hour and a half had vanished.

This was a cold night, especially down near the water, making it a hard place to truly relax. There was a kind of bone chilling dampness that should've made the time creep by slowly—not zip by quickly.

They tried to make sense of the time weirdness as they walked back up to the cabin. Both were well aware of the implications of missing time, and it scared them. It seemed that only minutes earlier the lakehouse had been loud and busy, full of people laughing around the fire. Now it was eerily silent.

The tent they were sharing for the night was set up in the middle of the yard in among a tight cluster of other tents. It was still dark when they unzipped the door and climbed in. When they set their heads on their pillows, Carol whispered to Pamela, "Before we go to sleep, let's ask the owl for a sign if we were really visited. Let's ask the owl to hoot for us."

Right as Carol spoke those words, there was an instantaneous owl hooting from somewhere in the woods. They both felt it was responding to them, validating their missing time experience. Then there was more hooting, this time it sounded closer, as if from a nearby tree. Everything went quiet for about 20 seconds, when they suddenly heard loud a set of booming calls directly above them. At the same moment, falling sticks and branches battered their tent. Carol said, "It startled me so much I felt numb." At that point, neither of them had any doubt that something had happened down by the lake.

Other folks were camping all around them, and the hooting was so loud it woke a bunch of them. Jack was jolted awake in the next tent over. He looked at his phone and the time read 4:20 a.m.

Later that morning, I sat with several people who had also heard the loud owl hooting the night before. I used my laptop to search out some recorded owl calls and they all agreed it matched the barred owl. They have one of the loudest calls of any North American owl. Their noisy squawking can sound more like a chimpanzee in the jungle than a bird in the Maine woods.

Jack found this loud owl hooting particularly personal. During the day leading up to this early morning owl event, he'd sensed the presence of his father. That afternoon he'd lamented, "I'm turning into my father." I sat with him while he explained that he was talking like his father, and even gesturing like him too. When the loud owl call woke him early that morning, the time of 4:20 was poignant. April 20 (4/20) was the day of his father's death, and he recognized that at the moment he looked at his phone. The owl echoed both missing time, as well as death.

One more interesting detail—Carol, Pam and Jack are all reiki masters. This is something I see so often in these kinds of stories that I've come to expect it.

This intertwined set of events presented itself with an owl as one of the key players. There is even a UFO in this story, even though it appeared as nothing more than a flash in the nighttime sky. The missing time event in conjunction with the loud hooting of an owl seems most prescient, but what does it mean? How do I, or any investigator, make sense of this mystical cloud of events? All I can do is document these stories. These mysteries seem to hang at the edge of reality, as if patiently waiting to reach out and intersect with our lives.

Chapter 4
Gypsy Woman and a White Owl

There is a curious harmony within the narratives of owls and death, it's not an exact play by play from one story to the next, but more a similar mood. It's this palpable feeling that repeats over and over in these accounts. In nearly all the world's mythic traditions, the owl is associated with death. It's a creature of the night, so this analogy is understandable. There are stories where an owl will show up, seemingly on cue, and its role as messenger is unmistakable. The story that follows was written by a great-grandmother right after it happened.

> Yesterday morning [Oct. 3], I woke with a start—didn't know why—just woke as if someone had shaken my shoulder or something. I sat up in bed and looked around trying to figure out what was going on... I was sitting on the edge of the bed and something out the window of my sun room door caught my eye.
> The property is covered in trees, but there's one tree at the end of the driveway that is, for all intents and purposes, dead. The limbs are always bare. I saw something in this tree, and whatever it was seemed really large. At first, I thought it was a helium balloon stuck on a limb, but it was probably as large as two or three of those balloons.
> I walked over to the window and saw that it was an owl, a very large white owl... It stayed there some time before flying off. So, all day, I've been puzzling about its message. I felt the message was ominous... I wondered who it was about, who it concerned.
> Fast-forward to this morning, October 4. I woke with a start and sat up in bed, just as I had done yesterday. Before I'm fully upright, my phone rang. It was my son, Stephen, calling to tell me he'd just gotten word that his ex-wife, Michelle, died this morning. She's the mother of my granddaughter Grace, who has three little ones, and is the same age as Stephen. She had been diagnosed with cancer some months ago but seemed to be doing as well as one would think after having had chemotherapy.
> Even though they've been divorced for a number of years, she and Stephen continued to stay in touch. And she stayed in touch with me, too, always updating me on things with Grace and her little ones.
> The other thing I find really interesting is that had the owl perched in any other tree, or even on a different branch on the tree he was in, I would not have been able to see him from my bed. One branch up or

down or to the side and he would not have been visible to me.

In all the years I've been here, I've never seen a white owl before... The only other owl experience I've had was when my brother died a number of years ago. The night I received the news of his death an owl came to a spot right outside my apartment. This owl stayed for a while, even coming around to the place I moved to later, and eventually disappeared and didn't return. [1]

This report was initially posted on October 9, 2013 in Synchro-Secrets, an online site dedicated to synchronicity run by husband and wife writing team Trish and Rob MacGregor. This story is mentioned on page 284 in *The Messengers*, an example of the ancient folklore of owls and death playing out in present day. I reached out to contact the author, and she patiently answered my questions. I asked what I usually ask; do you have psychic abilities, are you a creative type, have you ever had a NDE (near-death experience) and have you seen a UFO? I was wasn't too surprised that she answered yes to all of these questions.

She has been an active blogger under the pen name Gypsy Woman, and she sent me a set of personal essays. These were posted on her blog where, like me, she has been documenting her odd life experiences.

The stories that unfolded left me amazed, although at this point I should expect these kinds of esoteric connections. She described growing up in a family that was constantly traveling and moving for her father's job. During these car trips, her parents and siblings saw so many UFOs that it was perfectly normal to casually point them out in the sky. Most were seen at night, and often cigar shaped.

Gypsy Woman wrote about one dramatic event that took place in the late 1960s. It happened with her son and two daughters on a bus traveling a rural stretch of road in Louisiana, between Sterlington and Monroe. Her then six year old son was riding in the window seat next to her. She describes how he stood up and tugged her sleeve and pointed to a huge object pacing the bus.

> I remember being so startled that I closed my eyes and then reopened them to be sure I was really seeing what I knew I was seeing, and sure enough, the object was still there. The other passengers on that side of the bus were all looking at it and talking about it. I remember a lot of the passengers from across the aisle getting out of their seats and into the

aisle to see it better. By then, there was general commotion with passengers wanting off the bus, and passengers telling the driver to drive faster (which he did)... It was not high in the sky, but very low, well, low enough for us to see it out the window without straining to look upward. I cannot say how far away it was but I can say that it was close enough that the texturized surface of the body was visible.

She said it made absolutely no sound. It was definitely not a plane, there were no wings and no engines. She described it as at least the size of a football field, either oval or circular, with a domed top. There was a row of what appeared to be windows or lights encircling the bottom, the body of the object a matte grey akin to the color of a battleship. She clearly remembers a mottled texture to the surface of the craft, almost like an old cast iron pot.

There was absolutely NO doubt what this object was, let alone what it was not, it was daytime, the day was clear, there was no mistaking it... The UFO continued beside us for quite a distance, although I cannot say how far, but for more than just a few minutes, and then, just as suddenly as it had appeared beside us, it made a 45 degree turn to its right and upward and was totally out of sight just instantly... And still no sound.

She describes the bus driver trying to outrun the craft and how most of the passengers were hysterical. When the bus pulled into Monroe, they were greeted by news reporters at the station, an unusual detail in this era well before cell phones.

I remember wanting only to get my children and leave, to get away from it all. By then, I somehow felt extremely fearful about the experience, as if "they" were "looking for me," I don't mean that it was just a little feeling but an overwhelming one.

She had seen UFOs before, but for some reason this felt different. Her reaction was profound, literally wanting to flee with her children to a place where they couldn't be found. She took a taxi to her mother's house, and within minutes the phone began to ring with questions from reporters and the local police.

Several days later, several men dressed all in black (I kid you NOT) came knocking on the door to interview me, identifying themselves as being with Wright Patterson Air Force Base. I told them what I saw, they had me draw a diagram of the object, and I did, and they took it with them. I remember at least one of the men giving me a business card when I asked for it. I also remember that some time later, when I phoned the number on the card, there was no such number. I called Wright Patterson directly but no one had heard of the person for whom I asked.

Okay, something weird just happened as I was editing this post just now, the house phone rang (we don't use the house phone ever) and the incoming call was from Ohio. We don't know anyone in Ohio, have no business there, but the call was unidentified except for "Ohio." The only association I have with Ohio is that is where Wright Patterson Air Force Base is located. Weird. Oh, and when I answered, there was no one there, weirder. [2]

It's both weird and cliché, yet this kind of clandestine involvement is interwoven into the UFO mystery.

Here is another curious detail to this story—Gypsy Woman's father traveled constantly, and their family moved a lot, yet she never knew for certain what he did for work. All she was told was that he was a "purchasing agent" for the government, but he wasn't active military. She shared, "I can say that we kids knew that he could not tell our mother where or why he was going when he traveled without us, which was very frequently."

It was well understood by her mother that she could tell no one anything regarding her father's work. According to her sister, who remembers this event very clearly, their mother once, and only once, made the mistake of revealing something about their father.

Gypsy Woman said, "Something appeared in the news media and our father rushed home, demanding to know with whom our mother had discussed whatever it was that could not be discussed and was furious to learn that she had, in fact, divulged something to a friend. Then we moved again." [3]

This was from a man who would casually point to the sky and comment, "Oh, there's another flying cigar."

Like owls, UFOs have their own folklore. Within this mythology are endless claims of secret government involvement. It's common within UFO contact accounts to hear whispered hints that one (or both) of the parents of an abductee are involved with something secret. This might be easy to dismiss as paranoia, but most researchers hear this kind of thing a lot, enough to take these claims seriously. What this might imply is guesswork, but it points to something that leaves me unnerved.

Along with this and all the UFO sightings, Gypsy Woman had a near-death experience in 1966 at the age of 23. During surgery to remove gallstones, she heard someone in the operating room frantically exclaim, "She's going down, she's going down!"

> Then I began to rise out of my body (from my head) and was able to "see" everyone in the room, including me, the body of me, as I continued to move upward toward the ceiling. I remember looking down at me and feeling as if the "me of me" were being pulled away like a soft glove being slipped off... I knew that I was dead... I didn't want to be dead, I was young and had just begun my life with my children, I couldn't be dying!
>
> ... I began to feel surrounded by more white softness, a white softness that became an all-encompassing totally purely unadulterated whiteness of light, but this light had a seductiveness about it. It called me, it waited for me, I belonged there. I was still aware of the silver-gray cord from me to my body below, but I was slipping further and further away from my body below and soon gave into the "leaving." I realized then that the thing called "death" was not the end of anything, it was the beginning, there was nothing to fear, there existed only total peace and caring. Total peace.

She was giving in to this irresistible pull. The voices of long dead aunts, uncles and grandparents were summoning her. She approached a transition, a realm of pure white light, and a feeling of elation, joy, happiness and freedom—pure peace. Then she was again outside her body and above the heads of the doctors in the operating table. Sensing the doctors were bringing her back, she remembers feeling angry.

She wanted to go all the way, and completely surrender to the light. In that moment she heard a voice say, "But who will raise your children? No one but you can do that. You must go back!" Then she saw and heard the surgeons telling the staff not to take her to the recovery room, but to a room where her family could see her one last time. She explained:

> I followed my body in the bed down the hallway and into a private room where my family was. My in-laws had called in their own minister." She could plainly hear them making arrangements for her, and she was furious. "I knew that I was coming back—it was crystal clear to me—I was coming back to my children—no one else—NO ONE—was going to raise my children but ME—and then, in THAT moment, I surrendered back to my body.

She was unconscious for several days in the hospital, and when she finally regained consciousness her doctors said, "We almost lost you." She replied, "You did lose me, but I came back."

She explained what she'd seen and heard in the operating room, and her two doctors confirmed this was exactly what had happened. Neither of them had ever had a patient tell them anything like the experience she'd described. Her children are now grown, with children and grandchildren of their own. Gypsy Woman absolutely knows for a fact that these children were her destiny in this lifetime. [4]

It was because of her essay about seing that white owl out her bedroom window that I was introduced to Gypsy Woman. This was a sighting that foreshadowed the death of a close relative. This owl story takes place over two consecutive days, October 3 and 4 of 2013.

I have my own owl story which also takes place over the very same consecutive days, October 3 and 4, but of 2009. Although my experience doesn't involve death, it does include a wildly prophetic synchronicity with owls and a UFO. This kicked off a chaotic string of weirdness that hit me hard, and is the subject of the next chapter.

This other story also begins with a blog post about an owl on the Synchro-Secrets site, almost exactly four years earlier. Curiously, within that long list of comments was an account from Gypsy Woman. Here is what she said back in 2009:

> I'm reminded that when my brother died many years ago. On the night that I received word of his death, I went out onto my patio clutching a childhood picture of him—and as I stood there holding his image to my chest sobbing and crying out for him, across the drive, in a big pine tree, came an owl who sat there "talking" to me until I went inside—throughout the night, I heard the owl out my window—and for a very long time, I was never without the "voice" of the owl—for several years, actually, I was followed by an owl, even when I moved—and I lived in a city—there were times I asked other people to listen to be sure that I wasn't imagining it—but, sure enough, they heard it too—at some point, the owl or owls left me—but not for a very long time—I've always liked to think that it/they left only when my brother knew I was okay. [5]

These owl accounts match the folklore, both ancient and present day, from divergent traditions all around the globe. This same woman also talks about seeing multiple UFOs, including a close up daylight sighting and a visit from Men In Black. Add to that a profound near-death experience and a long list of psychic abilities. It's as if her lifetime of unusual experiences created an opening that morning for an owl to land on that bare branch. It could be that this owl was delivering a message, sad as it may have been, to someone with the life experiences that would allow her to receive it.

Chapter 5
Stacey, Owls and the Psychic

October of 2009 stands alone as the absolute height of my own synchro-mania. At that point in my life I was totally freaking out, it felt like the world was coming unraveled around me. I'm not exaggerating—it was grueling.

The story that follows was told on page 120 in *The Messengers*, and it defines my collision with this owl stuff. That version was whittled down to the bare minimum, and will be told in all its strange details here. This stuff got so weird that it might be hard to follow, and it was hard for me to write because every detail seemed so important. Some synchronicities can be life changers. The really good ones are all tangled within a web of other clues, as if each thread leads back to seemingly impossible connections.

The late summer of 2009 marked the peak of my owl sightings. I was coming unglued, and had been seeking out any kind of help in hopes of making sense of the baffling stuff going on around me. I played phone tag for over a month with a psychic medium in Los Angeles, trying to set up an appointment for a session. Her name is Marla Frees, and I felt drawn to contact her after listening to her conduct audio interviews on Whitley Strieber's website. She was often a guest host, focusing on psychic experiences.

Due to our conflicting schedules, we needed to book our one-hour psychic session over a month in advance, her first available time slot was Sunday, October 4 starting at 1 p.m. I had a good feeling about the whole thing, and was hopeful for some clues to help me understand the oppressive weirdness in my life.

On the morning of Saturday October 3, the day before the appointment with Marla, I was at my desk on the computer looking for anything relevant to my own experiences. I stumbled onto a site called *Synchronicity* (now re-named *Synchro-Secrets*), and one story caught my eye. This online post was the opening salvo for a cluster of strange events. Here's the post, titled "The Owl and the Money Clip." [1]

At the old place, Richard and his wife had lived with a single mother, an arrangement that worked great in some aspects, but also felt a little cramped, which tends to get worse during harsh Idaho winters. Both families had gone to look at a prospective larger house a few times. All four kids loved it, as did his wife and her single-mother friend. Richard wasn't so sure; his hesitation was understandable, as the new house cost more and he is the main breadwinner.

With the pressure on to decide soon, one evening Richard vociferously announced that he was "going fishing." He walked down to the river to spend some time alone and reflect. As the evening twilight progressed, an enormous owl swooped down over the water and dropped something shiny. Richard waded out to where the owl dropped the item and discovered an empty money clip. Examining it closer, he saw that the silver was emblazoned with his own initials!

Richard took the owl's message as a sign, which helped him, decide that his family would be better off in the end if they made the move...

This was exactly the kind of story that fascinated me, so I figured I would leave a comment, partially to share a link to my blog and my owl stories. I added a short reply, the thirteenth under that heading. Then I read down through the other comments and one of them caught my eye. A woman named Stacey wrote this:

> ... a couple years ago I had the privilege to spend time in a giant owls "nest" for lack of a better word, with over thirty barn and horned owls watching me... it was one of the most profound moments of my life!

Over thirty owls? Now this piqued my interest, especially since just a few days before I had posted a request on my site asking if anyone had experiences with lots of owls. So, it felt like I requested something, and got a wallop of a reply. Stacey's comment had a small picture next to it, clicking that sent me to her profile page. I clicked on her contact info and fired off a message. I wrote:

> Stacey, I gotta ask about that story. Here's why I'm asking. For reasons unknown, I have been awash in owls this summer (and in the last few years) and it's been really strange. I'll add that I have my own blog dedicated to my own paranormal and synchronistic events... I wrote about seeing a big crew of owls on my blog, and it's dedicated to synchronicity. I am intrigued!

Later that same day she replies:

> ...Owls are amazing and I have spent time with a few of them... LOL! I have just posted my story about the owls on my blog. Check it out... I'd love to hear your thoughts.

I went to her blog and read her story. It was originally a creative writing assignment, and she added it to her site after my owl comment. The text is written in a way that's overtly moody and mysterious. Here's a short excerpt:

> Above me, I heard a flutter. I looked up. A shadow flew. I felt I was being watched. I looked around for what it was. What was watching me? Then I saw it. A geisha faced owl staring down at me. We contemplated each other until another rustle distracted me. I slowly turned in a circle staring up into the canopy of trees, bearing witness to several owls camouflaged in the leaves keeping a watchful eye. There were too many to count. I had stumbled upon a holy shrine and I was the initiate.

Beyond what is written above, the story was filled with lots of mythic imagery, some real and some metaphorical. Things like a black beetle, an altar, divine guidance, a holy shrine, a friend named Christian, the longing for a first kiss, and a baptism in mysticism. Okay—now I'm really intrigued! Here's the final line of Stacey's short essay:

> It is said that owls are guardians of the afterlife and their nocturnal nature is a symbol of inner knowing. People are often called to their power animals because they share a mutual energy. With the doors of perception opened, perhaps I had been brought to the owls as a reminder of my intuitive powers and to be shown I was already riding the wave, I had just lost sight of it. [2]

Immediately, I added a comment to her blog. I wrote:

> Stacey, you said you saw a lot of owls in one spot. My request ... Please, tell me more. For some reason, my life has been inundated with owls lately. I can't quite understand it. There is something SO mystical about an owl, that I can't help but try and see the event as some sort of premonition—or divine message. I'll also add, there is a scary alien abduction movie (due out soon) that features a lot of owls in the trailer, followed up with, "Those aren't owls!" (The Fourth Kind).

Within minutes, I got this directly in my email inbox:

> Hi Mike ... Later that night Christian and I saw a "UFO"... I left that part of the story out ... I can't believe your comment ... that is hilarious! Maybe they are connected!

Up to this point the only hint about UFOs in our correspondence was my reference to the movie *The Fourth Kind*. I reply instantaneously:

> What?!?!? You saw a UFO the same night as the OWLS????? Okay, my blog is all about my UFO experiences! And the owls are intertwined with my experiences... Just so you know, this has been EXACTLY the kind of stuff that has been happening to me. Especially this funny email meeting. Now, you kinda need to fill me in on the UFO sighting (Pleeeeease), this is really interesting.

Then Stacey replied, "So funny! You are so surprised and excited, I love it. Nothing shocks me. I believe in EVERYTHING."

She explained that she'd already written about the UFO sighting, it was at the end of the essay that began with her and Christian seeing all the owls. She hadn't included the part about seeing the UFO when the story had been posted it online, only sharing the part about the owls. The UFO details were left out because she felt the readers of her blog weren't ready for that, but she included the missing ending in the next email to me. Here's an excerpt from her essay:

> We were back on the two-way highway when I saw what looked like a streetlight up ahead but as we approached it, I realized the light wasn't attached to anything and then it flew over our heads.
> "It landed back there," Christian said as his head snapped back around and his eyes lit up like he had just seen a ghost.
> "What was it?"
> "I don't know."
> "Do you want to stop?"
> "Yeah."
> I stopped the car and backed into a vacant lot that was used for selling produce during the harvest season. It was pitch black and we were out in the middle of nowhere surrounded by olive groves. As we got out of the car Christian asked, "If they want to take us would you go?"
> "Yes, as long as time stood still," I said not sure if it were true.
> We walked down the middle of the two-lane highway cloaked in darkness when we heard a loud rumble like a semi-truck heading straight for us. We looked at each and ran for our lives back to the car. As I opened my car door whatever-it-was flew over our heads and then vanished into thin air.
> We got back in the car and drove away, gazing out into the night sky where it had been. We were silent, not knowing what we had just seen and thinking it was too fantastical to be named. Naming it, owned it and

we weren't ready to own it. As we got back on the Interstate Five, Christian put his hand on my shoulder. It felt familiar like it had been there my entire life. I felt supported and loved beyond a first kiss like we had been married for years. Christian fell asleep and I wondered how many dragons he'd slain that day.

That essay, now read in completion, certainly got my attention. At the bottom of the email, Stacey added this cryptic little aside: "So funny, I thought I was abducted the other night...it happens all the time."

This seemed like a playful line written in jest, but still. This was happening right when I first sensed that owls and UFOs were somehow connected. Now I just had read an essay where these two elements were clearly linked. Beyond owls and UFOs, there was so much mythic detail in what she had written, dragons slain, harvest season and time standing still. But it was what Stacey told me next that really blew my mind.

> My friend Marla (who interviews for Whitley Strieber on Unknown Country) has great stories to tell ... she's tapped in.

What? She just mentioned the psychic who I would be having a session with—the next day. I reply:

> Okay - this is getting strange... I am going to have a phone session with Marla Frees tomorrow! And you bring her up in this email!

To say I was astonished would be an understatement. I was suddenly dragged under, drowning in synchronicity. I went on to write:

> ... I wanna ask more about the UFO event, but email is a funny forum for that... I'm having such intense deja vu that I am not sure what I'm trying to say. Did you ever post that text about Christian putting his hand on your shoulder anywhere on the net? I feel like I've read it before...

At this point I'm wigging out, the cryptic power of what was happening was too much for me to handle. I was right on the edge of what I could endure. Taking it in stride, Stacey responds:

> That is great. You are going to love Marla. My friend Christian is a great guy who is also on the leading edge of all this stuff. How strange we have met through here... and that you're speaking with Marla tomorrow.

The entire day was swept up in a frenetic email exchange with Stacey. Beyond the Marla thing, there was a long list of other mythic plot points that fascinated me: owls, UFOs, abduction, and the overt religious symbolism in her essay.

My appointment with Marla was scheduled for 1:00 p.m. the following day. The phone rang at around 10:30 that morning. It was Marla, and she sounded angry.

She said, "I just got a call from Stacey saying she had met my one o'clock appointment. What is going on!"

This took me by surprise. It seemed like she'd assumed I'd been trying to snoop or something by contacting Stacey behind her back. I tried to explain that yesterday was a weird mess of synchronicities, and I was baffled by what it might mean. It took some time, but Marla realized I wasn't snooping and that something else was at play.

She sternly told me, "Okay, but something weird is happening here. You need to come to this session with an open heart chakra!" That wasn't a suggestion—it was an order.

My head was spinning after we hung up and I wasn't really sure what to do. I just sat on my couch, closed my eyes and repeated "open heart chakra" over and over for a few minutes.

At some point a little bit before noon the phone rang. It was Marla again and she sounded agitated, "I can't stand this, we are starting right now!"

She explained that something weird was happening, and it was making her all crazy. She had just finished one of the worst psychic sessions of her life, and she implied it was my fault. She said she gave this guy a reading, but it wasn't for him, everything that came through was about me. She had to stop in the middle and reschedule it.

Our session wasn't for another hour, but from how she sounded, it seemed like she was about to burst. Marla said the information was insistent and she needed to talk to me right then. I didn't know what to think, so I said okay let's start. She took a deep breath and began talking in a slow steady cadence. This was a big change from her frazzled voice just seconds before. It took a moment, but I realized she was now fully in her psychic mode. Then suddenly she was crying. All I could do was sit there and listen. She explained that something was terribly wrong, and I needed to take these experiences very, very seriously.

I wish I had recorded this session, all I can clearly remember was that the intensity of it was overwhelming. I have a single piece of paper with notes from that hour, but reviewing that page all these years later doesn't fill me in on much. The one thing that stands out on that page was something she said and I wrote down: *You are here for profound reasons*.

What started on a Saturday morning with me commenting on a blog post about owls ended on a Sunday afternoon with a crying psychic. I was both freaked out and amazed.

Later that night I talked on the phone with Stacey. I think we were both a little stunned at the whirlwind of what had been happening. About a half hour into our call there was a click on the line and Stacey said she needed to take the other call.

She called me back after about 15 minutes later and asked me if I knew who'd interrupted our call. I said it was Marla and I was right. We talked for more than a few hours, but she never told me what Marla had said. We spoke again the next day, and Stacey hinted about what Marla had told her when our call had been interrupted the night before. Marla had implied that something important was going to happen to Stacey in October, and I was somehow connected.

This flurry of synchronicities with Stacey and Marla could never have unfolded like it did without the internet. Cyberspace seems to have its own mystical powers, as if there is a global expanse of electronic brain neurons running everywhere; in the air, into space and even into our own consciousness. It's as if we've gotten entangled in a new form of synaptic fiber, allowing for a deeper web of synchronistic happenings. I wrote about it in my blog the next day, and so did Stacey. [3] [4]

Another curious similarity is the romantic subtext to both Stacey's owl story and my initial owl experience in October of 2006. Stacey writes about a "first kiss" that doesn't happen with a fellow named Christian in the owl story posted on her blog. I wrote about a very similar longing with a young woman named Kristen in my very first owl posting on my blog. I mean, Christian and Kristen, these are similar names, right? Each story is about seeing multiple owls in the company of one other friend—two mystical stories paired with a theme of an unrequited yearning. I didn't actually write anything about a first kiss, but the implications were right there in the text.

This was where I first started paying attention to people with some variation of the name Chris, and how they seem to show up so often in these owl stories. [5]

Stacey and I met later that same month. I was attending a two-day conference hosted by Whitley Strieber at a retreat center in the dusty town of Joshua Tree, California (while there, an owl crossed my path). Stacey lived in Hollywood, so after the conference was finished I drove the few hours to meet her.

I went to her apartment where she lived with her 9-year old son. She made dinner and we all ate together. Later, we all sat on the floor and played Go Fish. Her son repeatedly called me John, and each time Stacey would correct him, "No, this isn't John, this is Mike."

When it came time to leave, I stood at the door and said, "Listen, I realize this had the build up of a first date or something. I just want you to know that I don't feel anything romantic here, but at the same time, something is going on. I feel like I need to play detective and try to figure out what it might be."

She understood exactly what I meant. We hugged and I left. As I walked to my car, I was struck by how much this all felt like a movie, the whole strange drama with this scene actually taking place in Hollywood. I thought to myself, if this were a movie, I would be playing the role of the gay next door neighbor who comes over once a week for dinner.

The next morning, I emailed those very thoughts to her, and she wrote back: "LOL! That's John!"

About a month after returning from California I had another psychic session, this time with a woman named Anya Briggs. I was desperate for any insight into why these things were happening. I asked her about all the weirdness surrounding Stacey, and without skipping a beat she explained that she and I had lived a charmed life as brother and sister in a past life in 19th century Paris. I was flamboyantly gay and Stacey was my confidant, and I would escort her to parties in the high society social scene of that bygone era. Anya made it very clear that I was, "quite a dandy and wore ascots with particular flair." Now there is no way of knowing if this really happened, but on some level it just felt right, something about it was oddly familiar. When I told Stacey about this psychic reading, and our lives as siblings, she laughed and agreed—that's what it felt like to her as well.

It was almost a year later when I sat alone at the microphone and tried to document how intensely weird October 2009 had been for me. That month was without question, the most bizarre and oppressive thing I'd ever endured. This podcast was my attempt to make sense of all the meaningful stuff that happened during that month. I also interviewed Stacey, Marla and Anya, including them in the final audio document. It took me a few days to record and edit my thoughts, and I had multiple owl sightings (where they crossed my path) during this process. [6]

A funny synchronicity in the audio time counter emerged during my long winded verbal essay. I need to begin by saying that the numbers 123 and 1234 have been plaguing me, showing up at odd synchronistic moments. But I really pay attention when the numbers 12345 show up. When I finalized this almost two hour long audio file, I checked the time count numbers to see if there were any clues at 12345. It's very strange that I would check these numbers at all, and doing it was a sort of unconscious reflex.

The digital MP3 player on my computer counts up on one end, and counts down on the other. That means the number 1:23:45 shows up two times on the counter. And at both points it lines up perfectly to the funny story about me feeling like I was Stacey's gay neighbor! This story gets told twice—once by me, and again during a recorded conversation with Stacey about our meeting in October. And both times, forwards and backwards, it lines up exactly to that curious number, right when I quote Stacey's email where she wrote: "LOL, that's John!" [7]

During one of my conversations with Stacey, I asked the big question, "Do you think you are an abductee?" She was very clear in her answer, she is not, yet she made the playful comment that she thought she had been "...abducted the other night...it happens all the time." These were her exact words from our initial day of emails. She rejected having abduction experiences, but she's no stranger to powerful synchronicities—and this one detail implies a lot. I see her as a seeker, in the best sense of the word.

When I met Stacey she'd had a successful career with a major movie studio in Los Angeles, yet she left all that security to follow her dreams. She is now acting as a life coach, spending time with clients and horses as a way to foster a trust in one's own intuition. Like so many others, there was a major change in the direction of her life, and she is now working to help people.

Like Stacey, Marla also left a successful career in Hollywood to start a new life helping people. I've spoken with Marla many times over the years, and sought her out for two psychic medium sessions after each of my parents died. She's been very supportive during my times of confusion over the UFO issue, and how it had consumed my life. She is well aware of the subtleties and challenges that come with this type of contact. She speaks with a sort of insider's knowledge, so I asked if she'd had any experiences.

Marla speaks straight. She told me that her mother was terribly abusive, and believes her psychic abilities had been fostered out of that trauma. She spoke about her childhood, "I prayed to be rescued by someone or something, even aliens in a spaceship. Since that didn't happen, I had to intuit ways to survive."

Marla then told me about an event in Sedona Arizona in 1997. She was with another gifted psychic, James Van Praagh, and they were taken out into the cold desert night to watch for UFOs. They were driven in a van as part of a tour, their destination was Boynton Canyon, a spot just outside of Sedona known for UFO sightings.

At that point in her life, Marla wasn't interested in sightseeing for UFOs. She was skeptical of the whole thing, to her it just seemed ridiculous. James chided her, "Marla, you thought talking to dead people was nuts until you started doing it." She admitted he had a point.

When they got out of the van, they were all alone in the desert looking up looking up at the stars. They passed around a Russian night vision scope that allowed them to see the heavens above with an eerie clarity.

She said, "Nothing could have prepared me for what I saw when I lifted up my little telescope. Behind the puff of a cloud the object sat motionless. It appeared to be a dome top with a saucer-like bottom. It looked exactly like objects I had heard so many people describe. There it was and I was witness to it." [8]

The first thing Marla did was try to rub off any thing on the lens that might have created that image. When she looked through the telescope again, the craft had flipped on its side and it was now aimed so she could see its bottom. She announced to the other sky watchers, "It's mooning me!"

Marla was looking at a hovering lifesaver shaped object, and her distinct feeling was that it wanted her to see it. Her next memory is sitting at a bar in Sedona. Years later she connected again with James Van Praagh and asked what he remembered of that night. He said the same thing, they were all out in the cold looking up at the starry sky, and then they were at the bar without any memory of how they got there.

I asked what she thought might have happened, and she was clear with her answer, "I had contact."

What she saw that night was a lifesaver, and it's hard not to see that as symbolic.

Both Stacey and Marla have played a role in my life, and perhaps in previous lives as well. It's as if October 2009 was a kind of reverberating distress signal. During that feverish month, I'd lost any ability to make sense of what was happening. I was on the verge of crumbling. It seems as if the scriptwriters of reality sent these women into my life, they arrived to help me.

Chapter 6
Kenneth Arnold and the
Dawn of the Modern UFO Era

The dawn of the modern UFO era can be traced back to June 24, 1947, the day Kenneth Arnold saw something unusual in the sky while flying alone in his private plane. Although his wasn't the first sighting of its kind, it was the one that exploded onto the national stage, ushering in the flying saucer craze that forever changed the popular consciousness.

And here's something delightful—Kenneth Arnold had a pet owl!

Arnold's daughter Kim was driving at night with her older sister when they saw a young owl that had fallen from its nest. The little bird had an eye injury, so they took it to a veterinarian. Afterwards they brought it home, and Kim put ointment on its eye each day for weeks until it recovered. Kim's father built a beautiful cage for the wounded bird. It was a great horned owl, one of the largest species of owls in North America. As it grew it got stronger and more difficult to deal with. Eventually it became so large that it felt dangerous to handle, so they ended up donating the adult owl to the local zoo in Boise, Idaho.

Looking back, Kim says she thought it was quite incredible her father would allow her to keep such a wild creature, much less build a cage for it. She described his handiwork as a reflection of his loving character; the cage was magnificent.

Kenneth Arnold unwittingly coined the term flying saucer in 1947. He radioed a report from the cockpit to the tower that he'd seen nine silvery objects flying at tremendous speeds while piloting his small plane near Mount Rainier in the state of Washington. The airport staff contacted the local papers, so there were eager newsmen waiting when he landed. He described what he saw to these reporters, "they flew erratic, like a saucer if you skip it across the water." The iconic words flying saucer ended up in the headlines, and from that moment on Arnold became a reluctant celebrity.

Curiously, he did not report seeing anything shaped like a

saucer—what he saw was a chevron or crescent shaped craft, and his description of their motion made the term flying saucer the catchphrase for the entire phenomenon. What seems peculiar is that in the follow up media circus and public hysteria, flying saucers are exactly what people around the world began to see.

Kenneth Arnold was the perfect UFO witness. He was, by all accounts, honest, trustworthy, and entirely believable. He had nothing to gain and everything to lose by coming forward with what he'd seen. In an era where the cowboy was our national icon, Arnold's home was a ranch in the dusty plains of Idaho. If a Hollywood director needed someone to play the part of a stoic citizen in a western town, casting Kenneth Arnold would be the perfect choice.

He had a follow up sighting just one month later on July 29 1947, over La Grande Oregon. This involved a cluster of about 25 small brass colored craft seen while flying his plane. There was another UFO sighting in 1952, again from his plane. He saw two distinct craft flying below him, one was "as solid as a Chevrolet," and the other was semi-transparent like a jellyfish. He could look down on it from above and see the pine trees on the ground through the center of the object. [1]

Here's what he said to Look Magazine in a special edition about UFOs:

> The impression I had held after observing these strange objects a second time was that they were something alive rather than machines—a living organism of some type that apparently has the ability to change its density similar to fish that are found in our oceans without losing their apparent identity. [2]

Arnold was changed by what he'd seen. No longer satisfied with the prosaic stance of the time, he was opened up to some of the more esoteric ideas about UFOs. This was a bold stance in an era dominated by nuts and bolts ideology. He wrote about his beliefs in the November 1962 issue of *Flying Saucers*:

> After some 14 years of extensive research, it is my conclusion that the so-called unidentified flying objects that have been seen in our atmosphere are not spaceships from another planet at all, but are groups and masses of living organisms that are as much a part of our atmosphere and space as the life we find in the depths of the oceans The only major difference in the space and atmospheric organisms are they have the natural ability

to change their density at will. (3)

Arnold experienced something very strange during his initial sighting over Mount Rainier—he felt as if these craft had interacted with his consciousness. He never hinted about this psychic aspect at the time of the event, but he eventually spoke about it with journalist and researcher Bob Pratt. What follows in an excerpt from that 1978 interview:

> I think that this (the June 24, 1947 sighting) was the first indication that... there was some intelligence somewhere that was able to read my mind. I think other pilots have felt the same way about it... It was a rather frightening experience due to the fact that when you actually felt inside that somehow your mind was being controlled or being read in some way by some unknown entities that were apparently making use of it. It didn't really make any sense.(4)

Telepathic communication is consistently reported by UFO witnesses and abductees, but mind control in relation to UFOs was unknown at that time. It's understandable that Arnold would hold back on this psychic aspect back in 1947. His story was already difficult to comprehend, and declaring his "mind was being controlled" by UFOs would never have been believed. It was over thirty years later that he finally spoke about it during an interview. Over the decades he'd talked to a lot of other pilots who had seen UFOs, and he implied that many of them had also experienced direct mental telepathy.

This level headed man wasn't just seeing things flying in the sky, his life was plagued with even more strangeness.

At the time of his 1947 sighting, Arnold had been searching for the wreckage of a large military transport aircraft. It had crashed the previous January on the glaciated flanks of Mount Rainier—presumably killing all thirty-two Marines aboard.

Arnold had his famous sighting on June 24, 1947, the crashed aircraft was found on July 24 and the memorial for the dead Marines was held on August 24. Three interconnected events, each separated by exactly one month. This numerical coincidence took on a special meaning for Arnold. What began as a fascination with these types of synchronicities eventually became an obsession. He also claimed that the crashed transport aircraft was found on Mount Rainier essentially intact, but with the entire crew missing. He describes it as an irrational mystery:

> [When the search team] reached the fuselage, the fuselage was almost intact and all the luggage of everyone was still aboard, and their parachutes had never been used. But he said there was no blood, no bones and there were no bodies! ... I just thought it was a very unusual thing and there was no way they could say [the thirty-two Marines] walked off from it.

This plays out with an eerie similarity to the *Mary Celeste*, a British ship found empty of its crew in 1872. Arnold questioned the meaning of his role in these events, along with his UFO sightings, and it frustrated him. He initially expected some explanation, but none ever emerged. [5]

The 1947 Maury Island incident was a UFO account every bit as important as Kenneth Arnold's sighting. This event took place on June 21, just three days before his sighting at Mount Rainier and less than 50 miles away.

Multiple witnesses saw a doughnut shaped craft supposedly eject molten aluminum, some of which was collected by witnesses at the site. Some researchers contend this was all an elaborate hoax, but there are details too bizarre to dismiss. Arnold became involved in this event when he was hired by Ray Palmer, editor of the pulp magazine *Fate*, to play the role of investigative reporter. Arnold soon found himself entangled in a perplexing cloak and dagger mystery with a cast of nefarious players, and yet another military plane crash.

On August 1, 1947, two officers died when their B-25 crashed, supposedly carrying the mysterious residue from the Maury Island UFO. Both officers had met with Arnold in the hours before the crash, and the news of their deaths disturbed him greatly. [6]

Two days later on August 3, Arnold's own plane crashed. He wrote: "I reached an altitude which I would judge was around fifty feet. My engine stopped cold. It was as if every piston had been frozen solid. It never even gave a dying bark. To take off and have an engine stop at that low altitude is probably the most dangerous thing that can happen in an airplane."

His plane hit hard at the end of the runway, but he managed to land it on all three points. He was unhurt, but shaken. Shortly after, he found what caused his engine to stop—the fuel valve was shut off.

Arnold wrote:

> I knew instantly there was only one person who could have shut that fuel valve off—and that was myself." He speculated that he could have been influenced by some form of mind control and this caused him to shut off the fuel valve before the flight. [7]

Arnold met the very mysterious Fred Crisman as part of his Maury Island investigation, who claimed to have witnessed UFOs the day after the initial sighting. Crisman was later subpoenaed by New Orleans District Attorney Jim Garrison during his investigation of the JFK assassination. He was Garrison's key suspect for the trigger man on the grassy knoll. [8] [9]

Some of the unusual aspects of Arnold's 1947 sighting impacted him deeply. He described a pulsating light emanating from the surface of each of the nine silvery craft, and he felt this matched the rhythmic beating of the human heart. This blue white light was so bright that it lit up the interior of his cockpit, even though the objects were many miles away. He was cautious about what he said at the time, but the power of what he saw influenced his core beliefs.

Arnold's daughter Kim said that after his 1947 sighting, "He spent the rest of his life standing by his story. He had a devout belief in God, and he felt that he had these experiences for a divine purpose." She also said, "My dad believed they were alive, they were not mechanical craft in any way shape or form." [10]

Kim has recently shared something that had long been a family secret. Shortly after the 1947 sighting, a glowing ball of light appeared in Arnold's home. It was first seen by one of their daughters in her room, then it floated down the hall and appeared in his own bedroom. Arnold was so frightened that he fell to his knees and began reciting the Lord's Prayer. [11]

This wasn't his first experience of seeing a glowing orb. As a boy of seven, he and other witnesses had seen a globe of light in the room where the body of his deceased grandmother was lying in state. [12]

Kim Arnold spoke about how the beliefs of her father had been affected by his experiences, "Near the end of his life... he believed it was possible that the flying saucers were the connection between the living and the dead." She said his sightings changed his view of dying, that death wasn't an end and that we lived on. [13]

In 1981, UFO journalist Gregory Long visited 66 year old Arnold at his Idaho home to conduct an interview. As a way to express his exasperation with the narrow views of most researchers, Arnold handed Long a copy of *The Complete Works of Charles Fort* and said, "I was astounded when I read Fort's books. There were similarities between what I'd investigated and what Fort had collected."

Publishing four books between 1919 and 1932, Charles Fort chronicled a wide range of extremely bizarre and unexplained phenomena including odd things seen in the sky. Fort's books are dense reading, and his conclusions are well outside the conservative norms of both his time, and ours.

Long wrote:

> As Arnold spoke, he revealed an unyielding, critical attitude toward science that ignores, ridicules, or attempts to rationalize away the "damned," Fort's term for anomalous data that do not fit established scientific views. This attitude is readily understandable given the treatment he has received at the hands of the press and the skeptics. [14]

That Arnold would not only read, but identify with an author like Fort says a lot about his outlook not just on UFOs, but how it overlaps with other paranormal phenomena.

Well known as a trustworthy man, Arnold was often approached by both military and commercial pilots. These men would share UFO sightings that they couldn't tell anyone else for fear of being grounded. These testimonies allowed him an insight into firsthand details few researchers would have heard. He also had military intelligence come to his home with high quality photographs of odd craft in the sky, asking if they matched what he'd seen. He also felt strongly that he was being watched by the government, his mail was being read and his phone was tapped.

Upwards of 10,000 letters arrived at Arnold's home, many of them from UFO witnesses. His sudden fame made him the go-to person in this new domain. In the early days of his sighting, two military intelligence officers visited his home and looked through the letters. They were particularly interested in anything from from religious groups and organizations. He was told the government was aware of the dangers of pious fervor, and they didn't want anything like that to well up around the burgeoning UFO hysteria.

Arnold said, "Governments are more afraid than anything else of Joan of Arcs, religious saints, or phenomena that cause their self-destruction."

There was a real concern of a mass panic overtaking the country. Arnold felt it was this fear that shaped the official stance on UFOs. [15] [16]

After his 1947 sighting, Arnold was interviewed often. He wrote a book, appeared in documentaries, and spoke publicly about his experiences. Before a presentation in Boise, he was approached by a team of military men. They spoke in threatening tones, telling him to stop talking publicly about his experiences. The presentation was suddenly canceled and no one told him why. This was followed by a friend from town driving him out into a lonely spot in the Idaho desert. This man then expressed the seriousness of that threat, including a cryptic remark that these men have killed their own to keep things secret. [17]

Shanelle Schanz, granddaughter of Arnold, felt that these shady run ins created deep misgivings of the powers-that-be. As a young girl she remembers her grandfather telling her, "Never trust the government." [18]

Arnold was by every account, an honest and decent man who never sought the attention thrust upon him, but there is so much more to his life's story. His experiences are like a mirror, reflecting the bizarre challenges within the overall phenomenon. What happened to him goes well beyond that initial event in 1947, admitting he'd had eight UFO sightings which to me seems astounding.

His story is a checklist of the same kind of high strangeness that is consistently reported by abductees. There is no way to know if Arnold ever had this kind of direct contact, all one can do is look at the long list of telling events that have invaded his life.

He described that some UFOs could read his mind, and that he and his family had seen a floating orb in their home. He also claimed his phone was tapped, and was threatened by the military to keep quiet about what he knew. This is standard stuff straight out of abduction literature.

Here is another curious addition to Arnold's life. It seems that his wife had psychic skills along with the capability to tap into past lives, her own as well as others. His daughter Kim said of her mother, "...she had abilities of mental telepathy, and that kind of perplexed the family..." [19]

Kim's daughter Shanelle said, "My grandmother... was somewhat of a psychic medium and telepathic, and they both believed in reincarnation."[20]

So, reincarnation and telepathy were talked about openly in Kenneth Arnold's home.

By the end of his life, Arnold came to see these experiences as something spiritual. As stated earlier, he was convinced that his many UFO sightings had happened for a reason, and that he'd been chosen for some divine purpose. All these mysterious incidents were transformational, changing his perception of reality. He was fascinated with synchronicities, especially number patterns. He believed the UFOs were alive, and that the phenomenon represented a connection between the living and the dead. He also felt strongly that he'd been at the receiving end of mind control from both the UFOs as well as government secret keepers! This is bold stuff, going well beyond what conservative UFO researchers, past or present, would dare whisper.

The strange experiences and spiritual beliefs of Kenneth Arnold are eerily similar to what many UFO abductees report, enough that one has to wonder if he really was chosen for a divine purpose. Perhaps he was meant to play an important role for these elusive beings—all this and a pet owl too!

Chapter 7
The Alan Caviness Report

UFO Investigator Alan Caviness was confronted with a cluster of reports that played out with a sort of illogical zeal. They all seemed to be connected in some way, but the why and the how of it is an unsolved riddle. There is a highly abridged version of these accounts in *The Messengers*.[1] What follows is a much more complete narrative of the same story.

Alan posted a very thorough pair of reports on his website describing these anomalous events. The initial incident involved Alan himself, putting him at the center of the story. I should add that he's had his own direct experiences with UFOs, and all the high strangeness that accompanies it. The first incident took place along a quiet residential road at approximately 6:35 on the evening of Tuesday November 12, 2002. This event and the others that followed all took place near the southern edge of High Point, a city in central North Carolina. [2] [3]

Alan was returning home from shopping with a 14-year old girl in the passenger seat, the daughter of a close lifelong friend. It was dark, and as the car crested a relatively shallow hill he saw a gray barn owl with a white breast in the beam of his headlights. It was standing perfectly still about 18 inches from the shoulder of the paved two-lane road. The owl squarely faced his car, and seemed to be looking directly at him. He used the word penetrating to describe the intensity of its glossy black eyes. With barely enough time to react, he swerved to avoid hitting it.

Alan had slowed down to just a few miles per hour as he passed the owl, and it didn't even flinch. The girl didn't see anything because she was digging through her purse the entire time. He stopped the car about 100 feet past the owl at the very bottom of the hill. Then he turned in his seat, looked through the back window and saw the owl frozen like a statue in the same spot. A few seconds later, it leaned awkwardly to one side and pivoted around like a penguin to face the woods at the edge of the road. Then the owl was motionless again, locked in an eerie pose. When he turned forward, he realized his passenger was still preoccupied with her purse.

Alan was immediately aware that seeing an owl might imply an abduction event. He had read enough UFO reports describing screen memories to know this was an unsettling possibility. An alien encounter might have just taken place, with the event erased from his memory and the image of an owl projected into his mind.[4]

His first thought was to get out of the car to see if the owl was actually real, but was worried he couldn't guarantee the safety of the girl in the passenger seat, so he drove to his home. Alan lived just around the corner (about 250 yards) from where the owl stood. When he got home, he checked the clock and saw no indication of missing time. About an hour later he left his apartment, got back in his car and drove past the site, but there was no sign of the owl.

He couldn't shake the feeling that this owl had been waiting for his car. He'd lived in the immediate area for over 50 years, and had never once seen an owl anywhere in the region. The bird he saw was big, but not unusually large, and it seemed to be in a kind of stupor, or trance. Yes, it was just an owl on the side of the road, but something just didn't add up.

From the moment Alan saw that owl alongside the road, he sensed this was somehow related to a long string of other strange experiences. He'd gone through several years of heightened paranormal events, and these all seemed to trace back to his initial UFO field investigations in 2000.

Alan recognized that the girl in the passenger seat appeared to act strangely during the event. She was focused on her purse as if it were the most important thing in the world. She began to compulsively dig through its contents in the moments before Alan saw the owl. Upon first seeing it he exclaimed for her to look up, but she continued searching for something. He even yelled at her, but she still refused to look up. After passing the owl and looking back behind the car, she remained oddly preoccupied with her purse and never saw the owl.

He returned the next day and walked the area taking daylight photographs. It was a large neighborhood with many houses nearby, yet where the owl had been standing was the only heavily wooded area in the vicinity. There was still one thing he just couldn't shake—the owl simply didn't look like it belonged in the spot where he saw it. Curiously, Alan never saw it leave the road.

He had tried to come up with other explanations, even considering that the owl might have escaped from a zoo, but the closest one was over 25 miles away. He even ventured into the woods about a hundred feet from the road and found an open field large enough to land a craft.

Alan is a competent researcher, and treated this owl sighting as if it were a UFO investigation. He returned to the site at the same time the next evening, parking at the bottom of the hill in the exact same spot he'd stopped before. He clearly remembered looking back at the owl through the rear window of his car the previous night and watching it make that odd pivoting turn.

Alan was suddenly confronted with a problem. It was nighttime, and without any streetlight nearby it would have been impossible for him to have looked back and seen the owl from that spot. He knew what he had seen, but it was simply too dark for the memory to be real, even with reverse and rear brake lights on. Something didn't make sense.

He was all too aware that his owl sighting played out like a typical screen memory, but if this had been an image projected into his consciousness it was eerily perfect. He couldn't know with any certainty, yet at that moment he felt that he'd probably experienced some kind of encounter with an alien being. This was terribly unnerving, and he knew he would need a lot more evidence before he could accept that conclusion.

Alan wrote a summary of the event, carefully noting all the details and abnormalities. That he would go to such lengths after seeing nothing more than an owl might seem like paranoia, but this wasn't the end of the story.

The UFO and the deer

Several days after Alan's owl experience, his lifelong friend Carson, a former police officer of many years and fellow investigator, dropped by to tell him about a local UFO sighting. His friend Jane (a pseudonym) had recently witnessed something unusual from her driveway.

This event took place at around 10:30 p.m., right as Jane arrived home from her second shift job at the local hospital in High Point. When she turned onto her driveway, she saw a relatively small light dancing and darting in the sky in the distance, just above the trees behind her house. The sighting only lasted a brief moment so there was no way to estimate its size or distance, but what she saw was enough to leave her astonished. She was delighted to see something so strange, and felt justified in calling it a UFO.

Although this had been her only sighting of this kind, Jane described feeling a connection to otherworldly happenings. She had felt this way her entire life, yet couldn't explain why. Months before her sighting, she'd told Carson that she wished one day she could see a UFO.

These elusive feelings can be tricky to pin down, yet it matches the emotional state commonly reported by abductees. This can be described as a feeling of urgency or as a powerful sense of mission, yet the source of these emotions is unknown.

Things got stranger when Carson told Alan the date of Jane's UFO sighting: it happened on the night of Tuesday, November 12. Alan looked at his friend with surprise—that was the very same night as his owl encounter.

There's more. After wrapping up their report on Jane's UFO sighting, Alan invited Carson on another investigation. They met with a woman named Peggy (a pseudonym) who also lived in High Point.

Alan found out about Peggy through her twin boys who'd occasionally worked with him at a nearby factory. The twins knew about his research and suggested that he should interview their mother, telling him she'd had a lifetime of strange experiences. Alan also recognized her last name was Native American, and that got his attention. He'd long suspected that these paranormal events might play out with a heightened frequency within that lineage.

Approximately two weeks after the owl and UFO incidents, Alan and Carson met with Peggy in her old neighborhood, known as the Allen Jay community of High Point (interestingly, an area with the same first name as Alan). They were at her former home to discuss an event that happened there back in the early 1980s, approximately twenty years earlier.

Peggy told them what she remembered. The event began in the middle of the night when she woke up feeling extremely thirsty. She got out of bed and walked to the kitchen to get a glass of water. While standing at the sink, she was astonished to see something huge outside the window in the night sky.

She described a large, dark, round hovering craft, which from her vantage point took up most of the sky. There were multicolored lights blinking in sequence around the rim, with colorful sparks and flares darting away from the craft.

She suddenly felt compelled to go to another window overlooking the other side of her property. Easing the curtains back, she was shocked to see a group of humanoid beings. There were between fifteen and twenty of them, all slowly walking in the same direction across her property. They were all similar, no more than five feet tall, skinny, with long arms—the nearest was no more than thirty feet from her window. Some of them wiggled their long fingers across the tips of the tall weeds, seemingly fascinated by what they were touching.

Peggy was terrified. Her immediate concern was for her twin baby boys asleep in their room. Right then, one of the beings closest to her suddenly stopped, turned and looked straight at her with large dark penetrating eyes. She sank to her knees in horror. After a few moments, she gathered her composure enough to rise and peek out the window, and was relieved to see the yard outside was empty. She stared in disbelief. At that moment, a giant blue electric flash rose up from a transmitter tower in the distance. Alan asked if this memory could have somehow been a dream, and her reply was resolute—she was certain it was not.

Peggy was no stranger to paranormal happenings, although this was her first clearly recognizable UFO related event. She went on to describe other strange incidents throughout her life; some seemed like they might be UFO related, and others were more akin to supernatural events.

It was during the interview on her old property that Alan decided to mention the unusual owl sighting he'd had just a couple of weeks earlier. But just as he began, Peggy interrupted and eagerly began telling a story of an odd experience involving a deer.

She told Alan and Carson that it had happened recently while driving home at night from her second shift job on a rural road on the outskirts of High Point. A few miles from her house she noticed a deer running alongside her car; it was a big buck with huge antlers, staring straight at her while galloping on the shoulder of the road, side-by-side with the driver's window.

When Alan asked her how fast she was going, she replied about 45 or 55 miles per hour, which was the posted speed limit for that stretch of road. The deer remained right beside her car for about a mile. She wasn't scared, just stunned because the deer was staring at her, their eyes locked the entire time she drove.

She slowed down and sped up to see what the deer would do, and it slowed down and sped up, accordingly. Finally, about a mile from her home, she came to a complete stop. The deer stopped too, and continued to stare at her for what seemed like a half-minute more. Then it turned suddenly, jumped a ditch, and ran into the woods. It was obvious to Alan and Carson that something wasn't right about her account.

Carson asked Peggy if she remembered the date of this incident with the deer. She thought for a moment, then said it was the night of Tuesday, November 12. Alan and Carson both did a double-take—this was the same night as both Alan's owl encounter and Jane's UFO sighting; like Jane's case, it happened sometime around 10:30 p.m. while she was driving home from her second shift job.

Here's where it gets even more bizarre. Both women work at the same hospital, but didn't know each other; Jane, a switchboard operator and Peggy, a nurse. The deer incident happened within minutes of the UFO sighting in Jane's driveway, and only four hours after Alan's owl incident. The UFO sighting occurred a little less than four miles to the west of the owl sighting, and the running deer was seen on a road just over four miles further west. All three events formed a tidy line running from east to west on a map, and all three witnesses were in a car during their sighting.

Stories from the Messengers

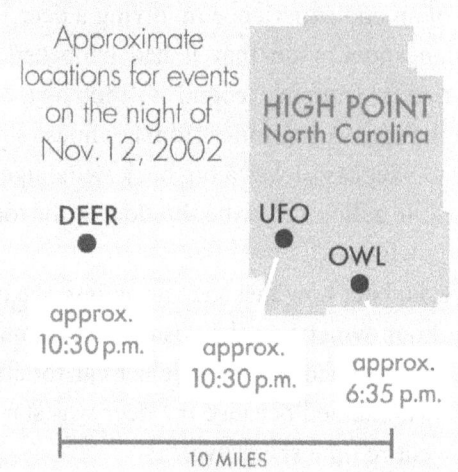

The owl and deer events each seem to play out like screen memories. Both Alan and Peggy had prior UFO sightings and other strange experiences. Jane had said it was her only sighting of a UFO, but she implied a deep lifelong connection to something otherworldly. Alan has a strong conviction that all three of these events are connected. He also knows that each witness from that night, himself included, could very well have been abducted without having any memory of what happened.

Carson knew Jane who saw the UFO from her driveway, and Alan knew Peggy who'd seen the deer. Alan feels that all these divergent elements ended up in his lap in a way that seemed significant. These details felt orchestrated, as if someone wanted him to play the role of detective and carefully piece together all these clues. But to what end? A mystery presented itself, yet nothing has been solved.

Sightings on Main Street

Carson had been friends with Alan since they were in elementary school together, and he's had his own curious sightings just a few miles away from High Point. The first event happened early on a Sunday morning while in his patrol car in the late 1980s when he was a police Sergeant. "My lieutenant was off that night and I had the shift and town to myself."

Carson was heading towards the station, driving at 'patrol speed,'

7: The Alan Caviness Report

about fifteen miles per hour. He drove parallel with a double set of railroad tracks running through town.

> I was almost at the intersection where the tracks cross over the street and as I approached, some movement off to the right caught my eye. I stopped the patrol car and observed what I can only describe as a plastic bag, or something similar, just a few feet above the tracks.

It was moving slowly in a perfect straight line, no side to side movement or up and down movement. It appeared to be the size of a large rectangular shaped pillow. The object had a silvery-gray appearance, like frost or fog, but he couldn't see through it.

He parked and jumped from the patrol car without calling his dispatcher. "I got on the tracks and ran several yards in its direction, when it suddenly stopped and slowly started to come towards me. I drew my service weapon and pointed it at the object, flipping off the safety as I took aim. The object stopped, then began moving away from me at a faster pace." Carson thought, "What's the matter with me, you can't shoot a balloon floating down the tracks! It's Sunday morning and I would just shoot right through it, sending a bullet flying downtown."

He holstered his pistol and started running towards this object once more. "I ran across the overpass and when I was on the other side, that's when I got the surprise of my life. The object suddenly lifted off the ground and was climbing at an angle away from me."

"I stood looking up in the sky as it got to perhaps a thousand feet, rough guess. Then, right in front of my eyes, I watched it change shapes." It was no longer a balloon, it was now a silver colored saucer shaped object. It was bright colored with a distinct ring-edge around it. He didn't see any lights or hear any engine noise.

He said, "This thing shot upwards at a speed I can't describe, moving away and becoming smaller. I watched for what probably was a matter of seconds, although it seemed longer. I don't know if it flew out of sight, or simply vanished before my eyes."

He smiled and thought to himself, "Well now you've finally seen one, and they are real." As he walked back to his patrol car, he noticed there were no vehicles or people on the streets. It was eerily quiet, even for a Sunday morning.

Carson had another sighting at exactly the same location over a decade later. This happened on clear, cold and windy Christmas Day. Same intersection, different object. He was alone in his car waiting at a red light right where the tracks cross over the street. He said, "Since that earlier incident I never pass there without giving the area a good once over."

After the light changed he saw, "something falling-spinning in the air. It appeared to be the shape and size of the hood of a car. It was a flat black color, no shine or brightness at all. The object looked like it fell by the street just to my right, close to where it intersects with Main Street."

He turned down that street expecting to find whatever this object was, but saw nothing. He said, "As I drove slowly down the street looking on both sides, I looked up and saw this craft climbing up in the air. It wasn't high, maybe several hundred feet. The object seemed to be metallic, rigid as far as I could tell, but on each side it appeared to have something flexible, similar to the flaps or ailerons on aircraft wings. This object would turn and spin, flip over and move sideways. There was no doubt, whatever it was, this was in a 'controlled' movement."

He watched its strange movements as it gained altitude.

"It would suddenly fall, then turn and spin, stopping in mid-air to turn or climb higher. I drove for a mile or two watching this thing, then parked and got out of my car and stood watching it until it went out of sight... I observed it for ten to fifteen minutes." It disappeared in the direction of Alan's home area, not far from the strange owl and deer sightings.

More owls

Alan was well aware that owl and deer are often reported as screen memories, but why an owl in one sighting, and a deer in the other? Is there some deeper reason why these two different iconic animals arrived for these two different people on that same night?

About two months after investigating this owl-deer-UFO trifecta, Alan spoke to a local psychiatrist, a friend he knew well and trusted. He shared an odd owl story with Alan, it was reported to him by one

7: The Alan Caviness Report

of his female patients.

The patient told him that while recently driving down a road in High Point, she kept noticing a big owl in a tree not too far off the highway. It was perched on a limb and staring at her. When the psychiatrist asked how long this had lasted, she said it continued for quite a while.

When he asked her how big the owl was, she confidently told him at least waist-high. The psychiatrist knew that was pretty much impossible—even the largest owl in the world couldn't be that big. Then he asked her if it seemed odd that she could continue to look at this owl on the same tree limb for "quite a while," even though she was driving down a road the entire time. She hadn't thought about this and she was suddenly confused. Yes, it was odd, but she insisted this is exactly how she remembered the incident. He didn't press her for more information. Although he was friends with Alan, a UFO investigator, the psychiatrist had never heard of anything like this.

A short while later the psychiatrist talked to another patient, also a woman, who mentioned that she had recently been followed by a big owl over a long period of time. She told the psychiatrist it was puzzling, but not scary. She wondered if, for some unknown reason, she might be experiencing hallucinations.

This woman also described what she had been seeing as far too large for any normal owl. It would just stare at her, seemingly very interested yet without showing any fear. She would see what seemed to be the same owl at different times and locations. She could never quite remember it arriving or leaving, just that it was there, staring at her. She recognized that this was very odd. Neither of these women mentioned UFOs.

The two women who reported their odd owl experiences to the psychiatrist did not know each other, yet out of all the psychiatrists in the area, both felt compelled to consult him when their unusual occurrences began. Also of significance, Alan had already told the psychiatrist months earlier not to be surprised if he ever gets abductee patients telling him weird stories about owls or deer. He mentioned this well before these women shared their unusual stories.

Alan made it a point to interview the psychiatrist at length, and it didn't take long to find out that this man had two UFO sightings earlier in his life. He described an unmistakable metallic craft of unknown origin seen at close range, both times with multiple witnesses. As an aside, it is exceedingly rare for anyone to see close-up UFOs, let alone twice. A little alarm should go off in the mind of any investigator—the implication is an unremembered abduction event.

Alan had complete trust in his friend; this psychiatrist was a highly trained professional with over 20 years in the U.S. Army as a medical field officer. He hadn't thought about either of these incidents in a long time, until Alan pressed him with questions.

One has to ask if all the players in this drama were UFO abductees. Alan has been open about his own contact experiences, but what about everyone else? Considering what they'd described, it certainly seems like most of them could fit into the role of an abductee, but is that even possible? The two women who'd both had odd events on the same night as Alan's owl sighting, the psychiatrist who saw close up UFOs, and his two patients who both saw unusual owls—could they all be abductees?

This story began with Alan seeing an owl on the side of the road, which on the surface seems pretty mundane. He could have dismissed it as nothing at all, but right from the onset he treated this owl sighting with the rigor of a UFO investigation. If it were a screen memory, it would seem to imply a hidden abduction event at the hands of forgotten aliens. This took place during a time in Alan's life when he was in the midst of frequent UFO-related events. These had been occurring for the previous three years, and would continue on for several more years.

Perhaps what Alan saw was nothing more than a normal owl standing alongside that dark road back in 2002. Yet it connects so cleanly with two other very strange reports, lining up both in time and their position on a map. If it were a real owl, its arrival at that moment seems to imply a sort of announcement to Alan. It's as if this mythic bird was there to give notice that a mysterious set of events were about to present themselves.

Was the owl something symbolic? Did it manifest for Alan to convey a deeper meaning? Seeing this owl might be more the province of a shaman, like a totem animal in a vision quest. Alan had the strong impression that the owl had been waiting for him. It presented itself to a UFO investigator, wanting to be seen, and this implies something even more complex.

I had been in close contact with Alan while working on this chapter, and during our correspondence he told me something I've come to expect.

He sent me an email telling me about an incident that took place in the follow up to some of our previous correspondence. Alan made mention of a message I had sent him two years earlier in 2014. He wrote: "Well, just 13 days later, I was approaching the same hill near my apartment where I had the original owl encounter." At that point we had not emailed each other in a very long time.

Alan was driving sometime between three and four in the morning, and just as he was about to arrive home, a big owl dropped down and landed squarely in front of him on the road. It immediately turned and looked into his headlights. He said, "It was as if the owl did not know why it had landed right in front of an approaching car that was plainly visible. Animals do not generally make blunders of this sort."

The owl seemed like it suddenly realized it shouldn't be there. It was quite animated, flying straight up in the air to get out of the way.

Alan wrote, "I continued on but immediately thought of how recent it had been that I had talked to you, Mike…"

The city of High Point, North Carolina had a cluster of unusual events in 2002, and there seems to be a tangled thread connecting all these elusive experiences. It's Alan's strong sense that these sightings, synchronicities and potential screen memories were all orchestrated to coincide for some unknown reason. His role as investigator was peppered with clues that found their way to him in ways far beyond mere coincidence, yet he is more than just an investigator—he is also an experiencer.

It's hard to find any significance in this jumble of strangeness. On the surface level, it all seems absurd. It's as if someone had carefully directed this odd drama from beyond the veil, but it's a performance without any meaning. Perhaps this was the intention, to create a deeper story that might bypass the rational mind. Reflecting back on those events from over a decade ago, Alan said, "I think it was all for me, possibly to encourage me to keep doing what I'm doing."

Something out there is attempting to get our attention, and it's imperative that we don't ignore these stories, no matter how bizarre. The message might be impossible to fully understand, but it won't serve us to look away.

Chapter 8
Owls and Drones

Owls and their connection to UFOs was the focus of a two-hour long interview on a radio show in March of 2014. I was the guest, and spoke about my research as well as my own experiences. This was a live interview, and along with the producer and host, there was a woman monitoring the online chat-room. Her name is Cindy Bailey Dove, and she contacted me right after the show concluded. She sent an email telling me she'd seen UFOs, as well as having some unusual owls sightings. We exchanged phone numbers and were speaking within minutes.

She's a young grandmother who's lived her entire life in Little Rock, Arkansas, and along with that came a delightful southern accent. She'd never heard about a connection between owls and UFOs, and was extremely curious about what I had discussed during the show. Cindy had helped produce a great many audio interviews for this radio network, but this was the first and only time she'd ever actually reached out and called one of the guests. She told me she'd had a lot of odd events stretching back to her childhood, and that the owl experiences were something new. What had been happening with the owls seemed to be part of a much larger web of UFO and orb sightings, along with paranormal ongoings.

The first story she shared was of a big owl swooping down out of the trees and passing directly in front of her, something she'd never experienced before. This happened in her backyard in full daylight just two days before we spoke. She felt that hearing me talking about owls and UFOs had been foreshadowed by that event.

She then told me about the first time she'd ever seen an owl. This happened at her home in August of 2011. She stepped out her back door and onto the porch to walk a friend to his car. It was dark as they made their way down the driveway, when something caught her eye in the shadows between her and her neighbor's house. What she saw seemed impossibly strange—a creature with wings of almost human sized proportions. It took a moment to realize what she was seeing was a very large owl, standing motionless on a garbage can with its wings outstretched.

They both cautiously approached this owl in the dark, and it stayed frozen in that eerie pose. Cindy got "uncomfortably close" to it, within about five feet, and it remained motionless the whole time holding its wings wide out to each side. She said its torso was as wide as a man's chest, which is absurdly large for even the largest owl.

They both talked to each other while standing within reach of the owl, but it never flew away. Cindy sensed that something was wrong, but her friend dismissed it as nothing at all, saying it was just some sick owl. After a moment they backed away, and she walked her friend out to the street where his car was parked. After saying goodbye, she walked back to the porch and passed close to the motionless owl. She kept walking, calmly entered her house and dismissed the whole thing as if nothing was out of the ordinary.

But Cindy knew something was wrong—the owl's size and behavior just seemed so bizarre. Her initial thought upon first seeing the big silhouette in the dim light, was that it was some sort of winged man. She actually thought it might be the Mothman. There was a wave of sightings over the entire year of 1967, where multiple witnesses reported seeing a winged phantom in the skies above Point Pleasant, West Virginia. This is an infamous case in paranormal history, and despite associated UFO reports, it sounds more like some sort of interloping demon than an alien from another planet.

Cindy drove home the next afternoon, and right as she turned into the driveway a large owl swooped in front of her car, almost hitting her windshield. Her first thought was that this was the same owl she'd seen the night before—it even seemed like it had just flown off the same trash can. She'd lived in this neighborhood of Little Rock her entire life without ever seeing an owl, and now she'd seen two.

These back-to-back owl sightings kicked off an intense string of unnerving events. She woke up a few days later with an obsessive drive to learn everything she could about UFOs and the paranormal. She started buying and reading stacks of UFO books, and spent endless hours online doing research on the subject. It was during this frenetic period that she felt the need to join the Mutual UFO Network (MUFON).

About a month later, she stepped onto the porch to let her dog out, something she did every evening around eight o'clock. She was facing north, and without knowing why, she turned completely around to the south.

She was shocked to see two glowing orbs floating above her driveway, right above where she had seen the big owl on the trash can. The orange orbs moved in perfect unison as if connected by an invisible bar, and were the size and shape of small car tires.

They were an eerie amber orange, a color so intense that she needed to carefully explain what she saw. "If you let a fire burn down to hot glowing coals, then put a frosted glass globe around these luminous embers," this was as close as she could get in her description, yet even though they were a dazzling radiant orange, no light would emanate from the floating spheres. This is commonly reported, that some orbs can be extremely bright, yet they don't illuminate anything around them.

"These orbs moved like nothing on earth that is flying." Cindy struggled to describe how strange they seemed, "They don't disturb the environment at all. It's like they are a part of the air. No wind, no light shining out, no sound. It's very hard to explain."

As she watched those floating orbs, all the dogs in the neighborhood suddenly started barking, including her own. She said, "I didn't want them to leave. I don't remember any other feelings but excitement and joy. No fear."

Right around this same time frame, she woke up in the middle of the night completely turned around, with her head at the foot of the bed. Even more disturbing, she was tucked in like a mother would tuck in a child. Her arms were straight at her side, and her legs were together with the blankets pushed in tightly all around the edges under her entire body with only her head sticking out. She was baffled, because there was absolutely no way she could have ever tucked herself in like that.

Some mornings she would find unusual scratches on her body. She slept alone, and was certain they weren't there the night before.

Although she doesn't remember anything happening, all these odd events suggest something took place during those nights. The source of all this strangeness seems to have the power to erase any memory of their interactions, leaving the experiencer with nothing more than a sense of unease. Any abduction researcher would be familiar with these clues and their implications. She and her family were also seeing orbs in her house, and it scared them.

It was during this time of heightened paranormal activity when Cindy's daughter drove through a neighborhood well outside of Little Rock, and without knowing why, she turned down a street she had never been before. She noticed a for sale by owner sign on the lawn of a nice house, and immediately called her mother. Cindy had been wanting to move to a more rural setting for years, but a wall of financial obstacles made it seemingly impossible.

Cindy called the number on the sign and asked a few questions. Without any planning on her part, the buying process fell into place with an exactness that baffled both her and her family. From that point on, everything seemed weirdly fast-tracked, and she was suddenly all set up to buy the house. The officer at the title company pointed out something she had never seen before, that the paperwork was written in such a way that the bank was paying all the fees. When Cindy asked about it she was told, "Don't look a gift horse in the mouth." She pressed with a lot of questions, but could never get a straight answer from anyone at the bank or title company.

The previous owner had the house on the market for two weeks, yet the only call he'd received was from Cindy. After all the papers were signed, he was suddenly hit with a flurry of calls offering nearly double what she'd paid, but at that point it was a done deal, and she was moving in.

She said, "Something in the universe wanted me in that house."

The Drones

Cindy began hearing owls right after moving, and she's heard hooting nearly every night for years. This detail got my attention, but here's something else—and it happened on the very first night in her new home. While in her yard, she watched two miniature helicopters

8: Owls and Drones

floating slowly down her street. These were about half the size of a normal helicopter, and abnormally quiet. Her first thought was that one of her neighbors must have some expensive toys, and she ran towards them for better look. She got close enough to realize that whatever these were—they weren't toys.

The next night the same little helicopters returned, and she made note of their line of travel. A quick look at Google maps shows a small airport in that direction, barely a quarter mile from her house.

Since moving into her new home, Cindy has been seeing a lot of unusual objects from her yard, and this has continued for years. These sightings include weird floating orbs, black helicopters and triangle craft. She also witnessed a small airplane hovering above her street, yet it wasn't flying in a way she could comprehend. Instead, it simply sat in perfect stillness no more than 30 feet in front of her. These objects are almost always seen at night and fly with an eerie silence, a common description of both UFOs and owls.

After all of Cindy's unusual experiences, it would be easy to jump to the conclusion that what she's been seeing are UFOs piloted by aliens from beyond earth, but their source may be much closer to home. Cindy is convinced she's been seeing man-made drones.

All these sightings created an obsession, and she began researching drones with a feverish urgency. The subject became the focus of her life, and this commitment has taken her from witness to expert. She's spoken to hundreds of witnesses of both UFOs and drones, conducted interviews with civilian contractors and military personnel, posted hours of video on Youtube, and hosted an online radio show called The Drone Report.[1]

There are aspects to what she's found in her research that match what she's seen from her yard. One example is the near total silence of these craft. In 2012, the Intelligence Advanced Research Projects Agency (IARPA) announced it had been working to develop a new class of quiet unmanned aircraft, aptly named the Great Horned Owl project. It's generally assumed that if capabilities of this sort are acknowledged publicly, it's likely they've already been in use for a long time.[2]

The specifics on how drone technologies are contracted and

developed has been central to Cindy's research. Looking at what's available in the public record, it's obvious that a massive amount of money has been pumped into drone development. The researchers trying to peer into these unseen programs are hinting that well over half the money involved is allocated to security. This means the actual research and design is left wanting. If money is the measure of value, then the secret is more important than the technology.

The cutting-edge drone technologies might appear so strange, that pretty much any witness would assume they were seeing something—well, alien. There's a longstanding contention that the government got its hands on a crashed flying saucer in the desert outside Roswell back in 1947. If that really happened, you'd expect the last seven decades would have been spent trying to figure out how it works. It's easy to imagine a super secret team of well funded technicians busily working to back engineer this alien hardware. It might be that some drones mimic the unusual flight characteristics of UFOs, because that's their source.

I can imagine a high tech little helicopter coming off an engineer's drawing board, but what about the weird glowing orbs—are they ours, or theirs? Perhaps the drone technologies came from nothing more than a lot of money and brainpower, and not from a recovered UFO. I have no idea what the truth might be, but I'm certain the secret keepers would want to manage the perception to their advantage. There are rumors that imply these technologies trace back to reverse engineered alien hardware, but this could be false information used to purposely muddy the waters.

Advanced drones are now mirroring UFOs to the point where it's difficult to untangle which is which, and even the $39 drones from the toy store float around with an eerie smoothness. Cindy is attempting to separate the genuine unknowns from the man-made technologies that are now dotting our skies. She's examined the UFO reporting databases, and has found more UFO sightings in states with documented military drone research and activity.

Cindy is convinced that the majority of what are now being reported as UFOs, are man made drones. She's been vocal with her conclusions, and this stance has put her at odds with many in the mainstream UFO

8: Owls and Drones

research community. There can be a religious zeal within this pool of enthusiasts, and it seems a lot of them don't want to hear what she has to say.

If people are seeing drones and assuming they are UFOs, then maybe the secret keepers would want to feed those fires. Better to have UFO enthusiasts looking to Zeta Reticuli as the source of these sightings, and ignore engineers at Lockheed Martin. Using the UFO community would be a perfect way to muddle any genuine investigation. We should expect a staff of "Mirage Men" to sidetrack the research by carefully seeding juicy tidbits of disinformation.

Walter Bosley is an author of both fiction and nonfiction, and his work explores some extremely arcane ideas. He shies away from UFOs, but digs deep into the esoteric and occult. He also served for over five years as a special agent in the Air Force Office of Special Investigations. I sought him out to ask what the higher ups might think of Cindy's outspoken drone research.

From his time in the Air Force, his initial thought was that they might be allowing her to speak openly "as a way to gauge the public reaction." They stand aside, watch what happens, then monitor the collective perceptions. My first thought was that the perception is pretty close to zero. It's sad to say, but for the most part no one is paying any attention. There's an awareness that drones are being used by the military, but on the whole the public seems uninterested, and this includes UFO researchers.

I told Walter what Cindy had shared about the small airfield near her home, and this piqued his interest. She said that Reynolds Metals had mined bauxite on that site for over 70 years, and this work left huge underground caverns. She said, "There are offices with beds and showers below this area. I know all this because my dad worked out there for thirty years."

Locals used to recreate on this land, but hunting and four-wheeling ended in 2007 when razor wire fences went up around the property. Cindy said, "Every time I go out to this airport, guys in white trucks are on me in seconds."

This small airport is surrounded by granite quarries and forest. Cindy's neighborhood is to the west, the only residential area bordering the site. There's one street that leads onto the property with just a small mobile home as the office. It closes everyday at 4 o'clock and, there are no lights on at night.

Hearing this, Walter speculated that there might be a non-governmental operation staging out of the site. Secret drone work run by a private firm would give the military a bit of distance and deniability should Cindy begin to get noticed by a larger audience. Better that a UFO researching grandmother with a southern accent is playing the role of drone whistleblower instead of a seasoned reporter at the *New York Times*.

There have been too many odd events in Cindy's life to dismiss them all as coincidence. The implication is that she's been moved like a pawn on a chessboard, set in position in a new house to see advanced flying technologies from her own yard. But who did it, and why? Could her personal obsession with drones have been influenced by an outside source? My research is awash with examples of events and behaviours seemingly orchestrated by an unknown force. Given all of Cindy's experiences, this might be exactly what has happened.

Ultimately we must ask, who is interacting with Cindy: the UFO occupants, or elements hidden within our government? The next question would be, are the drones spying on Cindy, or is she spying on the drones? Or is it both?

Perhaps the powers-that-be are genuinely curious about her, and simply want to better understand this mystery. A lot of experiencers claim they're being monitored by the government. In these studies, paranoid stories of tapped phones and tampered mail are par for the course. Maybe someone is using the latest gadgets to snoop on a UFO experiencer, and instead of an unmarked van parked down the block, there's a silent drone listening just above her house.

The more bizarre thought is that she was put there to do exactly what she's doing, reporting on the drones. I just can't ignore all the implications of direct UFO contact (not to mention the owls) in the lead up to her move. There is a sense that she was somehow chosen to play this role, to speak out about an issue clouded in deception. Is there something important enough about these drones that an alien intelligence would need to create a whistleblower?

I asked Cindy if her move to the new location near the airport, and her obsessive drone research, might tie into the owls and orbs events from 2011. Without any hesitation she said, "It sure feels that way."

She told me that accounts and details of this research have simply dropped into her lap, and the chain of synchronicities has left her astonished. This is something I understand, because the core of my owl research feels as if it materialized out of a similar cloud of synchro-weirdness. Whatever is going on, I get the sense it must be happening for a reason. What that reason might be is where it gets murky.

High Strangeness

During our long phone conversations, we spoke about more than just her drone research. Cindy described events and experiences that leave me baffled. These stories paint a picture of something much more complex than just seeing some orbs and a few owls. She told me, "The best word to use is high strangeness, because that's exactly what it is."

Cindy has been terrified of the dark since childhood. As a ten year old, she told her mother there were people looking in at her through her bedroom windows at night. She still suffers from a deep fear of being in a house after sunset, and looking out a window into the darkness. To this day, she still feels like she'll have a panic attack if a window isn't covered at night by tightly closed curtains.

Cindy's father lives with her in her new home, the site of all the drone activity, and he shares her fear of windows at night. Like his daughter, his bedroom windows are completely covered with aluminum foil taped to the glass and hidden behind heavy curtains.

These irrational fears have followed Cindy throughout her life. As a young adult, she sought the help of psychiatrists in hopes of finding some relief from these fears. Doctors performed a series of MRIs on her brain, and all the results were normal.

These fears made Cindy stop dead in her tracks the first time she saw the cover of Whitley Strieber's *Communion*. She had walked into a bookstore and was confronted with the image of a gray alien with its big black eyes—and it shook her to her core. There was an overwhelming sensation of knowledge, as if she'd suddenly remembered something profoundly important.

She sounded frustrated as she said, "I knew it was there—the memories were right there—I could almost get it, but I just couldn't bring it up."

It was 1987 when she saw that cover, but I could hear the emotion in her voice as she struggled to describe the intensity of an event thirty years earlier. In the end, all she could say was, "It changed my life."

This is nearly word for word what I've heard countless times from experiencers. The cover of that book has played a powerful role in this strange phenomenon. Those big black eyes have been a collective trigger, sending an electric jolt through a vast number of people. If alien visitors are arranging things as part of some grand plan, then one can assume they would want to orchestrate events for maximum impact. Both the hardcover and paperback edition of *Communion* reached the number one position on *The New York Times* bestseller list for nonfiction, with over two million copies sold. The image on the cover of that book produced a new archetype, as recognizable as Ronald McDonald or Santa Claus. Was that image a seed, purposely planted to someday yield a harvest?

There's something that occasionally shows up within this research that I recognize as a clear pattern, and I pay close attention when it does. I'll have long conversations with people, listening carefully as they share their experiences. There is a first set of surface stories, and sometimes it feels like they're on auto-pilot, telling things they've told many times before. At some point, and this might be after weeks of correspondence, they'll cautiously share more. These follow up stories dip below the surface into murkier waters, and each account seems to get progressively weirder. Collecting more information doesn't make the mystery any easier to solve, it only gets more confusing.

Cindy told me a lot, more than could fit into this chapter. What she shared seems to define the strangeness that pervades this subject. Here is a story that might seem vague, but it personifies the challenges of this mystery.

She had just walked out of a Walmart and was nearing her car, when suddenly nothing felt right. The normally busy parking lot was now eerily quiet, there were no people, and no sounds. She was standing in front of what should have been her car, but something was different—it wasn't her car. She was scared, and thought to herself, "I'm not getting in that car."

Nothing seemed right. The cars, the storefront—it all looked different. She thought she might be having a stroke. There was sudden sensation of *snap!* Then everything was back to normal, she was hearing ordinary sounds and saw people walking around. Her car was hers again, and when she got inside all she could do was sit shaking in the driver's seat. Something terribly distressing had happened, and she was swallowed up in waves of fear.

This story seems meaningless, and any nuts and bolts researcher would probably dismiss it outright. But this is the kind of strange experience people are sharing with me. It makes no sense, but it's precisely what I've been hearing.

Here is another baffling event that unfolded while Cindy was visiting her daughter's house. She was in the bedroom when she heard her daughter yell from the living room, "Stop it!" Cindy jumped up and ran to see what was happening. The room was somehow filled with little flashing orbs of light, and her daughter was terrified. The lights were too bright to look at directly, and could only be perceived by looking away and seeing their shadows. In that instant, the walls were covered in round shadows about the size of tennis balls. These dots of light seemed to all blink on and off in unison. There would be a glaring flash, then they would disappear. This bright blinking happened about every three seconds.

Cindy's immediate thought was, "Wow, this is cool," but her daughter wasn't having any of it. She was frightened and wanted it to stop. They turned off the lights in the living room and it stopped, but when they stepped into the kitchen and turned the light on, the weird blinking started up again. It responded each time the kitchen light was turned on and off, stopping with the light off, then starting again with the light on.

Cindy's daughter finally fled to her bedroom, turned on the TV without turning the lights on, and this seemed to keep everything calm. Cindy ended up sleeping in her daughter's bedroom that night.

During the final editing of this chapter I called Cindy to clarify a few points, and she excitedly described something that had just happened.

She was reading on her bed in the afternoon, when she heard three loud knocks coming from the wall. The noise startled her, it sounded like someone was outside pounding on the wall. Then the bedside table began moving, bumping into the wall and her bed.

Her first thought was that the dog was somehow stuck under the table and was trying to get out, but when she looked from the bed she couldn't see anything. The table was positioned between the bed and a tall stand-up wardrobe, and was hovering off the floor about five inches as it was being thrown around.

She jumped off the bed and yelled for her father. When he got to her door, he saw the table banging loudly into the wardrobe, bed and wall. Cindy said the sound of the table in motion wasn't right, it sounded like leaves rustling.

She asked, "Dad is there an animal under there?"

Her father found a flashlight, got down on his hands and knees and looked under the bed, all as the little table was slamming into things. He saw smoke coming from a power-strip under the bed, but before he could do anything it blew up, and sparks shot out from under the edge of the bed. At that instant the table dropped to the floor, and everything was calm again.

This weird event lasted for at least five minutes. There was a heavy Tiffany lamp sliding around on the surface of the table, but it never fell off. Altogether, the table and everything on it weighed around 40 pounds. Cindy was baffled how it could have floated off the floor.

She later went outside to try and recreate the sound of the three knocks that seemed to have initiated the entire event. The side of the house where the knocks came from is brick, and no matter how she tried, she couldn't duplicate the sound.

The big kitchen clock

Of all the accounts she shared, what follows was clearly the hardest for Cindy to tell. Her voice was shaky with emotion when she described the distressing events of a summer night at her house.

It was approaching midnight when her father burst into her room with a shotgun, ranting that he'd heard a loud noise. Cindy said, "I'd never seen him act like this, he was scared to death! He was convinced

8: Owls and Drones

there was a noise so loud that he thought the house was caving in. My room is right across the hall, but I never heard anything."

He went on and on about the noise, and thought a plane might have crashed in their yard. Then he said he'd seen multi-colored sparks, but was unclear if these were in the room, or outside his window. Cindy had no idea what he was talking about.

They crossed the hall to his room, and he explained that something was sending off red, blue and green sparks. He pointed to the top of the air conditioner in the window to a spot just above the unit where he had peeled back the aluminum foil to peek out into the yard. He was convinced something dreadful had happened, and that there were people just outside his bedroom window.

This didn't make any sense to Cindy, but she could see he was terribly frightened. She tried to reassure him that everything was fine, but he was insistent he had seen and heard something. He said said it had happened right outside the window.

She took him outside so she could show him everything was okay. They walked past the big kitchen clock on their way out out the door, and she saw the time was 12:02 a.m. He carried the shotgun out into the yard where everything was lit up by floodlights. They went to his bedroom window, and the air conditioner was humming quietly. There was no sign that anything had happened, it was calm and peaceful.

Cindy reassured him, "Daddy, there's nothing wrong, everything is fine."

When they walked back inside, the kitchen clock read 2:02 a.m. Seeing this, Cindy nearly panicked. They weren't outside more than two minutes, but somehow they had lost two hours to the minute.

I asked if she could have misread the clock on her way outside, and she was insistent that she read the time as 12:02. The clock is big, and she clearly remembered what time it was when her dad had entered her room. She was so upset that she couldn't sleep for the next three nights.

Sense of mission

I asked Cindy how she would define her sense of mission, and she told me her entire life had been weighed down with a feeling of unease.

It never felt like she was doing what she was supposed to, as if she were somehow off track, but everything changed about five years ago when she began her UFO and drone research. There has been a powerful sense that she was now doing what she was meant to do. It was while we talked that I realized this new chapter of her life seemed to begin with the owl sighting in her driveway. I told her this, and she agreed.

Why would owls have appeared at those points in Cindy's life? One thought is that they were alarm clocks to wake her up. If owls are messengers, then the message is probably important.

Cindy's owl sightings were a springboard to a long list of other experiences, and we tried to make sense of all this during our long phone conversations. Our stories are similar in so many ways, and we've both used the word *compelled* to describe the obsessive vibe of our research. It's as if a new purpose in life has been thrust upon us. I hesitate to say this because it sounds so ridiculous, but it seems like we've both been zapped by psychic laser beams, and are now compulsively documenting a very strange outlying aspect of the UFO phenomenon. And like me, a series of weird owl sightings seemed to usher in this new chapter in her life.

There are plenty of UFO abductees who've come forward with information. Sometimes the experiencer will say it straight up, that they've been told by the aliens to speak out publicly. Other times there's an urgency, but without any source. I can imagine the UFO occupants subconsciously urging someone to write a book about their contact experiences, and they unwittingly follow orders. I suspect there are a lot of examples of this, yet the authors might not know the source of their inspiration.

I've tried to pay attention to what is emerging from the abductee literature. In its simplest form, it's usually a message to be better global citizens. This can also play out as sermonizing about looming environmental catastrophes, how our technology has advanced beyond our spirituality, the evolution of our souls, and the need for universal love. You don't need aliens to know these are important messages, yet this is what's being conveyed.

It's one thing to hear an experiencer preach about universal love, but

8: Owls and Drones

it's altogether different to have someone with UFO experiences who feels compelled to beat the drum about the rise of military drones. If Cindy is a messenger, then we need to pay attention to her message.

Chapter 9
Denise Linn and Three White Feathers

Denise Linn was shot and killed when she was 17 years old. This happened in August of 1967, the Summer of Love. She was on her motorbike on a rural road in Ohio when a car rammed her from behind. As she lay injured in the ditch, the driver pulled up alongside her, then pointed a gun out his open window and shot her.

Some time later, a passing motorist found her. He stopped another car with two local teenagers, and they raced to a phone to call for an ambulance.

The nurses in the emergency room started to remove the bloody dress with scissors, and Denise shouted, "No!" She was afraid her mother would be angry if the dress was cut, so despite the searing pain she sat up as they pulled the dress up and over her head. Everything got dark as she laid back down. Denise remembers:

> The pain subsided, and I found myself being drawn into a womb-like darkness. Suddenly, the darkness burst, like a black bubble, to reveal a brilliant, golden light... Everywhere around me, into infinity, was shimmering light... [it] pervaded my being until I merged into it.
>
> I know it doesn't make sense, but I was made of light and sound flowed into eternity. And it all seemed completely natural and completely familiar. I was home.
>
> I tried to look down at myself, but I didn't have a body. My "self" was everywhere, without limits of time and space. I wasn't separated from the universe. Somehow that didn't seem unusual. Everything seemed more real than I had ever experienced. It was as if my teenage life up to that time had only been an illusion... a dream.
>
> There was no past and no future—each were folded into the golden light to form an infinite present. She felt an exquisite "now-ness" infused with perfect love.
>
> It was a love that goes beyond all boundaries, like a vast, unlimited ocean... If God is love, then in those few moments beyond death's door, I experienced divine love.

Denise saw a golden shimmering river of light manifest at her feet, and she stepped into its glowing warmth. She knew crossing that radiant flowing river meant she would never return to the trials and pain of her earthly life. This was a certainty.

> As I walked across the river, part of me wanted to let go and dissolve into it. I wanted to surrender to that powerful current, meld my being with its greater force… I knew that I had to make it to the other shore to be free. Every step took me closer to my true home. But before I could reach it, I heard a deep voice reverberate inside my mind: *You may not stay here. There is something you need to do.*
> I screamed, "No-o-o-o-o! No! No! … I don't want to go back. It's too hard. I'm not ready! No!"

She was suddenly being pulled back into her physical body, as if lassoed by a rope. In that moment, she had a spontaneous memory of her cousins practicing calf-roping on their Oklahoma ranch. She realized the rope around her wasn't what it seemed; it was an astral cord. The harder she struggled, the more insistent the pulling became.

Denise awoke in her hospital bed in harrowing pain. Fighting for her life, she was desperate to return to that beautiful place, grieving that she'd come back.[1]

Ten years later in January of 1977, Denise had what she refers to as "one of the major events" in her life. She and her husband David had spent a beautiful day fishing along a river in Northern California. The sun was setting as they began their journey home to San Francisco in David's old pickup truck. The night felt holy, every star was bright and clear. While sitting in the passenger seat, she fixated on an unusual light in the sky. She told David that it must be a satellite, but he seemed uninterested and continued their drive along the coast.

The "satellite" suddenly stopped, made a 90-degree turn and sped along high above them. She watched in astonishment as this light was now traveling parallel to their truck. It was flying on her side of the vehicle, hidden from her husband's field of view. To Denise, its odd motions seemed to imply that it wanted them to reverse course.

> "David, there's something up there that wants us to turn around," I said quietly.
> "What?!" He abruptly came out of his fishing reverie. "What are you talking about? Are you telling me that a satellite wants us to turn around?"
> "Yes, I am. I don't really think it's a satellite, but whatever it is,
> it wants us to turn the truck around," I said.

At first he refused, but Denise was insistent and they eventually turned around. They drove in silence on the empty road, and the "satellite" appeared again on her side of the car, still hidden from David's vantage point. She watched as it stopped in the sky, changed direction and headed inland. Denise abruptly announced, "It wants us to go east. Look, there's a road. Go up there." Gritting his teeth, David turned up the small country road. They drove for a while, the bright object staying just ahead and above the truck on her side.

From where David was sitting he couldn't see anything, but he eventually pulled the truck off onto the embankment and parked. He refused to drive on, saying he was tired. Denise pleaded, "Well, at least come outside and look at it." He stepped out of the truck and got his first view of the object in the sky. "Wow!" he said, suddenly not tired anymore. Denise writes:

> Maybe I'd watched too many B-grade science fiction films, but as I stood in the field, I put my arms up over my head and said, "Welcome!" I wasn't quite sure what else to do.
> In a whoosh, a large round ship came down and floated just above the trees. It was totally quiet and immensely beautiful in its silence. It was about 30 feet across and smooth in appearance, with a row of glowing lights around its middle...
> I gazed back up at the ship, and I felt a tentative presence touch my mind. "Oh my God! Whatever is up there can hear my thoughts!"
> If you can hear my thoughts, blink your lights. I silently projected my thoughts toward the ship... Instantly, the lights blinked off and on again. Could you do that again? I silently asked. The lights blinked again.
> Again, I felt a presence enter my mind so soft, kind, and questioning. It was like the feeling you get when someone comes up behind you; where you can't see them, but you can feel them there. This was much more intimate, however. A wave of love, homesickness, compassion, and wonderment all tumbled together inside me.
> Shouting in my mind, as loud as I could, I said, *Please help me be of service to others! Help me to help others!* Over and over again I mentally shouted this as tears streamed down my face.

At that point, the craft seemed to notice an approaching airplane and zipped away. After the small plane had passed, the UFO came back for a few moments, silently hovering over the trees before it hastily departed.

This aspect of her story might be ignored by a UFO investigator, but would be significant to a shaman. Denise had an amazing reaction while standing below the circular craft. Instead of being scared, or question who they were—she pleaded to the presence she felt in her mind. She was telepathically screaming: Please help me be of service to others!

This is exactly what her life would become. Denise is now an internationally known healer, writer, and speaker. She's lectured in 25 countries, written 18 books, studied reiki, meditation, massage, ancient wisdom traditions, native spirituality, and spent two years in zen monastery in Hawaii.

When Denise was in the presence of the craft, she described feeling a "wave of love," very similar to the near-death experience she had as a teenager. It's also interesting that she felt homesick. This is something an abduction researcher would be listening for; a desperate feeling of wanting to go home, or a pull to return to the stars. These emotions are commonly reported by experiencers.

That night, Denise and her husband saw something well beyond just a curious little light in the sky. Author and researcher David Marler has been calling these more noteworthy sightings unambiguous UFOs. This implies something far more telling than the tiny dots that make up the majority of the sightings reports. Marler says, "I came up with the term unambiguous UFOs to separate descriptions of large, low-flying, structured aerial objects from the ubiquitous and ambiguous 'light in the sky' UFO reports. I believe there is a huge distinction between the two that demands clarification."[2]

What Denise and her husband saw certainly fits the rank of unambiguous.

If an experienced abduction researcher hears an account that includes an close-up sighting, they might suspect something more had happened. The implication would be that an abduction might have taken place, but the memory of the event is hidden from the witness.

After the craft flew away that night in 1977, Denise wanted to get back in the truck and continue further up the road. She felt certain the object was beckoning them to follow, but David refused. As they drove back down the coast to San Francisco, they had one of the worst arguments of their entire relationship. Denise writes:

> I was angry that we hadn't gone farther down the road, and David was mad that I'd accused him of being scared. We went to bed still raging at each other; however, in the light of morning, all was forgiven as we

sweetly made love.
"As I lay curled up in his arms afterward, I said, "I'm pregnant."
"How do you know?"
"I just know."

Her certainty surprised them both. In the previous years, numerous doctors had informed Denise she would never be able to have children due to the severity of her gunshot wounds. Nonetheless, she absolutely knew she was pregnant, and nine months later her daughter Meadow was born. Abduction literature is brimming with accounts of mysterious pregnancies coinciding with contact events, so an unambiguous UFO sighting paired with the conception of a child within hours is significant.

Meadow has been doing spiritual work alongside her mother, and they co-wrote *The Mystic Cookbook: The Secret Alchemy of Food*.

It was ten years after seeing that circular craft above the trees when Denise read Whitley Strieber's *Communion*. She was reading his book at her kitchen table and got to the part where he's lying in his bed at night, then he's suddenly in some other place. He describes a strange round room with tiny beings moving around him with a disturbing quickness. What unfolds is a series of disjointed memories that have since been labeled as "alien abduction."

Strieber woke that morning, "...with a distinct sense of unease and a very improbable but intense memory of seeing a barn owl staring at me through the window sometime during the night."[3]

This passage was the very first instance in popular culture where an owl is clearly linked to UFO contact.

Right at that moment, Denise looked up from the book to see a great horned owl sitting together with a crow. They were side-by-side on a branch right outside the kitchen window, barely three feet from the other side of the glass. The owl and crow were perched about 18 inches apart, and they stared in at her for the next half hour. This took place during the middle of the day in urban Seattle, an unusual time and place to see an owl.

Denise told me this story during a phone conversation, and I interrupted her to say that I'd been hearing this same thing, or something very close to it, about once a day. People have been writing to me that they've seen or heard an owl while reading my book, so it should probably occur with other books as well, especially one as significant as *Communion*.

In 2013, I wrote to author David Carson who has written extensively on animal totems. I asked him about owls, and here's his response:

> Owls and crows are enemies. They say that crow sees night in the day and owl sees the day in the night.
>
> I had the experience of picking an owl up as roadkill and putting it in the trunk of my car and forgot about it. Then later, not thinking, I picked up a road kill crow. I tossed that in the trunk too. Didn't give it a second thought. A minute later in the clear night came the biggest blizzard I had ever been caught in. It was a white out. I made it to a motel and in the morning there was still heavy snow. I thought, what's going on. And then I thought of the road kill. I separated them, wrapped each in red cloth with tobacco. When I did that, the snow stopped. Later, I gave them a sort of scaffold burial nestled in the branches of different trees which is how they were treated in olden times. They are comfortable resting there, so some elders say.[4]

Researching the spirit meaning of owls and crows was easy because Denise has written a book titled *The Secret Language of Signs*. She has this to say about the crow:

> The eye of the crow was thought to be the entrance to the supernatural realms and the inner mysteries of life. The crow was also the bringer of messages from the spirit realm.... If this sign appears to you, take heed, for the crow is a portent of change in your life. This is a sign to step beyond the usual way that you view reality and look into the inner realms.

The spirit meaning for the owl is also addressed in this book (italics my own). These concepts were explored in depth in *The Messengers*.

> This is a very significant sign, as *the owl is a powerful symbol of transformation*. If this sign appears to you, there is probably a transformation coming in your life.... The owl sees into the darkness what others cannot see. If this sign appears for you, you are being given a gift of being able to see and perceive the truth. You will gain the ability to see clearly where things may seem dark.[5]

These are two powerful birds that arrived together on the same branch at the same moment. They were seen by someone at a point in her life when she was well aware of their spiritual implications. That this happened while reading about the direct link between UFO contact and owls makes this story all the more incredible.

There came a point in the late 1980s when Denise felt drawn to find her spirit name, or as it's called in some spiritual traditions—her true name. It was a hot summer afternoon when she walked into the cool shade of the forest near her mountain home, with the intention to discover this new name.

Denise stopped under a large old tree and closed her eyes. It was so still in that moment, even the usual birdsong and drone of insects seemed to disappear in a web of silence. With her eyes closed and heart open, she offered a prayer, asking that her true spirit name be revealed.

> When I finally opened my eyes, a great horned owl rested on a branch a few feet in front of me, so close that if I reached out I could touch him. He must have landed in the few moments that my eyes were closed. All I could see were his enormous eyes as he stared at me. It seemed an endless amount of time, but probably was less than a minute. Then, with a solemn blink, he lifted his massive wings and silently glided away into the forest.
>
> I looked at the branch where the owl had landed. Three small downy feathers were caught on the branch. I picked them up and held them in my hand. They were soft and white.
>
> I heard an inner voice say: *Put the feathers in your medicine bag.* The words puzzled me. I had a beautiful medicine bag, but it wasn't with me. Again I heard the voice say: *You are your own medicine bag. Put the feathers in your medicine bag.*
>
> Without a further thought, I put the feathers into my mouth and swallowed them. (I don't recommend this. Feathers are very hard to swallow and not sanitary, but that didn't occur to me at the time.) The inner voice continued: As you have taken owl feathers into your body, the spirit of owl has permeated your being and shall always be with you.

Denise gradually returned to the reality of the surrounding forest. With a calm certainty, she was now aware that her spirit name was "White Feather." There was a clear knowing that her destiny had been shifted with this experience.[6]

This is an account of an owl sighting, but in many ways it reads like a UFO report. There is a pattern of witnesses being in a place of yearning in the moments leading up to a UFO sighting, as if the craft itself is responding to their plea. Denise begins the story by entering the forest with a strong intention; to find her spirit name.

There was an eerie silence preceding the arrival of the owl, and a gradual transformation back to normal reality after it left. This almost mystical stillness is referred to as the Oz Factor, and is commonly reported in close-up UFO sightings. Witnesses will describe a distorted sense of time and space, as if reality itself is slightly altered.

She used the term "downloading" in a private conversation to describe what what it felt like to look into the eyes of that owl, something I've often heard in this research. She also describes an inner voice that plays out as telepathic communication. Telepathy is reported with near one hundred percent consistency in accounts where aliens interact with abductees. There is also a sense of transformation, as if one's life path had been fundamentally changed. Downloads, telepathy, and transformation are all aspects integral to the UFO contact experience.

But what is most fascinating was the request that she eat the owl feathers. There are repeated accounts in Celtic faerie lore, as well as modern UFO abduction reports, of people being offered food (sometimes unusual food), and being told to eat it.

Denise has Cherokee ancestry and draws deeply on this heritage in her work, traveling the world to spend time with other native cultures. There is always a heartfelt exchange in these visits; she is both teacher and student, and has been adopted into many of these tribes.

She went to South Africa in 1994 just before the election of Nelson Mandela, when the divided country was on the brink of civil war. This volatile time was the backdrop for her meeting with Credo Mutwa, the spiritual leader and prophet for the Zulu people. He is known as the sangoma (a shaman or healer) and high sanusi (clairvoyant and lore-master). Even his name implies something sincere—Credo in Latin means means "I believe."

Credo has been quite open about his own contact with UFO occupants, or as he calls them, the "fiery visitors." He is adamant that these small gray beings are real, as they've interacted with him throughout his life.

The late Harvard professor Dr. John Mack wrote extensively about Credo in his 1999 book *Passport to the Cosmos*, a study on how shamanic initiation parallels the UFO abduction lore. He spoke of the Zulu shaman, "Credo, like other indigenous people with whom I have discussed these matters, does not distinguish material or literal reality from mythic truths. This has made it particularly difficult for me to sort out what he may have actually experienced and what is part of African legend."[7]

Denise told me nearly the same thing, that many native people will speak plainly about interacting with entities from other realms. Even after her own lifelong experiences she finds this frankness perplexing. In contrast to Dr. Mack's statement that indigenous people often don't distinguish reality from myth, she feels they are simply open to beings interacting with us beyond our reality.

When Denise entered Credo Mutwa's humble mud hut, she was awestruck by his presence. She wrote, "Although I'd met many shamans and gurus on my journeys throughout the world, nothing compared to the energy emanating from this man."

She sat and listened to his stories long into the night. He showed her some traditional Zulu masks with large eyes and small chins.

These masks are representative of the aliens we have had contact with," he said, also mentioning that they'd taken him onto their ships.

> "Little Sister," he said, addressing me, "they have also taken you a number of times, especially when you were a child."
> I didn't want to disagree with this venerable man, but the conversation was beginning to frighten me. Even though David and I had seen a UFO the night before Meadow was conceived, the idea of alien abduction seemed unbelievable.
> "With all due respect, I think I would remember something like that. I'm sure that I was never abducted," I said.
> "You deny it because it frightens you to remember. But you were abducted, and they are still in contact with you," He said emphatically.
> I was getting really uncomfortable and steered the conversation away from me and aliens.

Here's where things get really strange—Credo Mutwa also claims to have eaten an alien. He tells of being given "a small lump of gray, rather dry stuff," by a friend, and was told it was the flesh of a gray alien, or the "sky gods." He and his companion ate this together in a ritual ceremony, and awoke the next day with swollen tongues and were unable to walk. They could barely breath and were helpless for several days. During this perilous time they were attended to by shamanic initiates. Credo said, "I came very close to death." What happened next sounds like a psychedelic trip lasting over two months.

Credo stated, "It was as if we had ingested a strange substance, a drug, and a drug like no other on earth… Every feeling was heightened, and it's indescribable—it was as if I was one with the very heart of the universe. I cannot describe it in any other way." Coming close to death followed by a blissful unity of oneness is similar to what Denise underwent during her near-death experience.[8]

Even stranger, the ritual of eating alien flesh is eerily similar to something Denise had done. She ate three owl feathers and then felt a "downloading of some kind of special energy." Throughout my research I have equated the owl with the gray alien. For me, these have become symbolically intertwined. Like Credo Mutwa, Denise had also eaten of a being steeped in mythic powers, and in doing so, felt she had taken on the attributes of the owl.[9]

Every Sunday, Christians around the globe partake in the rites of holy communion, the mandatory ritual of drinking the blood of Christ and eating his flesh. This sacrament is performed metaphorically with wine and bread.

Symbolically, this ties in with a long list of mythological traditions of eating the God. Beyond its Christian incarnation, these ancient rites are performed in different cultures around the world. By eating the god, you take on the god's attributes. In the dictionary, theophagy is the literal translation from Ancient Greek, meaning "the feeding on a god" or "eating/devouring god."

Dionysus, son of Zeus and brother of Athena, was worshiped as the Greek god of wine. He was glorified in the drunken ritual of Bacchanalia, a frenzied state of ecstasy where the celebrants' souls are freed from their bodies. The ancient rite climaxed with a live bull (the symbol of Dionysus) presented to the crowd, whereupon they would tear it apart with their bare hands, and devour it raw. After this symbolic feast of flesh and blood, the worshipers became possessed by Dionysus.

In the jungles of the Amazon basin, ayahuasca is known as the vine of the soul. Some tribes declare it to be the actual blood of the great cosmic serpent, resonating the wine in the eucharist, or blood of Christ. Some traditions see ayahuasca as simultaneously being a plant, a drink and a God. This powerful entheogen can induce transformative psychedelic experiences, often propelling the seeker into a new phase of their life. Like a UFO sighting, the ayahuasca ritual can change a person in profound ways.[10]

Credo Mutwa told Denise that she had been taken many times by the "sky gods" when she was a child. I have speculated something similar, that Denise might have been taken by the UFO occupants during her close-up sighting in 1977. There is no way to confirm if this was actually an abduction experience, and digging into what might have happened would only stir up more questions. There is a need to look beyond the preconceptions of what we think of as alien contact, and instead try to understand its deeper meaning.

If I suspect someone of having UFO contact, I ask this question: "What is your sense of mission?" I'll ask these folks to give me a number between one and ten, and quite often they'll pause thoughtfully before answering "eleven." I don't need to ask that of Denise; her monumental outpouring of books, recordings, videos, lectures, seminars, and retreats all paint a picture of someone on fire with a need to help people. Although she rejects the idea of ever having been on board a UFO, she certainly acts like someone who's had some sort of direct contact experience. She demonstrates this in her role as teacher and guide, ushering her students into a deeper realm, and urging them to confront these symbolic experiences with an open heart.

Denise used to lead a group she called The White Owl Seminar. She would take people to a secluded spot in the mountains, then guide them through a series of traditional rituals and lessons. The entire event culminated with a formal vision quest ceremony, where folks would sit alone in their sacred circle and ask for guidance. One woman sat silently while an owl repeatedly flew above her, swooping low enough that its wingtips touched the top of her head.

The owl is a symbol of transformation. Denise has said it plainly in her books, and this is my conclusion too. I go one step further and see the UFO as a synonym for the owl, at least symbolically. This transformation means leaving behind some older self and taking on a more vital role, often in service to others. There are rituals in place to represent this change, from the ancient rights of communion to sitting alone in a sacred circle.

In her lifetime, Denise has had a near-death experience, a close up

UFO sighting, and a mystical encounter with an owl. From my research, these three elements in one lifetime can pack a wallop. It should be no surprise that Denise is working as a shaman, healer, soul coach, past-life regressionist, and psychic. All of this seems to emerge from a place of deep compassion, as if her very being is fused with a mission of empathy and love.

Chapter 10
Adrienne and Owls

> I totally just SAW the owl. I went outside and called my BF on the phone (Shawn, the ufologist) and no joke I saw the Owl… It was off in the distance in a big tree but I saw it fly up into the tree and could see it sitting on a branch … I was telling Shawn, "OMG I just read Mike's essay!"

I received this from a friend, Adrienne Dumas, on the evening of July 3, 2013. She sent it via Facebook after reading my initial essay about owls and UFOs, which had been posted online earlier that same day. Her own experiences with owls and UFOs were featured in the very essay she was commenting on. This written work was the genesis of what eventually became the big book, *The Messengers*. I immediately recognized the synchronicity of her seeing an owl right after reading her own story of seeing owls! [1]

I've spoken at length with Adrienne about her experiences. She shared a story with me of a big owl swooping down over the windshield of her car, startling both her and her mother. This happened in the middle of the day while driving in rural Arizona. Her immediate thought was, "I knew it was some kind of sign that my life was going to change." A few weeks later, she met a UFO investigator named Shawn. They are now engaged to be married.

Adrienne has had other curious owl experiences. She told me about an owl living right over her at a point in her life when she was repeatedly seeing UFOs. I asked what she meant by stating that the owl was over her. She said that at the time she was working on an organic farm in southern Arizona and living nearby in a small RV alongside a row of trees. She would often see an owl on a branch directly above her little home. She said, "Whenever I would walk up to my house, that owl would watch me. It was eerie! Sometimes it gave me the creeps, but other times I felt honored to have it live near me."

Something strange took place while Adrienne was alone in that RV. It happened at around 2:30 in the morning while chatting on her

10: Adrienne and Owls

computer with a friend who shared her fascination for UFOs. At that same time she was reading a book about a woman having a spiritual connection with gray aliens. She described what happened next, "I looked out the window and I swear I saw what appeared to be a UFO 'parked' in a field across from my house." She was looking at a row of six extremely bright lights in the adjoining farmer's field.

What she was seeing was far too bright to be from a car or tractor. While looking out the window, she watched as a car drove down the road between her and the field. It stopped for a moment, as if observing the lights and then moved on.

She could gauge the glow of the car headlights in the foreground compared to the row of much brighter lights in the background. The car lights seemed normal, but there was something very strange about those other lights. She sat there staring at them for about 15 minutes, and then, "...as I was looking at them, they were suddenly gone."

This sighting left her feeling frightened. She sensed the grays were somehow related to those bright lights and there was a message from the experience. The event seemed to be telling her, "We are real."

Adrienne didn't sleep that night—she had an eerie feeling of being watched. The next day she went out into the field to see if there were any tracks or imprints, but she didn't find anything unusual.

She had another impressive sighting while living in that spot. It happened in full daylight with her brother Josh as they drove towards the farm where Adrienne's RV was parked. They saw a large old fashioned military cargo plane flying really low to the ground, leaving a trail of thick black smoke. It was close enough that she could see rust stains on the old fuselage. Adrienne laughed and said, "Maybe it will land at the farm and Mulder and Scully will get out!" She made an X-Files joke because something about the low flying plane seemed so strange.

The moment she made that comment, six shiny saucer shaped craft appeared in the sky. The objects were completely frozen, and seemed to be hovering directly over the farm where her RV was parked. Adrienne and her brother had an odd reaction to those the silvery disks, they were both giddy and laughing. She described feeling absolutely ecstatic at seeing these UFOs, and said, "It was one of the most joyful and happy moments of my life."

When they got to a stop sign near her home, they realized that all the craft were gone. Neither saw them fly off, and in that moment Adrienne thought they might have switched on some sort of cloaking device.

There was something peculiar about their sighting of the old military plane. I could hear a sort of awe in her voice as she spoke about seeing this aircraft. There was a heightened vividness in her descriptions; the black smoke, flying so low, and seeing the rust on the fuselage. All this sounded curiously intense, as if she were describing the details of a vivid dream. I have to wonder if this old plane could be some sort of screen memory. It's odd that her comment about the *X-Files* would mark the instantaneous appearance of the silvery disks, and it hints that there might be something more was at play than just a UFO sighting.

Adrienne had two UFO experiences while living at that farm. The one at night freaked her out, and in contrast the daylight sighting was joyous. During that same time an owl was regularly seen perched above her home, and it felt eerie that she was seeing it so often. Abductees will often tell of an owl taking up residence close to their home, often right outside their bedroom window, and often at a time of heightened contact. I don't understand why this happens—all I know is that this same story shows up again and again. This includes a palpable unease about the presence of these owls.

There is more to Adrienne's experiences. As a young girl around 11 years old, she had an intense sighting along with her entire family. This incident began with her mother while driving home at night in the family van. She was alone except for their dog.

Adrienne's mother saw an enormous bright light in the sky, and at the same moment the van's engine stopped. The light was so brilliant that her mother actually thought she was dying and this was the light of heaven! She gasped, "This is my time." She soon realized she was seeing some sort of enormous saucer shaped craft.

As the giant object slowly moved away, the engine started again on its own and she raced home. The dog was terrified as she drove, whining and cowering under the back seats of the van. The craft was hovering over their neighborhood when she burst into the house and exclaimed, "There's a UFO!"

At that moment Adrienne was watching an episode about UFOs on *Unsolved Mysteries*, and her first thought was that her mother was joking. But when the family went outside, they all saw the gigantic craft gliding away in the nighttime sky. She described the saucer shaped object as moving eerily slow, as well as spinning "in a very strange way." There were red and blue lights slowly rotating around both the exterior and bottom of the craft. Adrienne was mesmerized by the sight of this huge object, but her parents were terribly distressed. She'd never seen them act this way before, and it scared her. They then all watched several military helicopters approaching the craft. Adrienne said that these helicopters seemed to lose power as they approached the saucer shaped object, so much so that they needed to retreat to stay aloft. The event above her was close enough that she could hear the sound of the helicopter engines fizzle as they got close and return to normal as they eased away. The huge object and the helicopters eventually moved beyond their line of site.

So, we have three different UFO events, each directly foreshadowed by something she was doing or saying. Adrienne was reading a UFO book while chatting with a friend with a keen interest in UFOs when she saw the lights across from her RV. She made an X-Files joke before seeing the six discs with her brother. And she was watching a UFO episode of *Unsolved Mysteries* on TV when her mom burst in the house exclaiming about a UFO.

Adrienne has a few other odd stories. While living with her mother, she was in her room getting ready to go to sleep when their dog started barking. Then all the dogs in the neighborhood began barking. She was struck with a really sick feeling in her stomach, when all of a sudden she heard something strange above her. It was sort of groaning washing machine sound, a repeating, "vhummm...vhummm..." Then it all suddenly changed, the noise was gone, the dogs stopped barking, she felt fine, and everything was back to normal.

Within minutes her brother John called and asked, "Did you see the weird lights over the dry lake?" The dry lake is about a mile from her Mom's yard.

Everyone in Adrienne's family seems to have had strange experiences, and they'll talk about them when they get together. Her sister Kember shared something unusual at a recent holiday visit. She told everyone that whenever she hears a certain tone, she's overcome with a sudden vision of a giant gray alien woman pointing its long skinny finger at her. When her brother John heard this, he said the exact same thing happens to him. Then they both described the tone as the sound of the electric swamp cooler from the back of the house where they had grown up. It made a specific tone when it was switched on, and any similar noise will trigger the same memory in her brother and sister. They both recognized this was very strange, and each described the giant alien woman as being both vivid and dreamlike. Curiously, Adrienne had been collecting stories about giants, an interest that began after her own dream of a giant man. This was before she heard the near identical accounts from her siblings.

After hearing all this, I had to ask Adrienne the big question, "Do you think you are a UFO abductee?" She answered no. She was clear that she has no conscious memories of anything like being aboard a craft. She puts herself in the maybe category by declaring, "I do believe I have been contacted in some way or another." She went on to say that all her sightings and dreams seem to imply as much.

The next question I asked was how she would describe her sense of mission. She actually didn't understand what I was asking. I need to add that at the time she was running something called The Faeries and Angels Network. This was a collection of websites, podcasts, online videos, and until recently a paper magazine—all focused on new age spirituality. So, asking Adrienne about a sense of mission was like asking a fish about water. She said, "I can't even imagine not doing what I'm doing. It is just how I am. I've been like this as long as I can remember."

Adrienne radiates a glow of sincerity, so this was the answer I expected. Her kind hearted nature seems entirely genuine, and it colored her work. All of her online sites were filled with flowery adjectives along with pastel images of angels and unicorns. This is the kind of stuff that would make a nuts and bolts researcher cringe, and I'm certain the hard core pragmatics would dismiss her websites as silly, but I'm not so quick to judge. I saw her sentimental output as something heartfelt, an honest reflection of her spirit.

10: Adrienne and Owls

Like so many others connected to these UFO experiences, Adrienne worked as a psychic and healer. She also provided services such as angelic readings and private energy healings. So again we have a "maybe" person who has had multiple UFO experiences, some of them with an owl directly above her home. Even though she doesn't say as much, she is acting like a UFO abductee by sharing her truth so openly.

Our initial contact took place after I saw a youtube video where she spoke about the the UFO and the owl above her trailer. We've spoken on the phone a few times for my research, and she's always very helpful.

I've visited her website, listened to her podcasts and watched her videos. She's interviewed her family about their UFO sightings, and these audio postings helped me with this chapter. I would occasionally use her guided meditations, which were very peaceful and had the tone of an elementary school teacher reading a storybook aloud. There was something about the slow cadence of her voice that was almost hypnotic.

We've been friends on Facebook for nearly a decade, and this has allowed me to follow her life. I saw pictures of Adrienne walking her daughter to school, and the evolution of her relationship with Shawn from their initial meeting to their engagement.

There was a sudden change on Adrienne's Facebook page. All the new age stuff abruptly ended, and was replaced with posts about Christianity. This surprised me, but I also sensed a similar enthusiasm in her new found devotion to Christ, echoing the intensity of her new age beliefs. I contacted her with the same question from four years earlier when I first wrote about her owl experiences, I asked about her sense of mission. She replied:

> Oh man, at this time I am not sure what my mission is anymore—but I do still feel it is related to spirituality and God. When I left the new age, even though I feel it was right, I went into a temporary depression because I lost my sense of purpose, I am rediscovering my purpose in Christ and what that means. In Romans 6:8 it says, 'Now if we died with Christ, we believe that we will also live with him.' I literally felt like my old purpose died. It was a worldly purpose, covered up in 'spirituality.' What I mean by that is that everything I believed in and taught was a sugar-coated feel good message that the world loves. The world doesn't love the message 'take up your cross.'

She used the term "sugar-coated" to describe her new age beliefs, and that's a perfectly accurate way to describe her previous site. The imagery was mermaids and fairies floating around in waterfalls and rainbows. Her website had a healthy following with paying subscribers who would contact her for private oracle readings and long distance Reiki.

But her long time clientele wasn't very understanding with her new found conversion to Christianity. "I took up the cross. I was also 'crucified' by people who had followed me, because well they didn't like that I had changed. I really don't blame them for being in shock or feeling like they had been conned or something. When I was into the new age I believed in it one hundred percent. Everything I taught, I believed."

Adrienne said, "I used to be very anti-religion. I was tolerant towards people, but I used to think the world would be better off without religion. I didn't realize the new age is pretty religious itself." She laughed.

The change began with something unassuming—she would often see an image of St. Thérèse of Lisieux which was painted on the back of a truck parked in her neighborhood.

"So, I looked up information about her online and started to say her Roses prayer, and roses started to appear into my life. I also read her book, *The Story of a Soul*, which really touched me."

Saint Thérèse, also known as "The Little Flower," was a Roman Catholic nun who died in 1897 from tuberculosis at the young age of 24. She is best known today for her spiritual memoir, The Story of a Soul. Published after her death, this book became a modern spiritual classic. Alongside Saint Francis of Assisi, she is one of the most popular saints in the history of the church.

Adrienne said of St. Thérèse, "She helped me. I had said to her and to God that I wanted to completely surrender to God. I ordered my first Rosary, and started to pray with it daily, even though at the time I didn't even believe in the theology."

Adrienne began to lose interest in the channeled books and new age teachings that had been the focus of her life, yet she was still doing readings, reiki and dowsing for hire. She started reading the Bible, something she hadn't done for many years. She said, "It just hit me like a ton of bricks. I remember feeling a conviction so strongly that it nearly knocked me over. I just knew that the Word of God (scripture) was true, that Jesus wasn't just an ascended master but that he was and is literally God. I cried my eyes out knowing that I had turned away from him for so long."

As a girl, Adrienne went to church and read the Bible with her parents, but set aside this aspect of her life as a young adult. Curiously, it was Adrienne's interest in UFOs that played a role in her return to Christianity. She had been studying ancient megaliths, and from there began to research the myths of giants and floods. These topics brought her back to the Bible.

Adrienne is still very interested in both UFOs and the paranormal, "But I am leaning more towards various Christian viewpoints on these issues—so my interest in them hasn't changed. My perspective on what these things could be though is different."

She is aware that within organized Christianity there are divergent opinions; some say all ETs are demons, while the Roman Catholic Church has publicly addressed the idea of baptizing aliens.

She said, "I do worry that the new agers are believing too much in 'alien saviors' and I worry that if they arrive and try to convince us that we need them, that it could be the darkest deception of our time."

Adrienne's life was in turmoil because of her conversion. She had spent years building up a career, and let it all go with her new spiritual beliefs. At the same time, she lost her home and ended up spending a few months back in Arizona living with her mother.

On her first day back home she visited her father on his organic farm. He said there had been a wounded owl in the same spot where she had been living with the owl in the tree above her trailer. Her father called an animal rescue service from Tucson, but by the time they arrived, the owl was gone.

Adrienne said, "The day I arrived at the farm, the owl was back and looked healed. Very interesting. I've gone through a lot the past eight months personally, so coming home to visit family has felt healing. It almost seemed like the owl mirrored me."

She referenced a Bible quote from the Sermon on the Mount, where

Jesus refers to birds and tells his followers not to worry about their life, "Look at the birds of the air; they do not sow or reap or store away in barns, and yet your heavenly Father feeds them. Are you not much more valuable than they?" (Matthew 6:26 NIV)

Adrienne said, "God took care of that wounded owl, and he's taking care of me. That's a very comforting thought!"

Chapter 11
Blipping off the Map

While working at a restaurant in Boone, North Carolina, a woman noticed a stack of papers on top of a coffee urn. The image on the front was a great horned owl, and the title read "Owls and the UFO Abductee." This was a 41-page long printed copy of my original online owl essay, and the foundation of what would eventually become *The Messengers*. For some reason, she'd assumed I'd been there and left it behind. She wrote to me on August 2, 2013, and this set in motion one of the more elusive stories I've ever tried to untangle. Her name is Allison (a pseudonym), and here's a bit from her first email:

> I was working the day you left your essay with the big coffee urn. I have only worked at Green Jade for a couple of weeks, and had just revealed to a co-worker I trust that I have had contact. I noticed the owl photo on the front cover of your essay laying on top of the coffee urn. I continued to work. This same co-worker picks it up, and reports to me that she's gonna take it home and read it, explaining it's about UFOs and owls. My eyebrows raised. She later says she's overtired from staying up the night before. I'm thinking, she's not gonna read it tonight—so I asked to read it first.
>
> Many confirmations. Just wanted to say, hey. I resonate with your research for many reasons which are complex. Many synchronicities led to my profound experiences...
> — Allison, coffee barista/truthseeker

I had been to the Green Jade only once. My initial reaction was that I had left the printed essay at the restaurant while having lunch with Fortean researcher Micah Hanks. After thinking for a moment, I realized that our lunch would have been two months prior, but that was still one month before the essay had been posted online. The dates make it impossible, so I couldn't have left it there. I got in touch with Micah and asked if he had left a copy of the owl essay at that restaurant, and he said he hadn't.

I have another researcher pal in Boone named Alan Green. He's written extensively on synchronicity, and is exactly the kind of person who would have read that essay. I contacted him and asked the same question I had asked Micah, if he'd left a copy of the owl essay at that restaurant. He said no, but surprised me by saying his wife worked at the Green Jade. He asked her if she'd left it there, and she replied she hadn't. She also didn't know any barista named Allison. Also worth noting, Alan and his wife share the name Green with the restaurant.

Looking at my calendar, several key dates lined up in a way that got my attention. I had lunch with Micah at the Green Jade on June 2. The owl essay had been posted online on July 3. The message from Allison came on August 2. That's June, July and August. Three parts of a puzzle, each separated by almost exactly a month. Stranger still, I received the email while I was in North Carolina. I had been there for twelve days in June to visit my mother who was in an assisted living facility near my sister's home outside Charlotte. Her health was failing, and it felt important to see her. I was back again in August, this time for her funeral.

It's also strange that Allison would assume I had left that owl essay tucked behind a coffee urn. If I found a printed story in a restaurant, I doubt I would've jumped to the conclusion that the actual author had left it there. Someone left it there, but it wasn't me.

People contact me all the time with their owl and UFO contact experiences, but the timing of this message was curious. How and when she found my essay was synchronistic and confusing. It's hard to separate my own emotions from Allison's initial email, and its arrival just two days after my mother died. I'm not sure what the deeper meaning might be, but it somehow feels connected.

When I finally spoke with Allison and heard some of her stories, I realized that what had happened to her defied any easy categorization. She shared a lot, including one very strange account with both owls and UFOs. This event stood out as something truly bizarre, going well beyond just a sighting of an odd light in the sky. She called it a mystical experience, and I could hear the wonder in her voice as she tried to articulate what had happened that night.

A few days after the fall equinox in 2012, Allison and her boyfriend Eric had gone for a hike in the woods just outside of Boone. They were doing something perfectly ordinary, simply walking through the forest on a well maintained trail. Their plan was to walk a four mile loop and return to their car, beginning in the afternoon and finishing well before nightfall. During the hike Eric got a bit ahead of her, and at this point things became unclear. Now alone, she was overwhelmed by something she described as "profoundly spiritual." It felt like she was guided to leave the path and walk to a small meadow not too far from the trail.

What happened next sounds much like a psychedelic LSD trip. I asked about this, and Allison was clear she wasn't under the influence of any drugs, but was adamant that *something* happened. It was hard for her to describe, but it felt like she had somehow become a part of nature.

Allison sat down in a small clearing near a stream, a site she now refers to as a sacred spot. She heard the loud hooting of owls in the trees surrounding her, perhaps as many as five. She felt they were communicating with her, and at that point she felt as if she were "blipping off the map."

Then, for reasons she can't explain, she took off her clothes. The sun went down as she sat naked in the meadow. She watched as a series of four or five UFOs moved above her. These weren't physical craft in any way that we might understand; instead, they looked like the amorphous cloud nebulae photographed through telescopes. They were spherical with rings around them, evenly spaced as they moved slowly and deliberately across the sky. She described them as the size of airplanes.

Just like the hooting owls in the surrounding trees, she felt these formless craft were communicating with her. She was told that they knew she was there, and they had been looking for her. She described a clear telepathic message telling her they were making changes to accelerate a spiritual awakening.

While she sat there, her boyfriend Eric had no idea where she was, or what had happened. He anxiously hiked the loop, repeatedly yelling her name until nightfall. Allison says she never heard him, although she was quite close to the trail and should have easily heard his calls.

Eric saw a few other hikers on the trail and asked if they had seen anyone fitting Allison's description, and they hadn't. At some point, Eric contacted the sheriff and a search party was organized. A team of officers and multiple dogs arrived on the scene just as it was getting dark. They staged their efforts in the parking lot for the trail.

The forest was soon filled with a search party and rescue dogs, but it was Eric who finally stumbled onto Allison in the small clearing. He found her sitting contently, naked except for her shoes. He gathered up her clothes and told her to quickly get dressed. He asked where she'd been, and she replied that she'd been sitting right in that spot the entire time.

This didn't make sense to Eric. He was certain he'd already checked this small clearing more than once during his search, and then he told her she'd been missing between five and six hours. Allison was shocked—it simply couldn't have been that long. These unaccountable hours left them both confused.

This strange event happened during the evening hours in late September, and I asked her if she was cold. She responded strangely, like the thought hadn't even crossed her mind. Sitting still without clothes for over five hours at night would have been uncomfortably chilly, the local weather for that time of year puts the nighttime temperatures in the low-60s.

Before they returned to the trail and met up with the rescue crew, Eric needed to come up with a story that at least seemed plausible. He said they should tell the search and rescue team that she'd simply been lost.

Within seconds of them agreeing on a story, the sheriff, a dog handler and his search dog arrived in the clearing. The dog became extremely excited when it greeted Allison, and she sensed it was smiling when it saw her. The handler worked to control his dog who was jumping and yelping with joy. He said it was usually quite calm and he didn't understand why it was acting so rambunctious. When they arrived back at the parking lot, Eric apologized to everyone for the mix up and they left.

After this event in the woods, a lot of things in Allison's life felt different. She began to play music with a new intensity and passion, way beyond anything she'd ever experienced. It was during this time of heightened musical acuity that she realized she'd developed perfect pitch, something she didn't have previously. Eventually this intensity dialed back a bit, but she feels her talents are significantly advanced

11: Blipping off the Map

from what they had been before the events of that night.

I've heard similar things with other folks who have had close up UFO sightings. One woman who worked as a tarot reader described an increased ability to give readings. She felt her psychic powers had been boosted, and like Allison's musical upsurge, this woman's abilities lessened with time, yet were higher than before her sighting.

There were other changes after that weird night in the woods. Allison began to pursue alternative spiritual teachings with a deeper intensity, traveling alone to Arizona and New Mexico to attend the annual Star Knowledge conferences in order to meet with Native American elders. This urgency to follow a different path was something new to her, and she feels it was directly connected to her sitting in that small clearing in the trees.

Allison had another unusual owl experience years earlier when she was 22 years old. She was out in the woods at night with a group of friends, and they had all taken mushrooms together. Their intentions were both recreational and sacred. They were sitting in a circle, fully in the psychedelic throes of the hallucinogen, when a great horned owl landed in the center of the tripping group. It just stood there. Her description was that it was well over three feet tall, unusually large for any owl. Like Allison's event in the forest, we have another psychedelic experience where an owl plays a significant role.

It would be very difficult to put Allison's experiences into the confining box of UFO abduction. Her overall experience seems to include UFOs, missing time, an altered sense of reality, synchronicities and heightened psychic abilities—all that, and owls too. The problem is that in this case, these details don't fit together to create a tidy conclusion of abduction. Instead, it's blurry and hard to pin down. That said, the more confusing and complicated the story, the more I trust it. Something is at play, and it defies any easy answers.

What you've just read was the finalized chapter of Allison's experiences. It had been edited and tucked away in a folder marked as "completed" when I received a note from her.

She said, "Hi, Mike. I have been meaning to reach out to you. The stuff we talked about, back in 2013, about 2012, I have come to acknowledge and realize that I am bipolar. I was having some kind of psychosis at that time."

My heart sank when I read those words. I had spoken to Allison several times on the phone, and those were long conversations where she openly shared her experiences and emotions. I was concerned. I've suffered from a long history of clinical depression, and although my symptoms differed from her diagnosis, I knew all too well what it meant to be swallowed by irrational emotions.

She said, "I am getting treatment now. I am still trying to figure out up from down."

The core of her story is the missing time in the woods. Of this she said, "I was incoherent, hallucinating and hearing things that probably don't exist... perhaps my entry in your book is irrelevant."

She also said, "I did hear those owls." She was very clear about that.

I went back and reread her essay. I was aware that the tone of her story was outside the boundary of what might be a "normal" UFO contact report. These doubts were clearly addressed in the final paragraphs of what would have been the completed chapter.

I don't think Allison has tried to deceive me. Throughout our conversations and correspondence, she's always said the same thing—she doesn't know what had happened. The only thing she's ever told me with certainty was that "something" happened.

I tried to look at her account through the lens of a psychiatrist. From that vantage point it would be easy to see it all as some sort of psychotic vision, but doing so would mean ignoring the tangled web of synchronicities in her initial email. That note to me came at a tremendously significant moment in my life, just days after my mother had died. She signed her first email, Truthseeker. There was a lot to unravel in that one message—I was confused at the time, and I'm still confused. The synchronicities have a flavor I have come to recognize. There is a "vibe" to some of these things, and it implies something deeper. A string of coincidences connected to an email isn't proof, but for me it's a sign to take her seriously.

It was over a month after her message to me about her recently diagnosed condition before we spoke on the phone. She explained what had been happening, and that she was now taking several medications. I researched what she had been prescribed, and they seemed to be standard prescriptions for the treatment of bipolar disorder.

It was good to speak with her, but she was obviously worried and shaken. We had both initially agreed to use her own name, but now thought it would be better to use a pseudonym, and to change some of the names and locations.

A few points to consider. Allison is a performer and musician, and after the event she began playing music with a heightened intensity and passion. There is something joyous within the creative process, and it's heartening that this would be elevated after her experience. But this same fervor could be interpreted as some sort of mania—and a symptom of mental illness. Also, in the aftermath she said she'd developed perfect pitch, and this seems magical to me—something akin to the gifts of a savant.

It was obvious she was confused about the things that seem too strange to be real, yet she's adamant she heard the hooting of owls. Obviously people hear owls in the woods, but the timing is worth noting.

She also described hearing voices in her head. Again, a psychiatrist would see this as a symptom of delusions, yet a UFO investigator might attribute it to alien contact. Another viewpoint would be from a shaman, who might see this as a message from the spirit realm.

The voice in her head said they were, "making changes to accelerate a spiritual awakening." Tell this to a psychiatrist, and they would see it as psychosis. Tell it to a UFO researcher, and they would see it within a pattern of what a lot of other people have reported.

While sitting alone in her sacred spot she heard that same voice say, "Someone is coming to get you." Moments later, Eric walked into the clearing and found her.

Allison had participated in some Native American ceremonies during a weekend retreat about four days before her missing time event. This included fasting and a sweat lodge ritual. I asked if maybe these events could have left her fatigued in some way that might have caused her to black out for those hours. She said maybe, and I noticed some shakiness in her voice. If she had wanted to agree with my ideas about UFO contact she'd had every chance to do so, yet she never strayed from saying she didn't know.

There is no way for me to know what truly happened that night, but there are some subtle clues. She described her experience as becoming "a part of nature," and used words like mystical, spiritual and sacred. When I try to imagine a psychotic event, I picture something terrifying, but she saw it as something ecstatic.

That owls would show up for Allison seems important to me. My ideas about owls aren't confined to just UFOs. I've tried to make it clear that they show up in relation to plenty of other "highly charged" events or transformational experiences. UFOs, synchronicity, shamanic rites, psychedelic experiences and psychotic visions all have a transformative power, and somehow the owl appears as a totem.

Others have noticed this connection as well. Stanislav Grof has described synchronicity as a playful interaction between the psyche and the physical. Grof said: "Something happens in your dream or in your visions, and then the material world kind of plays it out. Let's say you have a powerful shamanic experience involving an owl, and you walk out after the session and there is an owl or a wounded owl and so on." He argues that these things truly happen. [1]

A young woman named Christina had been suffering from what seemed to be a total mental breakdown. She met with comparative mythologist Joseph Campbell, who had been her professor when she was a student at Sarah Lawrence College. He saw her experience as a kundalini awakening, a profound state of change described in Eastern cultures. Campbell put her in touch with Stanislav Grof, one of the founders and chief theoreticians of Transpersonal Psychology. She was amazed to find that many of Stanislav's research subjects had reported experiences very similar to hers.

This break from reality has been understood and respected by the sages throughout human history. She knew her suffering was real. Yet there was a conflict; aspects of her affliction were dismissed by Western psychology, but accepted by shamans. The term shaman sickness is used in other cultures to describe symptoms similar to what both Christina and Allison experienced.

Christina later became Stanislav's wife, and eventually became a respected clinician in her own right. She coined the term spiritual crisis (also called spiritual emergency) to define this "life-transforming process of growth and change." This malady goes by lots of other names; spiritual awakening, shamanic crisis, and more poetically, the dark night of the soul.[2]

In 1993 the Grofs, together with colleagues, were able to make a revision to the DSM-IV (Diagnostic and Statistical Manual of Mental Disorders, the bible of modern psychiatry). They managed to persuade the editors to acknowledge a distinction between mental illness and spiritual crisis.[3]

Joseph Campbell pointed out that one of the markings of the young shaman was this psychological break from reality. He didn't use the term spiritual emergency, but he's relating the same critical episode. He saw the role of the shaman as something vitally important within society, and described the patterns seen in the emergence of the young shaman, "as an overwhelming psychological experience that turns him totally inward. It's a kind of schizophrenic crack-up. The unconscious opens up, and the shaman falls into it. This shaman experience has been described many, many times. It occurs all the way from Siberia right through the Americas down to Tierra del Fuego."[4]

Campbell argued that there is an ecstasy interwoven within the trauma of these experiences. Christina Grof describes something similar, of feeling both depths and heights during her time of crisis.

What Allison described to me about that time in her sacred spot was both mystical and frightening, she called it "blipping off the map."

I asked again about the craft she saw, and she repeated the same description—they appeared as a moving amorphous cloud, and although she questions it, her memory of what she saw hasn't changed. The easy answer is that she was suffering from a clinical disorder, and these strange experiences were all in her mind.

I reviewed all of our email correspondence, and in her second message to me she wrote, "I'm still trying to make sense of my own experience, as I was in a natural, unaided altered state when it all happened. Perhaps that's why I find it challenging to fully articulate it, because I don't have it all figured out. Some of it sounds totally illogical when I remember back."

She's never wavered from that statement. Did I try to force the square peg of UFO contact into the round hole of a mental disorder? It's vital to follow these threads, but I am also aware of how easy it would be to get lost down a blind alley. I am deeply invested in this research, and I worry that I am mistaking the map for the territory.

In the aftermath of her diagnosis, Allison wrote, "There is so much I cannot explain but seems to continue to suggest unusual life experience, a lot of which I may never be able to explain or fully understand."

Something happened to Allison that night, and in an attempt to make sense of it I had overlaid my definition of UFO contact on top of her experience. A paper map is useful in how it represents a place on the earth, but the actual three dimensional terrain is infinitely richer. The map is small and well organized, yet the ground is vast and complex. Some things cannot be fully conveyed except through direct experience. I was focused on the flat paper with its well defined boundaries and labels, yet she described something that was both real and mystical, and ultimately unknowable.

The map is not the territory, and Allison made it clear that she had blipped off that map.

Chapter 12
Owls and Healing

Three days before her 25th birthday, Laura Bruno woke up knowing she would be in a car accident that day. She was in a New Jersey hotel room traveling for a corporate sales job, and knew how crazy she would sound if she called her boss and described these fears.

That afternoon, her car was rear-ended while stopped at a red light. She has no memory of the accident, only a slow awakening to the sound of honking horns. Her first thought was that it was her alarm clock, but faintly recalled a loud crash.

Laura saw a woman behind her flailing her arms with an "Oh, my God!" look on her face. It took her awhile to realize this was the driver who had hit her from behind. She thought, "She seemed so far away, though. *So far away, and I'm so tired. Just woke up. Why can't my car be my bed again?*"

After an awkward exchange of names and insurance information, she somehow managed to get back in her car and drove away. She remembers nothing after that, except for passing through a toll booth somewhere in New Jersey. Her only thought was, "If I were smart, I'd pull over and go to a hospital, but I want my bed. I want my sheets.... The next thing I knew, I was pulling into my parents' driveway in Bethlehem, Pennsylvania, trying not to vomit."

She'd suffered a traumatic brain injury, and every normal thing in her life came to a halt. The accident happened in May of 1998, and the severity forced her back into her parents' home to recover. She ended up spending six weeks in the house where she grew up, but a long list of unresolved issues made this return tense. Initially, she was unable to do much more than sleep; the rest of her time was a blur of nausea, confusion, and a perpetual migraine headache.[1]

Both parents worked, so her days were spent alone in a spiraling haze, alternating between excruciating pain and euphoria. By mid-June, she had developed a routine of getting out of bed in the afternoon, making a cup of tea, then slowly walking out onto the back porch. These few steps left her exhausted.

Things as simple as fluorescent lights were unbearable. Even the slightest stimulation sent her reeling into vertigo, so she was unable to read or meditate. And without any companionship or distraction, she felt unbearably lonely. She later wrote about this isolated time:

> Somewhere in the course of those afternoons on the back porch, I noticed what looked to me like an owl sitting on a branch at the back of my parents' property. Day after day it would return, and when the thought finally occurred to me that owls do not usually show themselves in daylight, I considered that I might be hallucinating. With intermittently double vision and all those painkillers, it certainly seemed possible. Still, I came to enjoy my afternoons with this owl, who so reliably settled himself on the same branch—always within a few minutes of my thud into the chaise. He was the perfect companion. Quiet, knowing, keen of sight. I never spoke to him, nor he to me, yet we developed an understanding between us; I could feel his presence, even with my eyes closed. Although the crows harassed him mercilessly, he sat with me for as long as I remained outside.

One Saturday morning later in the summer, her mother joined her on the back porch. Looking off into the trees, her mother suddenly gasped, "Laura, that looks like an owl!"

She ran into the house and came out with a pair of binoculars, and focused them into the trees, then stated it was a great horned owl. Laura nonchalantly explained to her, "He's my friend. He sits with me every day when I come out here."

Her mother was surprised and envious. Laura grew up in a house filled with hundreds of owl photos, pictures, string art, figurines, books, and knick knacks. Her mother was obsessed with owls, and had joined the Audubon Society in hopes of seeing more of them in the wild.

"Laura, why didn't you tell me?" her mother asked. "Because I wasn't sure if he was real," was Laura's reply.

Eventually, Laura recovered enough to return to her own apartment, and her mother never saw the owl again. Curiously, she did hear an owl on certain nights, but only when Laura was coming to visit. Over the years, her mother would joke that whenever she'd arrived, the owl would show up to welcome her.

Laura had a strange dream during a visit to her parents home in the

12: Owls and Healing

winter of 2001. She saw two dark catlike figures dance an elaborate S-pattern, then melt into one another. She explained, "I had no idea what the dream might symbolize, and yet it seemed important—like in dreaming it, I had participated in a ritual of wholeness."

That morning at breakfast, Laura described the dream to her mother, but neither of them knew what to make of it. Shortly thereafter, her mother went upstairs to fold laundry, and yelled for Laura to come up there. When she did, her mother was pointing out the window at some curious disturbances on the snow. There had been new snowfall the previous night, so the impressions they were seeing were obviously fresh. She told her daughter they needed to go outside and check it out.

They bundled up, left the house and trudged to the marked symbols they had seen from above. They were looking at two sets of graceful S-like tracks that made a what looked like an infinity symbol in the snow. Judging by the direction of the marks, it seemed as if a pair of large birds had dropped from the sky, swirled together on the crystalline surface, and then flew off. Laura wrote of the pattern in the snow:

> Of course, I cannot say with certainty that it was my old companion, but great horned owls do begin their courtship in late December. I like to think our bond remains. A true friendship: no matter how long the separation, we share key moments in our lives. [2]

Laura spent years recovering from her brain injury. Her initial diagnosis was that she would remain disabled. Conventional treatments and medicine weren't working, forcing her to find alternative healing methods. She eventually wrote a book about the odyssey of her recovery, *If I Only Had a Brain Injury*, which was published a decade after the accident. The book uses *The Wizard of Oz* as an analogy: Dorothy's journey begins with a concussion, and she heals along the yellow brick road. One reviewer wrote: "...a testimony of the power of believing in oneself, a true survival story."

The trauma of the accident left her helpless, and the summer spent at her parents house meant living in the dark shadow of things that happened in her youth.

The Devil Inside

When Laura was 14 years old, she awoke from a sound sleep to see some sort of being forming in her room. It was a cat-like figure in a hooded cloak, partially emerging from a chair, staring at her. The experience was horrifying for a young girl, yet in retrospect this "ghost" seemed feminine and benevolent.

Terrified, Laura ran down the hall and woke her mother, telling her there was a ghost in her room. Her mother spent the rest of that night ranting about demons, and before the end of the next day she was hospitalized. She had suffered a complete nervous breakdown and remained confined for the next four months. During this crisis, she spoke of seeing and feeling energies, yelling at invisible beings as if locked in a desperate battle with things in another reality.

Laura said, "It wasn't that she was crazy, I saw and sensed the same things she did, and it was terrifying." She felt her mother was fighting unknown forces, and was understandably afraid to tell anyone that she too had been seeing similar things. She feared if she spoke about seeing intruding energies, she'd also end up in a hospital.

The morning after seeing the ghost was terrible. She was up all night listening to her mom talking about demons, but still needed to be up early to compete in a swim meet. Her friend's mother picked her up, and the INXS song "Devil Inside" was blasting on the radio as she entered their car. Laura tried to act calm, but was she was secretly freaking out about the lyrics and how they tied into the night before:

The devil inside
The devil inside
Every single one of us
The devil inside [3]

Laura's mother saw these dark encounters through a religious lens, and was convinced her adversary was Satan. Laura said, "She and I spent all night on the couch with her telling me about demonic things happening in the graveyard behind their house." Laura later learned that right around that same time some of the graves had been disturbed, "…as well as some creepy seeming evidence of animal rituals going on in the graveyard."

Right around this time, Laura saw a UFO. It happened while driving home from a swim meet, again with the same friend and her mother from the morning after seeing the ghost. They all saw a glowing silver

12: Owls and Healing

disc moving above a farmer's field, but what seemed strange was that everyone in the car spoke so casually about what they were seeing. They simply muttered, "Oh, yeah, that's a UFO" while waiting for the traffic light to turn green.

Laura had her arm out the car window as they watched the hovering craft, when out of nowhere a freak bolt of lightning struck, seemingly six feet from her fingertips. Her hand was numb, and tingled for the next two weeks. I asked if she thought this may have any connection to her present role as a medical intuitive. She replied she didn't know the source, but says she now has healing abilities with that hand.

During the time all these strange things were happening, Laura remembers continually meeting people who were trying to convert her to Satanism. Barely a teenager, she recalls people following her at the mall and showing her certain verses in what appeared to be a Satanic Bible. They urged her to take this "bible" home, but she always refused. They would then congratulate her for "passing the test."

Being fourteen is confusing in pretty much anyone's life, yet beyond the normal teenage angst, Laura had to deal with added stresses of her mother's breakdown, a hooded ghost in her bedroom, a UFO, a close lightning strike, pestering Satanists, and an emerging psychic awareness.

Laura said, "It was the worst year of my life, it was like non-stop initiation."

Becoming a healer

Years before her accident, while in graduate school, people would stop Laura on campus and say, "I don't know why I'm telling you this, but I'm having these problems and I somehow know you can fix them." Laura would reply that they should do certain things; meet this person, move to this location, eat this food, or wear this color. She was also sought out for dream interpretation and life path questions.

After addressing people's concerns, she would add, "But don't tell anyone I told you this." She was desperate to keep these impromptu sessions secret, but before long became the go-to person on campus to help with personal issues and reluctantly began using her psychic skills.

Laura had been working in the corporate world in the two years leading up to the car accident, and in the weeks prior was preparing to return to graduate school. She'd completed a Masters Degree in English in 1996, and in 1998 received a scholarship and fellowship to pursue her PhD. Yet during this time she'd been having persistent dreams and messages that this wasn't her path. Instead, she was supposed to be doing spiritual healing work. There was an urgent feeling that she should quit her corporate job to become a poet and a landscaper. And when she did, her work as a healer would simply begin.

This urgency came to a head the morning she awoke in that New Jersey hotel room. She had the dream again, with the repeated message to quit her job and follow a spiritual path. The message of the dream was so insistent that she gave in and said aloud, "Fine, make it happen." Early that afternoon, while waiting at a red light, her car was struck from behind by another car.

The injury to Laura's brain was so severe that she lost her ability to read. This happened just before heading back to college to become an English professor, and she was fully aware of the irony. Now unable to read print, Laura tapped into her ability to "read" in other ways. Something happened in the car crash—all of her filters were ripped away. She began to feel people's energy fields even more intensely, and used this heightened intuition to better assess the mental, emotional, and spiritual patterns affecting their physical health. Laura feels she'd always had these psychic abilities, even as a child.

Long before her brain injury, people had approached Laura for intuitive health advice, but she wanted to keep it separate from her busy professional life. After the accident, it was impossible to ignore this deeper level of awareness. The source of these messages, whatever it was, became very insistent. She felt she was being told to put herself out there, and after years of bizarre synchronicities and nudges, she eventually gave in and announced that she'd be doing healing work. This has been her day job ever since.

The urgent message before Laura's brain injury in 1998 listed three requirements: to become a landscaper, a poet, and do spiritual work. She said, "At the time, poetry made sense, spiritual work some sense, but landscaping zero sense!" Yet now, almost twenty-years later, she has nurtured an organic garden on one-third of an acre that had been an urban wasteland. Her years of dedication have born fruit and nut trees, perennial vegetables, and vital habitat for bees and butterflies. She says that a shocking number of people have contacted her for medical intuitive or tarot sessions because of the garden photos on her website. Within the pool of people drawn to her, there seems to be a sense of urgency to heal the Earth. This same sense of mission is echoes through people who have had UFO contact, as well as near-death experiences.

By the summer of 1999, Laura had recovered enough to start working with a professional healer in Seattle who was a holistic optometrist, craniosacral therapist and herbalist. At that time he was in his 70s, and planning his retirement.

After nine office visits over three weeks, he casually mentioned that he would like to give his practice to her. Laura was shocked, and didn't understand why he would say this. He explained that after each of her visits, his next three patients would make quantum leaps in their recovery—he felt she was leaving a healing residue in the room.

Laura never took over the doctor's practice. Instead, she spent a year as his apprentice doing medical intuitive readings with his clients in exchange for guidance in the use of medicinal herbs. Since he only used the office three days a week, he insisted Laura use it on the other days to begin a healing practice, which she did, initially offering reiki and intuitive sessions to his clients. She gained confidence in the accuracy of her psychic skills during her time with the doctor, but she eventually felt led to leave Seattle.

The owl painting and the end of a marriage

Laura got married five years after her injury, but serious difficulties in the relationship came to a head in 2006. Her then husband was dealing with health issues, and used wildlife photography as a form of therapy to balance himself during these times. Laura often accompanied him on these outings, and he made use of her psychic abilities to call in animals. There was a day when he became obsessed with finding and photographing owls, and Laura joined him in a wooded park on the outskirts of Reno, Nevada. They hiked together with the intention of getting some pictures, and at one point she left him on the trail and went off on her own.

She walked up to the top of a hill, sat silently and began to meditate. Focusing her intentions, she asked the owls to please appear for him. It was a windless day as she sat alone and sent forth her call. Suddenly, a huge whirling gust of wind surrounded Laura. She sensed their arrival, thanked them and walked back down the hill to find her husband taking pictures of a pair of great horned owls up in the trees. This was the middle of the day, an unusual time to see nocturnal birds.

Laura made a print from one of the photos, using it as reference for a large painting. She began the owl painting in 2006, "But I could not, for the life of me, finish it. We moved every three to six months at that point, and I dragged this partially painted canvas around with me."

This was happening at a time when she was trying to find a way out of her marriage. There were personal compatibility issues between them, but for a long list of reasons, leaving seemed impossible. Four years later while living in California, she pulled out the unfinished painting of the owl. She painted over the background, changing it from day to night. Within twenty-four hours of completing the canvas, a whole series of events unfolded that allowed her to leave her husband and move out. Money arrived, a subletter appeared, movers showed up, and a new place to live revealed itself across the country in Chicago.

Laura had spent years in an unhappy marriage, yet was careful to keep these emotional issues hidden from her mother and father. It was right before filing for divorce in December 2009 that an owl showed up again at her parent's house, hooting loudly in the early morning hours. These calls awoke her mother, whose immediate thought was that something was wrong—her daughter needed support.

When Laura finally called and told her parents what was happening, her mother wasn't surprised. She felt the owl visits were a sign that her daughter was in the midst of major life changes. Her parents called it "Laura's Owl," assuming it was the same owl from the yard and her recovery. They considered its presence a sign that something important was happening with their daughter. Laura said, "It was like the owl showed up at key times in my life when I felt most trapped or vulnerable. I have always felt owls as a deeply kind presence."

Laura wrote a short story in 2006 and sent it to her parents. It later appeared as a story within a story in her novel, which would be published in July 2009.

Her dad read the short story and was completely enchanted. He proudly showed it to a bridge partner who took it home to read. Her father didn't know it, but this man was very ill and read Laura's story right before he died. Her father later found out that he had been feeling very positive at the time of his passing, saying he had received insights from Laura's story.

At the moment this man died, a big branch in Laura's parents' yard crashed down during a storm, destroying the neighbor's shed—the same branch where "Laura's Owl" had sat perched during her recuperation. Her father was awestruck by the synchronicity, and this dramatic experience became part of a gradual awakening for him. This was significant for Laura because her father had never been supportive of her writing fiction, but eventually became very interested in his daughter's work. He read her novel, a story of mythology and synchronicity at least twice, possibly more.

Meeting the Wizard

In September 2009, Laura and her friend Tania traveled to Mendocino, California to celebrate the completion of her novel. Tania had a mystical experience with a white owl that appeared in her mind's eye. It happened during a sound bath inside the Integratron, a domed building in the Mojave desert created by UFO Contactee George Van Tassel. She describes herself as a bridge between the humans, animals, and other worldly beings, both on and off Earth. Like Laura, she also performs healing and intuitive work as a Reiki Master Teacher, intuitive energy guide, sound channeler, and artist. [4][5]

During this trip, both Laura's computer and cell phone suddenly stopped working. "This is a theme with me, I blow out electronics." She felt like she was in an altered state for the entire trip. While in Mendocino, Laura felt compelled to get hemp lattes at a specific sidewalk cafe. She lead Tania off the main street and straight to a store neither of them knew existed, and as they sat down with their drinks, a man walked up to them when he noticed Tania staring at his necklace. She complimented it, and he said, "It's Atreyu's necklace. Do you know Atreyu?" They did—they had just been discussing *The Neverending*

Story, and Atreyu was a character in that film.

Laura described him like the wizard Gandalf, complete with a long white beard and staff. They bumped into him three times while on this trip. At one point he pulled out a notebook explaining he had what Laura sought, then he tore out several pages and gave them to her. The pages were filled with handwritten Runes, a symbolic alphabet thought to have emerged from ancient Scandinavia. He included corresponding numeric and word codes for these symbols. Some legends say runes were introduced to mankind by the Norse god Odin, and that the symbols have magical powers.

This happened at the same time that her marriage issues were becoming more difficult. Given Laura's psychic awareness, she's very sensitive to inharmonious energies, and her situation was becoming too much to bear. She began to have dreams with a very clear message—that she would die if she stayed where she was.

As things worsened, she called her landlord to say that she needed to break her lease. That call began with Laura blurting out that she had filed for divorce and she needed to find a way to leave California without the lease. After her desperate plea, the voice on the other end of the phone said, "Laura, I think you should call your landlord."

She replied, "Who is this?"

It turned out her phone had dialed the wizard from Mendocino instead of her landlord. She felt that the universe had rerouted the call or made her misdial the phone number. The wizard said, "You are family. You let me know what you need." When she explained the situation, he described how to use the runes he had given her.

Owl painting by Laura Bruno, 2010

12: Owls and Healing

Following his instructions, she pulled out the owl painting that had been unfinished for over three years. She got out her paints and started reworking it, changing it from day to night and then adding specific runes into the imagery. As stated earlier, within twenty-four hours of completing the canvas, everything aligned for her to leave. [6]

The unknown rattling sound

Laura spent a weekend in Bodega Bay California with two close friends, Tania and Karen, both of whom have had their own UFO experiences.

They drove together in Tania's Toyota Highlander Hybrid with the license plate HUNABKU, which is Mayan for Galactic Butterfly. They all joked it was their spaceship. Karen brought her cat Lily, and Tania brought her pet tortoise Gaia in her glass traveling case decked out with amazonite crystals. The house where they stayed was owned by Karen's family.

In the weeks leading up to this trip, Laura had been plagued by an ongoing rattling sound; her dishwasher would make this noise, then the dryer, followed by the washing machine. Every time one appliance or fan was fixed, the rattle moved somewhere else. Others heard it too, but only when Laura was near.

The same sound was later heard outside her apartment, and although it was loud, no one could figure out where it was coming from. It seemed everywhere she went, this curious rattle followed. It got to the point where she thought it might be a hidden message directed at her via some sort of rapid Morse code.

It was stormy during their first night at the Bodega Bay house. They all sat together as Laura explained her frustrations with this persistent noise, when suddenly Gaia the tortoise started making the same rattling sounds by rapidly tapping the glass of her travel house with her shell.

Laura said, "Now Gaia's doing it!"

Gaia was in a trancelike state, methodically bobbing her head, and making clicking noises. Tania referred to these taps as a binary code.

Then they heard the same rattle coming from the kitchen. They got up, ran into the kitchen and heard the noise coming from the stove. The clock on the stove had stopped at 11:11, even though that wasn't the current time.

Eventually the sounds subsided, and the women returned to the other room. Being intuitive energy healers, they all pulled out their pendulums as a way of seeking insights on what had just happened. Pendulums are simply a small crystal pendant at the end of a short silver chain, and are standard issue in these circles. The user will hold the chain steady, let the crystal dangle, ask a yes or no question and wait for an answer. The pendulum gently swings or rotates as a reply.

Laura said, "They just started spinning like crazy, like huge, huge arcs."

Tania described all their pendulums going wild, "They spun one way, then stopped and the other way... like little propellers, but all in sync with each other. This went on for quite some time, spinning, shifting, spinning, and then boom! Stopped all together."

Right then, Laura looked up and saw two gray aliens in the closet. She said they weren't doing anything, and just seemed to be observing. Then Karen's cat Lily ran over and started scratching at the closet door.

When Laura told this story, I needed to interrupt, "Wait, the closet door was closed? But you could see these two grays in there?"

She replied matter-of-factly, "I could see them in my mind's eye. I can do stuff like that."

Fair enough. She's a medical intuitive and is able to see health issues in her clients, so I kept listening. Laura said that once the grays in the closet realized they were onto them, they disappeared. It seems as if the presence of these spectral beings had somehow amped up their pendulums, along with the cat.

Tania spent the night in that room and said, "...they came out and visited... and I was paralyzed, as I usually am when this takes place, unable to move. Nothing bad ever happens."

The next day the women sat together again, this time in the front room overlooking the ocean. Laura led a guided meditation to explore their previous lives together in Atlantis, and strange things continued. Tania confirmed, "More things took place, like vultures showing up at the window in front of us during our experience... They were coming right at the window and looking in. We had to shoo them off and close the drapes."

This all happened on Halloween in 2008. I've collected a handful of accounts of owls showing up on Halloween, and it's striking how the folklore of that day plays out perfectly for seeing an owl. Laura's Halloween story doesn't have an owl, but it does have ephemeral gray aliens. In *The Messengers*, there are two similar accounts of women, both named Lauren, each seeing an owl on Halloween. So, two Laurens see owls, and one Laura sees two aliens. The name Laura, like Lauren, traces back to the laurel tree. The Latin meaning for laurel is "seer of second sight" or "gift of prophecy."[7]

Prior to the odd rattle sound showing up in her life, Laura had asked for inspiration to solve some issues in the first draft of her novel, *Schizandra and the Gates of Mu*. Specifically, she wanted to "bring the novel down to earth," and make it comprehensible to the preliminary editors who'd initially reviewed her manuscript. These readers were intrigued by the story, but also confused. After the 2008 Halloween experience and the 11:11 on the stove clock, she realized the rattling was some form of message. Seeing 11:11 on clocks had already been written into the novel, and at several points, characters see this timestamp just as paranormal events rip through their normal concept of reality.

Laura declared aloud, "Look, whoever you are, thank you for your input, but I don't speak rattle! If you've got a message for me, please give it to me in a book, a dream or some other way I can interpret it in English." Within a day or so, she felt that she'd received major downloads on how to fix the manuscript, and she never heard the rattle again. Her preliminary editors were pleased and satisfied with the manuscript revisions that followed.

There's more about this event worth addressing. When interviewing sighting witnesses, some UFO investigators will carry a clipboard with a pre-printed form. One of the questions on that page is about unusual animal behavior. Both Lily the cat and Gaia the tortoise acted strangely in the moments leading up to Laura sensing the grays in the closet. Also of note, Bodega Bay, California was the location of Alfred Hitchcock's *The Birds*, making this an apt setting for vultures to peer into windows.

Kundalini awakening on Easter Sunday

In our back and forth correspondence, Laura shared one account that might not seem like much, but it ties into a similar account in *The Messengers*. She had attended an Easter service at Rockefeller Chapel in Chicago, and said, "Something about the communion left me feeling way off balance—almost staggeringly drunk."

On the way home, she stopped at the little corner store in her neighborhood to pick up toilet paper, and had what she refers to as a kundalini activation. There was a nice fellow who worked there, and he walked with her to the toilet paper aisle, pointing to its location. Laura was already dizzy, and he accidentally bumped her, knocking her completely off balance. On the way down she managed to slam her butt on the metal shelves, one after another, before hitting the floor. Laura said, "I fell with my spine sliding down four shelves. Essentially, the fall was like a vertical crash the entire length of my spine, beginning at my sacrum, which hit every shelf, but then rising up my spine as I slid down."

The week before the fall, Laura had borrowed a moldavite pendant, even though her previous experiences of actually wearing this stone left her feeling ill. Moldavite is a green crystal that originates from one source—a meteorite that crashed into what is now the Czech Republic. She was in terrible pain after the fall, and something told her to wear the moldavite pendant. It seemed to relieve the pain, and she wore it for over a month straight. Then a day came when she heard, "the moldavite is done." It seems a crystal from outer space played a role in her recovery.

After her fall, Laura stated, "My sacrum was so bruised, I could not wear pants for at least six weeks! I recognized it as some kind of bizarre kundalini initiation…"

Laura's fall took place on Easter Sunday of 2010, the very same day a woman 800 miles away in Massachusetts left an Easter party in a panic. She fled because of a tremendous rush of powerful energy running up through her spine. She said it was like, "a Tesla coil going off!" This energetic rush up her spine is the textbook description of a Kundalini awakening.

This parallel account happened to UFO experiencer Susan Kornacki.

When she got home, she laid down on the backyard hammock, then watched as an owl flew above her, landing in one of the trees connected to the hammock. Another owl landed in the other tree that held the opposite side of the hammock, and a back and forth chorus of calls ensued with her lying between them. Susan explained:

> I just kind of surrendered. I laid back into the hammock, and I knew what was going on. I knew that they were taking this energy and calibrating it, they're helping me to ground it, to have it be more complete. The sound of the owls, and the energy was moving back and forth, and I was right in the middle. [8]

Laura said, "I, too, got some kind of freaky download that day... Not sure what happened on Easter 2010, but I was having downloads for weeks prior and weeks afterwards, along with seeing almost nightly UFO's from my ninth floor apartment right near Lake Michigan."

Both women, Laura and Susan, are now working as energy healers.

Healing and her mother

For nearly three decades, Laura felt that waking her mother the night of the ghost sighting had triggered her nervous breakdown. The question, "What if?" resurfaced a lot, and with it came a deep sense of guilt. Laura felt responsible for something terrible that affected both her family and her own life. She said, "My emotions were not exactly straightforward. The rational side wanted to dismiss everything as my fault, because I wasn't ready to deal with the broader implications.... Because if it wasn't me, then it meant that there really was something bigger and potentially much scarier and disturbing that occurred."

It was after her father's passing twenty-eight years later, when Laura learned about worrisome behavior in the weeks leading up to her mother's 1988 emotional crisis. There was a long list of warning signs, and hearing this freed her from the grim sense of responsibility, allowing her to move forward with her life.

I first spoke on the phone with Laura in the summer of 2015. I immediately recognized that her experiences played out with the kind of tangled narrative I've come to call the paradox syndrome. Too much, too weird, and too hard to believe. All this chaos points to it being real, at least to me. [9]

Laura replied with a polite "no" to my initial request to tell her story in this book. At the time there were issues involving other people that were too personal, yet we still cautiously proceeded forward. There was an unspoken knowing that these challenging life events needed to be addressed.

Our back and forth correspondence for this chapter lasted over a year, and a lot happened with Laura during that time. She was her father's caregiver during the final weeks of his life. He died peacefully as she sent him Reiki energy. After his passing, she stayed with her mother. She helped her move into a new home while preparing the old house for sale, all while providing healing support as she adjusted to her new life. They are closer now than they've ever been, reunited as mother and daughter in a deeply heartfelt way. In addition, Laura was happily married during the final edits of this chapter.

During our early conversations, much of what she shared about her mother was weighted with cautious concern. She made a full recovery after her breakdown in 1988 and has been emotionally healthy ever since, yet for Laura, the burden of that traumatic time remained with her for decades. Laura said this about her mother in one of our initial emails, "It's just NOT the same person... as a teenager, I could never accept her as my 'mom.' She was an imposter."

Over a year later, she shared this about her mother, "I most recently visited with her at her church. Many people there told me sincerely, 'Your mom is a saint.' " During the year of our correspondence, I've witnessed a transformation within Laura. With what she's shared, it's evident that although she's struggled with a harrowing childhood, a newfound friendship with her mother has begun.

Laura said, "It's like she came back to herself finally after twenty-eight years, except she is stronger and livelier than ever before. Such a relief!"

I sent this chapter you've just read in an unfinished form to Laura over Thanksgiving weekend in 2016. She needed to review what had been written for accuracy, including a series of questions about her mother. She replied that the email arrived with a "ping" while her mother was visiting. This was at the exact moment they were talking about an owl. Earlier in the year, her mother heard the hooting of a great horned owl outside the window of her new home. This happened on Laura's birthday while she was missing her daughter and feeling sad.

Laura said, "She received the owl's hoots as a sign that I was still with her and that everything would be okay."

Laura's mother does everything within the context of her deep Christian faith, and provides a genuine healing presence for people. Although Laura doesn't frame these issues the way her mother does, she's aware they've both had a lot of similar experiences. In the last few years, a great deal of relevant information has emerged, often through synchronicities and owls, and these revelations have deepened their connection.

After recovering from her 1988 breakdown, Laura's mother received her Master's degree in Counseling Psychology. She doesn't officially work as a counselor, but has been a compassionate listener for hundreds of people. Laura describes her mother as one of those people who is able to sit with someone who "never talks about themselves," and then listens attentively as they pour out their life story. Laura says, "Everywhere she goes, people connect deeply with her, and those connections are always loaded with synchronicities and opportunities for healing."

Like Laura at the clinic in Seattle, it seems her mother would also leave a healing residue in the room, and they are both playing similar roles. Each suffered terrible trauma; Laura with a brain injury, and her mother with an emotional breakdown. Both have also gone on to do healing work, and each sees the owl as a companion along this path.

I include myself in this pattern. I went through a debilitating episode of severe clinical depression in 1992, a malady of brain chemistry. Those dark days were terribly dangerous. I stood alone at the edge of suicide, and the threat of oblivion was real. From these personal experiences, I now see depression as a potentially fatal illness.

This took place during a bleak winter in Maine. Despite the crippling mood, I managed to get out a few times on my cross country skis. While touring the woods out along the Saco River, I found something beautiful—a large owl had touched down and plucked a mouse from beneath the snow, the tips of its outstretched wings had left a graceful print on the sparkling surface. There was a small hole and a dot of blood in the very center of this marking. Death had come in the night to take a fragile little soul from its hiding place below the snow. This was more than a decade before my obsession with owls, yet in that moment I stood in awe. There is an eerie power to this elusive predator, and I recognized it.

Being swallowed by depression and then returning was, for me, a death and rebirth—I say that in complete seriousness. The previous person died, and a new self emerged from the ashes. I don't consider myself a healer, but I've tried my best to offer solace to those who've endured the trauma of UFO contact. Many hours a week are spent returning emails and phone calls to people who are struggling with their experiences.

It's worth noting that the very popular book, *Wesley the Owl*, also tells of an owl playing the role of caregiver while a woman is dealing with a life threatening brain issue. The author, Stacey O'Brien, suffered from debilitating migraines due to a brain tumor, and her pet owl Wesley was a constant and faithful companion.

The story that began this chapter was posted in 2010 on a site aptly titled *Laura Bruno's Blog*. This was the account of an owl that would sit each day with Laura in her parents' backyard. None other than Stacey O'Brien left a comment on that post: "I had a connection with Wesley that was spiritual and even telepathic, which I never expected, since I came into raising Wesley as a biologist trying to learn more about barn owls." Again, we have an author with a near fatal brain malady who has a companion owl during her convalescence.

Laura said, "My mom loved the book *Wesley the Owl* and requested I paint her a picture of him, which I did during my visit in 2010." This happened while in Pennsylvania right after she filed for divorce. "So, actually, there were two owl paintings: Wesley the Owl for my mom and then I returned to California to finish the other owl painting." It was that second painting that seemed to play the catalyst for leaving her husband.

Stacey made the comment on Laura's blog just weeks after Laura finished the painting of Wesley for her mother. The comment right below what Stacey had written is a nice thank you from Laura, added the same day. And the next was my own response, written two days later. On February 3, 2010, I wrote, "So strange... I have a blog with a weird collection of owl synchronicities." This was very early on in my own awareness of these connections. What is striking is that I made this comment on the very day everything clicked for Laura to leave her husband in California, and right after completing the other owl painting.

These overlapping details are as confusing to follow as they are to write. Yet we have three authors, myself included, who've written about owls, endured dangerous brain disorders, and we all commented on an owl story on Laura Bruno's Blog.

"They are using the owl symbolically." This message came from the spirit of an owl. It was channelled for me by Jacquelin Smith; and by they, she meant the aliens. Jacquelin is a soft spoken psychic with UFO contact experiences, and this dialog is featured on page 338 of *The Messengers*. Here's more of what she shared, "There is an archetypal image that is mirrored to the humans, this goes in on a subconscious level and connects with the human's genetic memory bank. Because humans think with symbols, they are touching us on that level, and that goes back to the beginning of humankind, and how we see owls."

Jacquelin then channeled something that really hit home for me. She spoke of the spirit role of the owl, "What it does is to demystify [these concepts] so the fear can dissolve, which I love. So, their intention is positive, I love this, to announce initiation." [10]

Laura reflected on the profound changes in her mother, "It's not just that my mom never had another episode. She now really shines... She is sought after to lead healing related groups and retreats at her church..."

The nightmare of her mother's 1988 breakdown was a defining moment in both their lives. The four months spent confined in a hospital must have been emotional agony, yet Laura said that her mother sees it as something positive, and to this day "considers it a spiritual initiation."

Laura was raised in a house full of owls; the hundreds of pictures and knick knacks were there because of her mother's compulsive owl collecting. This is something I've heard a lot in my research. Someone who's had experiences with both owls and UFOs will tell me that their mother collected owls, often obsessively.

These obviously weren't real owls in Laura's childhood home, or the homes of many other young experiencers. Yet these children were surrounded by symbols, and it seems as if a subtle form of initiation might have been underway.

To be nurtured in the presence of something symbolic, then as an adult to have real owls manifest in highly charged moments—this feels important. If this is an initiation, the question is, an initiation into what?

Chapter 13
Between Two Bridges

I'm friends with a man who has patiently shared a lot of his experiences. I'm familiar with what he's told me, because I've experienced much of it myself. We share something else, the very common first name Mike. For anonymity, this chapter will use only his first name and the first letter of his last name. Like me, he is also Mike C. Synchronicities are interwoven into this story, and our similar name is the least of it.

Mike was driving home from work on an afternoon in the early autumn of 2015 in West Springfield, Massachusetts. He'd just crossed the Connecticut River on the Memorial Bridge and was merging onto southbound Route 5 when something unusual happened. "A huge barred owl almost slammed into my windshield. Its image burned into my mind because it scared the shit out of me!"

This happened during full daylight in a busy urban area, an unusual time and place to see an owl. Then, a bit less than a half mile further down the road, he looked to his left and saw something even more unusual—he had a clear view of a huge disc hovering above a industrial area known as Bondi's Island. It was a tarnished copper color, roughly 100 feet wide and floating low over the buildings. He watched it slowly rising as the traffic carried him along, and soon lost sight of it.

This could be just one more account of an owl and a UFO seen within moments of each other, but it gets weirder. Mike was listening to an audio of a lecture of mine that he'd grabbed off of YouTube where I spoke about owls, UFOs and synchronicity.

I replied immediately, "Wait, you were listening to me—AND you saw an owl—AND you saw a UFO?"

I was totally astonished—*an owl, a UFO and my voice!* He told me this story in a series of frantic back-and-forth messages over the Facebook chat box on September 20, 2016. It wasn't too long after when I noticed my message, what you read above, was time stamped at 1:23 p.m. I pointed this out to Mike in a follow up message, and he got back to me with, "Dude! I just looked at this message at 11:11 a.m.!"

I had previously met Mike at a small conference in Maine in 2016. He bought a copy of my owl book, and we talked briefly as I signed it for him. This Facebook correspondence happened a few weeks after we'd met in person, and almost exactly a year after his owl and UFO event near the bridge. Mike said, "I never picked up the connection until reading this book." That connection is owls and UFOs—and sometimes myself.

Within the pages of that book are repeated accounts of people seeing or hearing owls while watching the video of that lecture, the same one he'd been listening to while driving south on route 5. There's one story of a man seeing a UFO out his window while watching this video. I don't understand why or what it means, but I've been interwoven into some these accounts. I'm not actually present, but my words seem to be.[1]

On September 30 of 2016, about three weeks after our initial flurry of messages, Mike wrote me about another owl sighting, "Dude, remember the barred owl? Memorial Bridge, Route 5 and Bondi's Island? This happened at almost the same spot."

He was stopped in traffic and looking at the car in front of him and, "This dude has this stuffed owl in his back window. I did not, however see any UFOs."

He took a picture with his phone, and it shows a fluffy little toy owl staring into the camera. Later, he checked the image and the photo was time stamped 3:33. These number sequences might be easy to dismiss, but they seem to show up at highly charged moments within the lives of experiencers. The events between the two bridges generated 123, 1111, and 333.

Mike and I talked a lot on the phone during all this. The UFO sighting was impressive on its own, but we were both overwhelmed by all the synchronicities surrounding that one event. There are more that overlap into the next chapter, and these all seem tied into this same tightly knit web.

This is a powerful set of events, and I was involved—or at least my voice was. Because of this, I was fixated on the details of what had happened. I scrutinized maps, and did my best to measure the distances between the three points along Route 5. The two owl sightings, one real

13: Between Two Bridges

and the other a toy, took place about a year apart in time and almost exactly a mile from each other in distance. And as best as I can determine, the copper colored saucer was seen at the halfway point between these two owls.

But the one thing that leapt out at me was that, for both owl sightings, Mike had just crossed a bridge. This is meaningful, at least to me. If someone told me they'd had a dream of seeing an owl after crossing a bridge, I wouldn't be tied down to the literal. Instead, I'd be free to interpret the symbolic meaning of both the owl and the bridge.

I was at a paranormal conference and had the opportunity to talk with George Hanson and Rosemary Ellen Guiley, two researchers well versed in esoteric studies. I asked each of them, "What is the symbolic meaning of crossing a bridge?" They both told me the same thing, a bridge is liminal. It is neither here nor there, it is the nether world that connects two different places. The Latin word limen, means "a threshold."

In anthropology, liminality is the disorientation that occurs in the middle stage of a sacred ritual. It's the point when the participant no longer holds their pre-ritual status, but hasn't yet transitioned into their post-ritual role. The initiate "stands at the threshold" between their previous identity and something new.

A river can be seen as an obstacle, and crossing it means overcoming a challenge. The road is the path, symbolic of the life journey. In both cases he had just barely crossed the river, as if the rear wheels of his car were still on the bridge when the owls appeared.

I've come to see the details and themes of these experiences as playing out with a sort of dream logic. Instead of asking a pragmatic UFO investigator to make sense of what happened, maybe you should ask someone who interprets dreams. Those arcane skills might be better suited to analyze Mike's experiences near that bridge. I am now at the point where it's become normal to scrutinize reality as if it were a dream.

I spoke with a woman experiencer who told me that the owl should be seen symbolically in the context of UFOs, its role being to "announce initiation." I love that phrase, and it fits well with Mike's owl sighting as he crossed the bridge.[2]

About a month later, Mike contacted me with another account from that same stretch of highway. "Last Friday, on route 5, I was passing the landfill after the electrical station on my right. A bag flies into my windshield. It was a Wise Potato Chip bag. It got stuck on my wiper long enough to identify it."

Wise is a regional brand of potato chips, and their logo is the lone eye of an owl. The wise owl traces back to Athena, the Greek goddess of wisdom, as she was often portrayed with a companion little owl. Also of note, there's a Hooters on route 5 right near the Memorial Bridge. Again, more owl and goddess imagery.

A few weeks before this book went to press, Mike snapped a photo of the car in front of him while on route 5. The licence plate read 333, and it happened at 3:33 p.m. on the winter solstice of 2017.

Sketch drawn by Mike C to describe memories from childhood.

Mike sent me a drawing with two owls to capture what he remembers seeing from his bed as a boy (above). This illustration depicts two different memories from around the time he was 11 or 12. One is a smaller owl walking back and forth across his desk, something he remembers seeing fairly often. The other memory is something he only saw a few times, that of a much larger owl staring at him right up close to the bed. Both owls were blue.

My first thought was these images seemed terrifying, especially the big blue owl, and I asked how he felt. "That never terrified me. Weird, huh?"

There is a haunting power to this drawing. This is something that I've heard a lot, that people will wake to find an owl staring at them. It might be looking in through the window, standing somewhere in the room, or hovering as a sort of holographic apparition. Why an owl, and what it might mean is at the heart of this mystery.

Owls and orbs

Mike wrote to tell me about something that had happened the previous night in his son's room at bedtime, when he was nearly two and a half years old. He said, "As I was reading to him, I heard an owl chitter, plain as day. I then saw an orb. I debated telling you."

I pressed for details, and he said it happened while he was rocking his son to sleep in a big reclining chair. As he sat there, he heard owl sounds coming up from the floor, right at his feet. Then he looked up to see a faint orb materializing right in front of him, close enough to touch. It was about the size of a golf ball and traveled slowly across the room, then passed through the wall directly across from where he sat.

I asked a lot of questions about what happened. It was tricky to explain verbally, so Mike shot a short video with his phone. It was a hand held point of view as he walked from the hall and into his son's room. He showed the reclining chair, then pointed to a spot on the floor as the exact location of the owl sounds. Then he described the motions of the orb as it floated up and traced its path with his finger to the spot where it passed through the wall. You can hear the tension in his voice as he tries to articulate what he had seen the night before.

There's something more. I counted twenty-one little orbs passing across the frame during this two minute video.

We both tried to come to terms with what these glowing dots might be. He hadn't used a flash or light on the phone while recording, so there wasn't a light source close to the lens. Perhaps it was nothing more than dust or tiny insects, but it was mid-December, a time of year without flying bugs. And the dots didn't have lazy floating movements of dust particles in an air current, they were more frenetic.

After we considered a long list of mundane possibilities for what the orbs might have been, he got his phone again. His intention was to try and capture something more on video. This follow up clip was 1:29 minutes long, and it opens as he carefully sat down in the chair, declaring out loud that he didn't want to stir up any dust. After a few moments of sitting still, he began talking to the empty room. He was addressing the orbs themselves, and they seemed to react. Here is a transcription of what he said, and what can be seen along with the time count.

> (00:24) "If that entity is around that… Oop!" He starts asking a question, but before he can complete the sentence something appears. A slow graceful orb shows up, he sees it and exclaims, "Oop!"
>
> (00:31) "Hey there… You kidding me?" This seems to be the same orb from seconds before, it floats about mid-screen, fades out and the reappears just as he says, "Hey there."
>
> (00:36) "Okay… Oh, you flash at me now?" At this point his voice is playful. An orb zips up from the bottom of the screen at the word "Okay." Another crosses along the bottom left of the frame at the end of this statement.
>
> (00:46) "Well, can you do me a favor and do it again?" There's an immediate tiny flash, as if an answer to his request.

Right in the moment he was aware that these little dots of translucent light were performing in response to his words, but after watching the video multiple times I realized it was more than that. These small orbs were appearing *before* he could finish his question, so it's less a reaction, and more a simultaneous event. In both videos, he was only seeing the orb activity on the screen of his phone. This was unlike the night before when he had seen one with his own eyes.

The specks of light in those videos could be easily dismissed as nothing at all, but the timing is curious. I am cautious to declare anything, but I can't help but feel those little orbs were consciously interacting with Mike. It was both obvious and playful.

Another thing was that these videos were shot for me, as if these little orbs were appearing for both of us. Again, this might seem pompous, but I cannot separate myself from this mystery.

When Mike and I speak on the phone, we end up talking over and interrupting each other. We've both been struggling with the same thing—how do you actually deal with this weirdness? It's one thing to see a UFO, but it's something altogether more oppressive to get inundated with non-stop synchro-weirdness. He was overwhelmed and said so. Then he asked if I had any advice. I suggested that he might just ask the phenomenon to back off.

13: Between Two Bridges

I told him what I did when it got too overwhelming for me. There was a point in 2009 when I was seeing so many owls that I needed to find a way to dial it down. It was simply too much. I walked into the woods alone, and stated out loud that I would no longer pay attention to just any owl. Seeing an owl off in the distance in a tree, or on some fence post didn't count. I declared to the universe that I would only pay attention if an *owl crossed my path.*

A few days after making my plea, I was riding my bike through my little home town at twilight. While coasting down the middle of the street, I noticed an owl perched on a telephone line off to my left. As I got closer it dropped down, flying slow and smooth, passing right in front of me at eye level. Then it floated up and landed gracefully in a tree on the other side of the street. I had a few more sightings like this in the weeks that followed, and each time the owl would blatantly cross my path, as if demanding my attention. It seems someone heard my plea. (3)

He got back to me a few days after our phone call, "Dude, I just tried something and got some success!"

He told me what he had done. A lot of little signs had been piling up in his life, but it wasn't enough. He needed something more definitive, so he went out to the backyard and stood alone facing the woods at the edge of his property. He spoke aloud, "It's not enough." Immediately, an owl hooted in the tree off to his left.

He said, "Really?!"

Then there was a slow eerie hooting coming from the tree right in front of where he stood. He told me, "A couple seconds later I saw a bright flash at eye level a little to the left of the tree where I'd heard the ominous hoot. Seeing as I might have inadvertently insulted someone, I apologized and said thank you."

He snapped a few photos with his phone, aiming at the site of the flash and hooting. He sent me the three images, each showed a rural yard at night. Looking closer, one had swooping pale blur across the lower part of the frame. At first glance, the other two didn't have anything worth noting. Yet after adjusting the brightness and contrast, each had a thin straight line of dim light. We considered that these lines might be the motion of an insect caught in the picture. The problem was that this was a cool spring night in April in New England. A weather check for his town says it was in the low 60s, making bugs seem highly unlikely.

Trying to examine photos and videos within this research can be problematic. There might be an odd blur or speck in a picture connected to an unusual event. Sometimes these pictures are burdened with an emotional neediness, and I've seen people convince themselves that they've caught something paranormal when it might be nothing at all. To his credit, Mike has been even keeled about his photos and videos, he's mindful to consider the more likely causes. These experiences are often fraught with both paranoia and an eagerness to see alien clues everywhere. There might be a mundane explanation, but it's difficult to know for certain.

The call of the eastern screech owl

People will often contact me with their owl experiences, asking if I've ever heard of anyone else with the same story. This is tricky to answer because it's rare to hear the exact same account, yet it's common to hear stories with the same flavor or mood.

Here's a similar story involving Suzanne Chancellor, and it was through the twists and turns of these events that I eventually met Mike.

Suzanne and her partner Jack and had both been hearing an odd high-pitched whinny sound outside their bedroom window. They heard it many evenings for over a year. After some online research, Jack thought it was most likely a baby raccoon. Months later, Suzanne found a website with various owl sounds posted within an article. When she clicked on the call of the eastern screech owl, she realized that's what they'd been hearing.

A few nights later, Suzanne heard the noise again and went outside in hopes of recording the audio on her phone. She told me, "I was going to record it to share with you, so you could hear what I've been hearing."

Suzanne clearly heard two owls communicating to each other from adjoining trees in the neighbor's yard. She approached the closest tree and, "I suddenly saw an orange light/sphere/orb appear right where I was looking. It blinked on and blinked out, then the hooting stopped!"

It looked like an orange flashlight shining through the leaves of the tree. "It was pretty high up, maybe 30 feet. It was a bright orange light, about the size of an orange." She waited awhile, but never found the source of the light. After the flash, the owls remained silent.

Suzanne told me this story in the days leading up to a small UFO convention in Maine. I was to be one of the speakers, and wanted to include this story in my talk. I added a nice photo of her and Jack to my Powerpoint presentation. Then I found an audio clip of an eastern screech owl, and played for her it over the phone. She confirmed this was what she had been hearing, both outside her bedroom window, and just before the orange flash in the neighbor's tree. [4]

I needed to download that audio from the birding website and onto the Powerpoint document. This should have been easy, but something wasn't working. I stayed up late trying to get that owl call into the presentation, but couldn't. Andrea and I would be getting up early to travel from upstate New York to the conference in Portland Maine. I was frustrated, and eventually gave up. I went to bed knowing there would be a long drive the morning.

Sleep was fitful, and it seemed the sun was rising too soon. I was in a half awake state when I was jolted by the sound of an eastern screech owl right outside the bedroom window. It was unmistakable—I'd listened to this same call dozens of times the night before while attempting to load it into the presentation. Andrea heard it too, and blurted out, "Was that an owl?"

I said it sure was. I got out of bed and opened the window and tried to listen for more. We heard it just once, and this was the one and only time I've heard that call coming from a real owl.

The message was clear, I had to figure out a way to plug that audio into the presentation. I went to my desk and tried a few things, but nothing was working. I finally played the audio on my laptop while holding it up to the mic on my desktop. This was the only way I could manage to get the audio transferred.

The next day, I stood in front of an audience and gave my presentation. I told the story of Suzanne trying to record the owl sound and seeing an orange flash in a tree. To accentuate the story, I played the eerie whinny of an eastern screech owl to a room full of UFO enthusiasts.

I hadn't met him yet, but Mike was in the room, and when he heard that sound he nearly fell out of his chair. A year later at that same conference, he walked up to me and told me about his emotional reaction to the recorded owl calls in my presentation. He nervously explained that he had heard that same eerie sound coming out of the baby monitor that had been set up his son's room.

This is scary stuff, and my heart sank hearing it. I've listened to parents struggling to describe the fear that their child might be involved with the phenomenon. Within this research, this is the one thing that I find most challenging—how can I offer any solace to a parent with these kinds of worries? The emotions are unsettling, and I have no meaningful advice. [5]

There was very little I could say to Mike. I wrote about these emotions on page 41 in *The Messengers*.

> Parents will explain that their children are telling them about big owls that come into their bedrooms at night. Most of these giant owl stories are part of a larger narrative, one that includes UFO sightings or an outright abduction.[6]

Mike later took a photo of this page, circled the quote above, and posted it on a UFO group page on Facebook. That picture, and the synchronicities surrounding it, plays an important role in the next chapter.

This story began with the call of an eastern screech owl outside Suzanne's window, and it looped around until I woke hearing that same call. All this eventually connected me with Mike.

What struck me about these two stories was that Mike and Suzanne were both in their yard at night trying to record an owl. Suzanne tried to capture audio on her phone, and Mike tried to get a photo—and they were both doing it for me. I feel a powerful responsibility, not just to them, but to all the people reaching out to me.

During the writing of this chapter, Suzanne had been in the backyard sitting around the fire at night with Jack and their dog. She saw a curious orange dot in one of the trees along the edge of the yard. It was a small glowing point of light about the size of a marble, and she watched it for about 40 seconds. Her first thought was that it was something in the sky behind the tree, perhaps an airplane. But it was windy, and anything seen through the moving leaves and branches would have flickered. She considered it might have been a firefly, but it was too large, motionless and an orange-yellow color, unlike the typical pulsing green glow of a firefly.

A little while later, she saw a nearly identical orange dot in another tree. After a moment, she and Jack both heard the loud whinny of a screech owl coming from the closer of the two trees. She got out her phone to try to record the call, and as she approached the tree she realized there was a second owl hooting from the other tree where she had seen the second dot of light. The two owls seemed to be communicating with each other.

Though obviously not the same exact thing, Suzanne's story of owls and orbs in her yard has a very similar flavor of what Mike has described.

"Wake them up"

Like me, Mike talks very fast, and during one of our phone conversations he sort of slipped in the line, "I was told to wake people up."

I barely caught it and interrupted, "Wait, who told you that?"

He replied cautiously, "Uhmm, you know who."

I needed to hear more, and asked how it happened. Was this in a dream, or a real event? He said, "It was at night, but I wasn't asleep. I heard my son stirring, and I got up to go to the bathroom. I opened my bedroom door and saw a four foot blue gray being in the hall, I got in my head 'wake them up' and then I watched as it gently slid to my left through the wall."

He knew exactly what that message meant— that people are sleep walking, and he needed to do something to wake them up. "It's as if I saw the words and saw the world at the same time."

Mike has been using Facebook as a platform for this newfound purpose. Some postings have an urgent undertone, and you can sense his amped-up emotions. He explained his frustrations with mainstream UFO research and its focus is on sighting reports. "There are occupants in those craft. That's the real story, and it's being ignored. They're talking about objects, not about communication."

Facebook is a curious place to try and change the world. Here's one of his posts, "Everything that is happening right now is a result of my wanting to better myself. The visitors knew I wanted to change. When they knew I was open, they began the awakening."

I've spoken with Mike extensively, and also followed him on Facebook. He's been hit with a lot in the two years since we've met, and I sense he's on an edge; some of these experiences get brushed off as mundane, and at the same time it's clear that he's been struggling. This conflict isn't buried, it's right on the surface. Things happen that most people would rather ignore or deny, and coming to grips with these issues might only generate confusion and doubts. Trying to make sense of these experiences can be terribly difficult.

I've listened to Mike describe the intensity of some of what's happened, and I'm at a loss to offer up much. Here is an example of what he's been experiencing.

It was the middle of the day, and he saw a small orange being looking in through his kitchen window. He ran out the door and watched it running for the edge of the yard, then it just faded away. Not too long after he was in the backyard with his son and saw a gray being at his bedroom window, but this time it was inside the house looking out at them. He ran in the house, but there was nothing. Both these sightings seemed terrifying, and I asked if he was frightened. He said again, "None of this stuff has ever been scary."

It might not be scary for him, but I sense it's a lot more intense than seeing 333 on a licence plate.

He was told to "wake people up" by a telepathic being in his hallway, and then he started doing exactly that. This could be seen as a sinister order meant to deceive, or an important message to help humanity. Mike is a healthcare worker, and he is helping people. There is nothing about him that is new-agey or fluffy. He's intense, compassionate, and doing the hard work to heal people. At the same time, he's working to heal the world.

Here's one of his Facebook posts: "I have been trying to make waves....waves of awakening."

Chapter 14
The Owl and the White Buffalo

> I guess I'm just following the synchronous bread crumb trail in an attempt to get to the bottom of my experiences.

Those words arrived in my email inbox in November of 2011. They were part of a letter from a woman named Brenda, who said she'd had a "very strange owl experience."

I contacted her right away, and we spoke on the phone for several hours. She shared two stories that were extremely unusual, one of which involved an enormous owl staring at her through a window. We eventually lost touch, but the strangeness of what she'd shared always stuck with me.

I wanted to include her owl account in *The Messengers*, but I couldn't get in touch with her. I ended up doing something I didn't like—I used her account without permission. It was told in a sparse way with very few details, so I didn't feel there were any ethical issues. But it was unlike me.

I received an anonymous comment on my blog on September 17, 2016. In it was the line, "I spoke to you back in 2011 regarding the huge owl on the back deck after a night of a weird visitation." I immediately knew it was Brenda, and put up my own comment on the blog along with my email address and asked to speak with her again.

She got back to me by email the next day, and I replied with an apology for using her story without permission. Included in that message was the single paragraph of her account from page 41 of *The Messengers*. The passage began, "There are also stories of what seem to be real owls, but the context is so strange that it is hard to truly know."

In her follow-up email, she said she didn't mind that her experience was in the book, and I was relieved. The reason she'd reached out to me again was that she saw an image of a page from my book. It had been recently posted on a Facebook group page dedicated to alien abduction, and she felt pretty sure that the guy who'd added the image had his own contact experiences.

Three days later on September 21, the autumnal equinox, Brenda sent me an email with an image attached. She wrote:

> Also, I don't know if you remember me saying that there was a guy on Facebook who posted a page from your book, which was another one of those significant coincidences. After you quoted the part where you included my owl experience (pg. 41), I went back to that guy's photo of the page from your book. The page he posted had my story on it, haha! I've attached the photo... The guys name is Mike something. His last name starts with a C.

I knew instantly that it was Mike from the previous chapter. It was the day before when he had sent me the message about seeing both an owl and a huge UFO while listening to my voice. This was personal; it involved me, and because of that it feels like one of the most powerful owl stories I've ever encountered. The book is nearly 400 pages long, and he'd circled a passage that was important to him. The very next line was Brenda's experience.

I should be used to this kind of thing by now, but this went way beyond coincidence—it felt like I was being shaken by something that was demanding my attention.

When I replied to Brenda that I knew him, I added this: "Holy crap, my right ear started ringing as I typed that!"

I will occasionally get a loud high pitched ringing in one ear, and it seems to show up when I am talking about UFOs. This time it happened for just the few seconds that it took me write out that I knew Mike.

Reviewing the timeline of all these messages made me feel that something has been orchestrated. The web of connections is woven too tightly to ignore. There are two different people with two different stories, but they overlapped in a way that shook me to my core.

Mike C and I spoke on the phone for the first time the same day I received Brenda's letter with the image of page 41. He needed to tell me the entire story of the owl and the flying saucer as much as I needed to hear it. The next morning, he sent me a cell phone video of something strange hovering above his house. There wasn't much to see, just a small dot of light in the predawn sky, but the anxiety in his voice was palpable.

For the next few days, Brenda's messages were overlapping with

14: The Owl and the White Buffalo

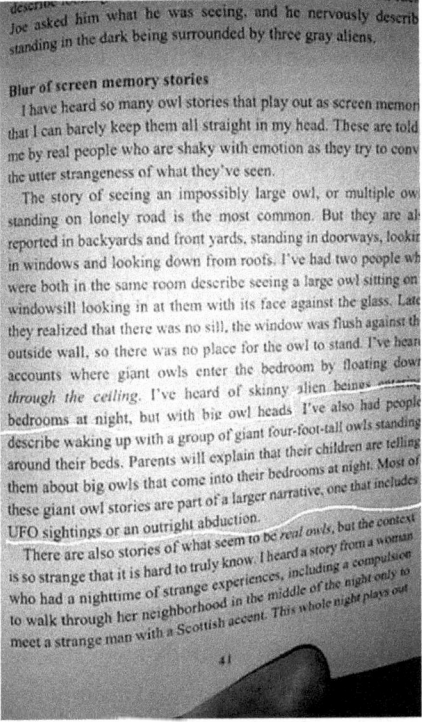

The circled text is quoted in the previous chapter, and the line below describes Brenda's experience

Mike C's. It would be nearly six months later when I finally spoke with Brenda again. She retold the two stories I had first heard six years earlier in 2011.

An owl out the back door

Brenda's owl experience began on Halloween night when she was 22 years old. She was at her mother's house with her boyfriend; they were getting ready for a costume party, and were both dressed as goth vampires. They ended up getting in an argument and he left. She was upset and wanted to talk to her sister. She said, "Somehow I got it in my head that I was going to walk to my sister's house, even though it was a twenty minute drive."

I interrupted and asked if she had ever walked to her sister's house before. She laughed, "Oh heck no, I had decided to walk even though I knew that I never would have made it, and at that point it was past midnight."

She'd had a few wine coolers and thought it would be better not to drive, but I could hear in her voice that might not have been the reason. Looking at a map, this would have been about 12 miles. She knows it doesn't make sense, but she left her mom's house and started walking.

She hadn't walked very far when a car pulled over and big guy with a Scottish accent offered her a ride. She was wasn't sure what to do, but he said he was a jazz musician as if that somehow made it okay. Hearing this, she got in his car.

Something about this seems so unsettling, and I asked about her impressions, now over twenty years later. She's very aware of how odd this sounds, getting in a strange man's car in the middle of the night is something she would never do. She described him as a big man with red hair and a red beard. He talked about being a musician, and she felt really awkward the entire drive.

He dropped her off at her sister's house on a quiet suburban block that backed up to a dense forest. Nobody answered when she knocked, and all the doors were locked. She walked around to the back deck and sat alone in the dark for what felt like two hours. She spent that time waiting, all the while with the strong feeling she was being watched.

When her sister finally arrived home, she turned the on the light in the room next to the deck and Brenda stood right up against the sliding glass door and knocked. This scared her sister terribly, and it took her a moment to calm down enough to let her in.

Brenda desperately wanted talk about her relationship problems, but it was after two in the morning and they were both tired. They got the couch set up for Brenda, and said goodnight. Her sister's bedroom door was within view of the couch where she was sleeping.

Brenda was jolted awake when the television suddenly came on. She was instantly fully awake, but her body felt heavy it was hard to move. The clock on the VCR read 4:19 a.m. Her first thought was that her sister's husband was getting up early for work, and that the TV was on some sort of timer. It was a talk show with two women in conversation. There was sound, but the image on the screen was weirdly dark as if the brightness was turned down.

Electronics acting strangely is commonly reported in UFO visitation accounts, so the TV turning on by itself is a red flag that something more might have happened. She was seeing two women talking on the TV, and this is precisely the reason she had gone out into the night. She wanted to talk with her sister about her relationship issues, and that's what was presented to her—two women in conversation.

Brenda turned the volume way down on the TV, then noticed an odd amber glow coming from her sister's bedroom. There was a shuffling sound, and a shadow moved within the strange light. The couch was right next to the door to her room, close enough to hear easily.

She said, "I got this weird feeling. Something was really wrong. Something about the color of that light wasn't natural. Whatever comes out of that bedroom, I don't want to know what it is." Brenda was suddenly overwhelmed with fear, "I closed my eyes really tight and suddenly felt that dropping off the cliff feeling. It was sudden and powerful, like I was forced into sleep. I never drop into sleep that fast or that heavy."

She awoke facing the window, and saw the fading light of dusk. She said, "It was was really pretty, the clouds were streaked with pink and purple."

Her only thought was that she must have slept the entire day, and it was now evening. She stared at this lovely view for about five minutes when the phone rang, and was suddenly seeing a bright blue sky. She struggled to try to explain how jarring this was because the view went from sunset to full daylight without so much as a blink. I asked, "Could it have been dawn? Could the sun have been rising and not setting?"

"No, because I was facing west, so it had to have been sunset. My body had already adjusted to the wakeful state. My eyes didn't blink, it was set off by the phone ringing. It was just BAM! Noon with no clouds in a bright blue sky. I was like, that didn't just happen."

She answered the phone, and it was her mother asking to talk to her sister. Brenda frantically tried to explain what had just happened, how it had jumped from sunset to noon. Her mother seemed interested, but couldn't stay on the line.

Just before hanging up the phone, she noticed a gigantic owl just off the back deck. It was on a branch, and its weight bent the branch down so low that it was almost resting on the side railing of the deck. She said there was something creepy about this owl, "It looked three foot tall, it was white with wispy gray feathers. The eyes were pitch black. It was so spooky because as I was pacing back and forth waiting for my sister to come home, its eyes followed me everywhere I went. It never took its eyes off me."

The owl stayed there all afternoon, staring at her through the sliding glass door. When her sister arrived home from doing errands, Brenda hurried her to the big window and asked, "Are you seeing what I'm seeing?" Her sister saw the owl too, and remarked that it was enormous.

About ten minutes later, they both watched the owl fly off. Brenda said, "I remember the branch rising up. It was quite a large branch, so it bounced up and down really heavy and slow."

I asked if she thought this was a real owl, or some sort of screen projection. She answered in a shaky way as if she wasn't sure. She remembered it as a real owl, yet it seemed too big, she described it as the size of a small child. In the days that followed our conversation, she searched through pictures for an owl that looked like what she had seen, but couldn't find anything that matched. She recently sent me photos of great gray and barred owls, and said these were close.

After that owl flew off, Brenda spoke excitedly with her sister about all the strange things that had taken place the night before. First, she asked if the television had been set on some sort of timer, and she replied that it hadn't. Then Brenda tried to describe the eerie orange light coming from her sister's bedroom, and asked if her husband was up early for some reason. Her sister said that he was out of town, and that she'd slept soundly through the night.

During the writing of this chapter, Brenda asked her sister what she remembered of that night. She remembered the owl, and that it was huge. Brenda also told her about having "real dreams" all through that night. Another thing she shared was that it didn't make sense that she didn't get home until after two in the morning because she never stayed out that late.

Brenda said, "The whole thing was really weird and for the next two or three days I felt off kilter. It was like a non-reality, almost as if I was in sort of shock."

Kundalini awakening

It wasn't long after these events that Brenda broke up with her boyfriend. In the aftermath, she went on a health kick which began as a way to distract herself from getting depressed.

"I began a discipline of mind, body and spirit alignment." This meant yoga every day, meditating, exercising, eating a vegan diet, affirmations and reading spiritual books. There wasn't any profound reason for this change, she was just doing what felt right to keep a feeling of peace.

She said, "After about six months... I came into some kind of body soul spirit alignment and I had a powerful Kundalini awakening."

She described waking one morning with a low vibration in the base of her spine. The next morning it happened again and this time it lasted a couple of minutes. The sensation scared her.

There is a slow calmness to how Brenda speaks, so it was disarming to hear what she said next. "The third time it happened, it wasn't going away and it was growing in intensity. Only this time I had the distinct feeling that something was about to shoot up my spine like a rocket! I had the immediate urge to sit upright in bed and just let it happen—I really had no choice. Well when it did, it was like liquid sunshine shooting up like a geyser through the top of my head!"

This intense surge seemed to push a mass of black tar out through the top of her head, "I could see it dripping down my face before suddenly dissipating into nothing."

> Then the light burst forth and poured through my entire body... My whole body became luminous with these sparkly golden white lights and everything became a hologram... I was lit up from the inside out and became translucent. I knew this because I held my hand in front of my face and saw that I could see right through it! And there was light pouring out from the inside! Also, as I looked around the room I realized that I could see right through the walls to the trees and houses outside. There was this ocean of light... and I wasn't prepared for it and I was scared.

Despite this profound experience, she still had to get up and go to work. She worked at a medical office doing their billing, updating patient files and answering phones.

> I always knew what the date was because that's how my day began. I started up my computer and while I was waiting for it to come alive, I started going through the stack of patient files on my in-bin. And I noticed that they were all the same files from the day before—Tuesday. I thought maybe there was a mistake or maybe they all needed to be updated again.

She knew it was Wednesday the eighth, so she checked the day and date on her computer monitor, and it read Tuesday the seventh. Maybe the computer hadn't updated, so she shut it down and restarted it. When it came back up, it still said Tuesday the seventh. She turned to a coworker in the next cubicle and said her computer was displaying yesterday's date. They got into an argument, Brenda said it was Wednesday and her coworker said it was Tuesday. Eventually Brenda gave in, reliving Tuesday and updating all the same files as she had the day before.

She said, "The phone calls were pretty much all the same as the day before, each was like deja vu. I knew exactly who was calling and what they were going to say. Also, everyone in the office who came within a ten foot radius of me began acting strangely. I thought maybe it was the residual effect of this strange brilliant energy that was still emanating through me from that morning. They would start to giggle and smile and say that they felt so strange. They said they felt tingly all over and it felt really good."

She said, "I'm not sure what happened but I am absolutely certain that I repeated that Tuesday."

At this point the synchronicities were overwhelming, and it frightened her. Things were happening that she didn't understand—she would have a thought about God while driving, and at that same moment the DJ on the radio would say God, and at the same time the word God was on the billboard in her line of view.

> It was like boom, boom, boom, it was synchronous, like right now, right now, *right now!* Everything was like that and I became so scared because I didn't know what was happening. The best way that I can describe it is that I was aligned and filled with the Christ Light, and anything that was not resonating with this energy caused me tremendous discomfort. I had to go away, I had to get out of the city.

She saw a world filled with illusion, as if everyone were wearing a mask; the corruption and dishonesty around her was completely transparent. And there were things about her job that required her to be less than truthful to the people she spoke with on the phone. "I could not abide by that. Not in the state that I was in. It was like lying to God's face. I couldn't live in any kind of untruth or deception. So I wound up running away with the gypsies."

She described how everything was, "...in some sort of perfect alignment to abruptly close out my old life and begin an entirely new life."

Things were falling apart, but she saw it as necessary. She lost her boyfriend, lost her job, lost her house. "The universe was moving, it was driving me. Like the stars had aligned, and they all point with a huge arrow saying go this way!"

The double-edged sword

It was during this chaotic time that she took a weekend job at an outdoor renaissance festival. This was carnival of free spirits and eccentrics, old world music, food, artisans, fortune tellers and tarot readers. The job meant wearing a costume from that era, and she spent her days dressed as a medieval peasant.

While at the fair, she spoke with a troupe of gypsy musicians and tried to explain the strange recent events in her life. One of the performers stood nearby and overheard their conversation. He approached Brenda and handed her a white rose. Speaking in a beautiful romantic tone, he asked her to leave everything behind and travel with him in the caravan.

I interrupted, "Wait, you mean you really did run away with gypsies? I thought it was, like, some kind of metaphor."

"Yeah, I went with them. I closed out my bank account, packed up and left. It was the most magical experience of my life." [1]

Brenda was now part of the tightly knit community that worked these traveling festivals, and they called themselves "Rennies."

This next story took place during the down time in between renaissance festivals. Brenda and her traveling companion Luke were staying at the home of his friend in Texas. They had also worked the traveling fair circuit, but had recently settled down.

On their first night, they all sat together. The scene was pleasant; there was a fire in the fireplace, and a football game on a small television. The lady of the house asked Brenda if she would like some Turkish coffee, and without knowing what it was she said yes. It was served in traditional little cups, and she was surprised at its strength. A gracious guest, she drank it all.

Luke's childhood friend Jacob arrived at the door. Brenda was meeting him for the first time, and he was very soft spoken and shy. Both Luke and his friend went outside. She sat and made conversation with her hosts, a husband and wife, all while drinking two more cups of the strong black coffee. The husband was watching a football game.

Luke and Jacob came back inside after about twenty minutes. They were were oddly quiet, and Jacob had a sword in its scabbard hanging from his belt.

I asked her, "Wait, where did he get a sword?"

She said it's the kind of thing "Rennies" have lying around, so it wasn't really unusual.

Then Jacob positioned himself with one foot on the raised fireplace hearth and spoke to the room in a deep theatrical voice. He said, "Long ago came forth the story of the White Buffalo, and how the power of its light and shall be one day return to earth…"

His voice was different. Instead of the gentle whisper when they met, he sounded like James Earl Jones reciting Shakespeare.

He delivered a long mythic parable about the secret meaning of White Buffalo, and how it embodies the light of Christ. His words were booming, full of authority and power. He explained that there was an energy affecting the world on a grand scale, and its power is too concentrated and would throw things out of balance. He said that evolution must happen slowly, and The White Buffalo must be brought down. It wasn't cruel to bring down a symbolic creature—it's that our lives and our world depended on it.

As he spoke, the energy of the room seemed to change. It felt eerie, and Brenda felt the need to avert her eyes. She turned and caught a glimpse of the television, but instead of seeing the football game on the screen, she saw the living room where she was seated. It was as if there were a live video feed of all of them as they listened to Jacob's melodramatic sermon. She looked back and forth, between what was happening in the room and the television, and it was the same scene. The image on the screen was from her point of view, as if the camera was in her mind.

The speech reached its crescendo. He unsheathed the sword with dramatic flourish and spoke the line, "The White Buffalo has been reborn, and the Christ has returned. So the hunt is on!"

Then he turned and pointed the sword at Brenda. He looked her dead in the eye with a fierce expression and declared, "If you think the sword was sharp last time, now it is twice as sharp and doubled edged."

After delivering those final words, Jacob calmly put the sword back in its sheath, sat on the hearth and fell silent. He looked down at his hands and appeared to be totally confused, like he had no idea what had just happened.

Everyone in the room was quiet for a long time. Eventually the lady of the house broke the silence and said, "Well, I'm going to bed." The husband added, "Yep, some of us have to work in the morning." Then everyone left the room.

Brenda said she couldn't sleep that night, partly because of the Turkish coffee, but more because of the strange drama that played out in the living room. "There was someone roaming around the house, I was sure of it. I had the feeling of my hair standing up, it was the feeling of being watched."

She awoke late the next day and found Luke and Jacob playing a video game in the living room. She asked, "Okay you guys, what was all the shit about the White Buffalo last night?" They were both confused and didn't seem to know what she was talking about.

Their response angered her, and she said, "You guys are messing with my head and I don't appreciate it!" They acted clueless, and she demanded, "What was this story about the White Buffalo?"

She pressed them, and they got angry. Confused, she backed down and stopped asking.

A couple of hours later, after Jacob had left, there was a knock at the door. Luke answered it and Brenda overheard the conversation. There were two Jehovah's Witnesses asking to come into the house to talk. Luke was very clear that it wasn't his house and they couldn't come in.

They kept pestering and finally said, "Well, actually, some of the members of our church saw a UFO hovering above your house last night and that's what we wanted to talk to you about."

At that point Luke shut the door in their face.

She said, "It was really weird. There was a UFO above the house that none of us knew about. And the whole thing about the White Buffalo that neither of them seemed to remember. I was the only one that remembered and they said it never happened."

Brenda was freaked out and scared. She had the feeling that that this tale was meant for her, that she was the White Buffalo. It felt like she was being told her kundalini awakening has caused some disturbance in the grand balance of humanity. She had the thought, "I had better tone it down quickly lest I be forcibly brought down!"

Jacob ended his heavy-handed speech with the line about a new sword being twice as sharp and doubled edged. In the New Testament, the word of God is described as a sharper than a double-edged sword.

> For the word of God is alive and active. Sharper than any double-edged sword, it penetrates even to dividing soul and spirit, joints and marrow; it judges the thoughts and attitudes of the heart. Hebrews 4:12 (NIV)

The phrase double-edged sword means something that "cuts both ways," something both advantageous and detrimental. That strange monologue was summed up with a paradox, both a blessing and a threat.

The two Jehovah's Witnesses who came to their door said something else, implying that the UFO above the house was a sign from Jehovah that they were chosen. Brenda said, "Over the years I have wondered if they were really Jehovah's Witnesses, or if they were from one of those organizations who show up on your doorstep after a UFO visitation. I feel that this part is relevant because it ties in with the whole biblical context of the double-edged sword."

A few things seem noteworthy from these experiences. One is that it all seemed to begin on Halloween, an appropriate date given all spooky incidents. Brenda and her boyfriend were dressed as vampires, and the ancient mythology had Lilith in a very vampire like role. This ancient goddess could transform into an owl, fly through the night and drink the blood of babies. Brenda didn't see the owl on the back deck until the following afternoon, but the timing is curious.

The second story also begins with Brenda being in a costume. She was dressed in medieval peasant attire when Luke handed her the white rose. I'm not sure if this means anything, but it's a funny little detail. Brenda described Luke as being powerfully psychic, "He was one with the spiritual realm, it flowed through him like water." She remembers they had on old radio, and it would crackle with static every time he walked by, even though it was unplugged and without batteries.

Three UFO events

"I've been seeing tons of UFOs since I was 17." Brenda told me this in one of our long phone calls. To anyone outside this field of research this might sound absurd, but it's common within these studies.

Brenda left her sister's house at sunset, the same house where they'd seen the big owl out the back window. There had been a birthday party for her sister's son, and she was on her way to visit her grandparents. It was a clear evening in October, and it would take an hour and 15 minute to get to their house.

The drive took her north on a main highway as the sun was dipping below the horizon. Looking to her left, she saw bright dot of light low in the western sky. Her first thought was that it was a planet, but it was moving slowly upwards. Her route took her on another highway heading east, and the bright light was now off to the right. It was difficult to focus on it and drive at the same time, but she tried to keep an eye on it. There was something about it that seemed so strange. She thought, "It can't be an airplane."

Brenda carefully explained her route on the big grid of farm roads. She would be traveling north, then make a right angle turn east, then back north again, and with each turn the dot of light would be seen from the opposite side of the car. It was confusing at the time, but after looking at a map she realized that the thing in the sky seemed to be moving in one direction, but that was hard to perceive in the moment with all the turns on the roads.

She lost sight of the object after leaving the main highway and traveling onto smaller farm roads. It wasn't long before she saw it again, and now it seemed to be moving toward her grandparents' house. Seeing this she pulled over, turned the engine off and rolled down the window. She watched as it moved across the twilight sky, listened for any noise, but heard nothing. As far as she could tell, it was flying in total silence.

As it got closer, she could see a single bright headlight in front, which must have been what she thought was a star when she'd first seen it in the western sky.

It moved in low until it was above the road where she was parked. She said, "It came right over my car and shifted its angle to where its underbelly was facing me… it was like it was looking at me."

Until that moment she hadn't seen its shape. It seemed to be intentionally showing itself, tilting in a way so she could see the entire underside of the craft. It was a triangle, but the three long edges weren't straight, each were slightly bowed. She said it looked somewhat like the insignia on the uniforms in the original Star Trek series. It had a single large green light in the center and a strobing red light on the tail end.

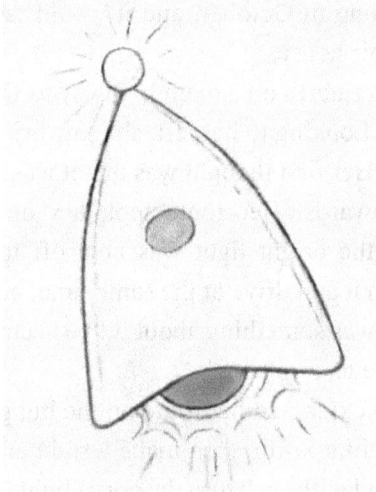

Witness drawing from Brenda.

As it slowly leveled out, her teeth began to hurt. She was feeling some sort of painful high pitched sound, and it scared her. She rolled up the windows, locked the doors, and watched the craft pivot and change direction.

It slowly traveled above the road ahead of her car for about a quarter mile, then tilted and rose up. She was looking at the strobing red light at the tail as it moved away from her. It continued rising upwards, getting smaller and smaller in the night sky, until all she could see was a small blinking red dot. Eventually it disappeared completely at what she assumed to be a tremendously high elevation. She'd seen odd lights in the sky many times before, but this was the closest and longest sighting she'd ever had.

After it was gone, she looked at the clock. She was aware of missing time in UFO reports, yet there was no sense of anything unusual, the time and travel seemed normal. We talked about this event, and she struggled with one odd detail—she remembers looking up at the underbelly of the craft from outside the car. Yet at the same time, she feels she only rolled her window down to look up, and never left the car. This would have been on the last stretch of road before her grandparents' house.

I asked if anything had happened after she'd arrived. She replied that a lot of odd things happened at that house, then shared curious story. "It wasn't the same weekend of seeing the craft, but I had a dream of being anointed with rose oil. I woke up at their house to a very pungent aroma of crushed red roses. The fragrance was all over my nightgown and embedded into the fabric of my bed linens. I know this smell did not come from the perfumes of detergents. My grandmother only used Tide and bleach to wash her linens. She did not have any kind of perfume and neither did I, especially rose oil."

She also shared a story from the spring of 1994. Having heard about a recent flap of UFO sightings on the western coast of Michigan, she convinced a friend to drive around looking for things in the sky. They ended up seeing something near the Miracle Twin Drive-In theater outside of the city of Flint. [2]

Brenda commented when something passed high over their car, and her friend said, "It's just an airplane." At that instant it stopped, then backed up until it was directly above their car. It held its position while they scrambled to get the binoculars they had brought with them.

They looked up to see a silver triangle with a red light in the center with four "Tic-Tac" shapes on the bottom of the craft. But what seemed most bizarre is how it sat so perfectly still above them.

Brenda said, "It was so eerily still, it gave me the creeps." She struggled to describe the strangeness of it. "It was like our world was a hologram."

This was difficult for me to follow, so I pressed her for more. She said, "It's hard to explain. It's like seeing a person standing still on a stage with a movie screen behind them showing the sky. The person in front is 3D and the movie is 2D, they are totally separate. You see both, but they're not the same. It's like the rest of life was moving, but that triangle was too still, and my brain was struggling to accept it."

Brenda had another sighting that began with an unsettling dream where her best friend from childhood was in danger. When she awoke, it was clear to her that this was something more than a dream—it was some sort of clairvoyant message. Her friend was in an abusive relationship, and might be in serious trouble.

Brenda was concerned but wasn't sure what to do. It was the middle of the night, and she didn't want to call her on the phone. She was wide awake and worried and didn't feel like she could get back to sleep, so maybe she should just drive to her friend's house. She got up, grabbed her car keys, walked out to the driveway and saw that her car was blocked. Someone had parked behind her.

It was normal to have extra cars at the house, and she thought maybe someone had a friend over. What seemed weird was the car that had blocked her in was a very similar make, model and color as hers, enough to confuse her in the dark.

She could see silhouettes moving around inside this other car as she approached. Getting closer, they were suddenly gone—the car was empty. She peeked in the window, close enough to see the flowered Hawaiian print seat covers. Something was terribly wrong. An eerie feeling flooded over her and she backed away from the car. But it wasn't a car, whatever was there was shifting into something else.

She turned to run back inside, and was suddenly aware of something pointy and black looming above the roof of her house. She stood frozen as she watched a hovering triangle slowly glide into view. It was low, just above the treetops, and although it wasn't illuminated she could see what she assumed was a red light in the center of the structure. There was something unnatural in the way this thing was moving above her—its sliding motions were creepy, and she was scared.

It positioned itself directly above her, and looking straight up she saw big block letters that read USAF. These were printed on the underbelly of the craft in some sort of reflective text. She said, "My body got so heavy, I fell to my knees, I was trying to stay awake but I just collapsed."

From this point her memories are blurry, and she ended up lying on the driveway next to her own car. She could smell the grass and feel the pebbles pressing against the side of her face. She was looking at the underside of her car, "All I could think was, it's so dirty and I really need to wash it. Then I blacked out."

When she woke up the next morning, she was backwards in bed, and her head was where her feet should have been. There was no sense that what had happened the night before was any kind of dream. It seemed entirely real, as if all her senses were fully engaged. "I know when I am dreaming. But this wasn't like that. It was reality as far as I know reality."

Sometime later, a vision from that night popped into her mind. She remembered seeing a blue holographic screen hovering in mid air, it happened when that triangle was positioned above her. She was staring at some kind of transparent projection with a long list of names on the left and numbers on the right, and they were scrolling fast.

"It felt like it was somehow being downloaded into me, but I don't know what it was all about. All the other things felt real, but suddenly remembering that blue screen is a mystery to me. I don't know if it really happened, I'm skeptical."

The trauma of not knowing

I had sent emails and phone messages to Brenda in the years after we spoke in 2011, but never received a reply. There was something unsettling about the two stories she shared, and I wanted to check in. Another reason I'd tried to contact her was that my notes from our one phone call were sparse. The key details were written down, but it felt unclear. I was doubting my memory.

Brenda explained the reason she never replied in the years after our first conversation. She wrote to me: "That's such a shame that we didn't connect back then. I vaguely remember you trying to contact me, but I had a pretty wicked spell there a while back. I was suffering from debilitating clinical depression and I cut off contact with pretty much everyone and didn't check my email for a long time. I apologize for missing your communication."

I understood. I've suffered terribly from depression and have spoken about it elsewhere in this book, my previous book and in my blog. Over the years I've met with a lot of abduction researchers, many of whom are practicing therapists, and each has listened attentively as I've described my long history of dark moods. All of them seemed to treat this as something normal, the connection between UFO events and depression. It's hard to determine the source of depression, but trauma can certainly be a cause. Even if it's been forgotten, trauma would still have the same power to influence one's emotional well being.

I've talked with a lot of people who tell of experiences very similar to what Brenda has shared. Many will confide about anxiety, insecurities or bouts of depression, but these personal issues won't come up in the first phone call. They'll only emerge after long hours of conversation. I am not a psychologist, so there isn't much I can offer in the way of advice, all I can say is that I know how hard it can be.

Looking back on her experiences, Brenda sees them strung together all along her life path, as if arranged for some purpose. "The Halloween thing with the owl and my sister led to the Kundalini awakening, which led to running away with the gypsies, which led to the night of the White Buffalo and the UFO. It's almost like things were set on a roll."

Brenda told me, "I've had a life of high strangeness, but even after all of the UFO sightings… I've never once seen one of those beings that they all talk about. I just don't understand what it's all about. How can I share so many similar experiences, and yet have no clear involvement with these beings?"

There is a misconception within our popular culture that alien contact means one thing—tiny gray aliens entering bedrooms and whisking people up to their flying saucers. This might be part of it, but I feel it's only a small facet of something much more complex and far-reaching. The phenomena is capable of hiding itself by erasing or altering memories. This makes it terribly difficult to comprehend what might be at play, and a lot of people are suffering from not knowing what has happened.

Much of Brenda's story is hard to categorize. One example is the morning of her Kundalini awakening. She described liquid sunshine shooting up out of the top of her head while black tar dripped down her face. This is not a UFO event in the way we think of them, yet it's precisely the kind of bizarre thing that shows up in the lives of people who've endured these experiences. In her youth, she suffered from a debilitating paranoia that the people around her were "going to find out that I'm not human." This curious detail is quite commonly reported, one more clue in the column of proof. But proof of what?

Brenda's story is echoed by many others. Her confusion and the need for answers is at the core of what I hear, and what I feel myself. I'm

14: The Owl and the White Buffalo

playing a role in all of this as an author and researcher, but also as an experiencer. This is personal for me, and I feel an obsessive need to chronicle these stories. I've surrendered to this work, and it's both baffling and inspiring. Over the last decade I've connected with a lot of people, and listened closely as they recount what they've endured. After hearing so much there should be some new insight, yet all I've come away with is an awareness of the monumental difficulties within this subject. I want to offer some solace to the people who've shared so much with me, but it's a helpless feeling not being able to provide the answers they so desperately seek.

Chapter 15
Kristin in the Desert

I received an email in June of 2014 from a woman named Kristin, and she told me that her first ever sighting of an owl coincided with a UFO sighting. She even hinted this might have been an abduction event, then added, "But I don't remember anything but the breadcrumbs."

I wanted to hear more and told her so. There was a follow-up email the next day, and here's what she said:

> I had to tell you about this morning. I have been trying to meditate for five minutes every dawn. Today I was able to clear my mind for almost two minutes (this is exciting to me since I could only do it for seconds at a time at first). Anyway, afterwards a song bombarded me out of nowhere (I am clairaudient) so I looked it up on YouTube. I had never seen the video, but I knew the song. I had been thinking about communicating with you and the whole UFO issue (before meditating) so this was such a delightful nod. I love it when the universe is playful. You will like the last few seconds. Delicious.[1]

I clicked the link and watched a short animation set to the Cat Stevens song *Moonshadow*. The imagery was stylized to match the cover art from his 1971 album, *Teaser and the Firecat*. It's a timepiece of trippy storybook illustration with a boy and cat. The song plays while they ride around on the moon past watercolor rainbows, twinkling stars, and psychedelic spirals. The last few seconds shows five red owls with bright yellow eyes lifting the moon out of a tree. The moon is no longer a sphere, but suspiciously saucer shaped, and the owls spin this disc upwards into the night sky.

It seems that Kristin was "bombarded" to watch a cartoon of owls and a flying saucer right after I asked to hear her owl and UFO experience. In our follow up correspondence, Kristin went on to describe something very familiar to me:

> For about 15 years I was absolutely compelled to hike the harsh desert terrain of Big Bend National Park here in Texas. I would go out for days and sometimes weeks by myself. Those days of lonely hiking are some of my most cherished memories. . . I wonder now if I was having abductions/contact during that time since I was so often alone miles away from other humans and had many mystical experiences.

She told me all those years of hiking alone was more than walking through a barren terrain, it was about meditating. This chapter of her life is now in the past, yet she still longs for that state of being. She cut her teeth on extreme desert travel, a place with scarce water, thorns, rattlesnakes and scorpions. But more dangerous than anything was the brutal heat; traveling on foot in a barren wilderness with temperatures over 100 degrees can be fatal if you underestimate its power. She said after that, hiking anywhere else seemed boring, "It seemed that I couldn't be satisfied by an environment if it wasn't trying to kill me."

She described herself as absolutely unafraid of this kind of travel. Instead, it was something she thrived on. This might come across as reckless to most people, but I understand it deeply. I've had this same compulsion for long ambitious trips alone, and like Kristin, I'd surrendered to it for decades. I've also wondered if I'd had unremembered UFO contact during my solitary time in the mountains.

Her very first sighting of an owl happened sometime in the early 1990s. This was the chapter in Kristin's life when she was hiking and camping alone in the desert. She spent her time deep in the backcountry of Big Bend, a huge expanse of remote wilderness along the Mexico border in southwest Texas.

Her best friend JoAnne (a pseudonym) had joined her on one of these trips. They stayed with close friends Gracia and Eladio, a married couple who lived and worked in the park. Their home was among a small cluster of government employee trailers along a dusty loop road hidden behind one of the visitor centers. They shared a bedroom in the back end of the last trailer. The room had one large window, facing out onto the vast desert wilderness and the big open sky.

Kristin and JoAnne had been sleeping there and doing day hikes in the rugged terrain nearby. They had spent the early part of the evening at the local hot springs, and drove back to Eladio and Gracia's trailer where they would be spending the night. Just as they were about to park, they saw an enormous white owl. It flew right up to their windshield, opened its wings and swooped off.

This was the first time Kristin had ever seen an owl, and they were both talking excitedly about it when they entered the trailer. Gracia told them she'd recently seen a big owl and assumed it must be the same one.

Their plan was to get up early so they could hike before the heat of the day. They went to the back bedroom with the big window where they shared a king-sized bed, and set their alarm for 5 a.m. The next morning they were unusually tired and having a hard time getting ready for the day. It was still dark when they sat and had coffee with Eladio, who was already at the breakfast table dressed for work in his ranger uniform.

Suddenly, Kristin remembered why she felt so tired. She complained to her friends at the table that she hadn't slept well because of the moon. She said, "For what seemed like hours, the full moon had been shining brightly in my eyes through that damn bay window."

JoAnne agreed, "Oh right, that was bothering me too. It was so bright!"

They were both grumbling about losing sleep because of the moon when Eladio interrupted, "Umm, there was no moon last night."

They looked at the weather section in the newspaper, checked the phase of the moon, and realized he was right. The moon couldn't have been visible at any point the previous night, yet they both remembered the "moon" shining brightly into their room. But if it wasn't the moon out that window, what was it? Big Bend is an enormous, desolate park, and there is nothing out on that desert floor for a hundred miles.

It was still dark when they left the trailer and drove to the starting point of the day's hike. The sky was just beginning to get light when JoAnne noticed something odd—she saw a golden light coming from beside a bluff. It was small but extremely bright, and only lasted a moment. Unfortunately, Kristin was facing the wrong way, and by the time she turned around it was gone.

Looking back at these events after two decades, Kristin is savvy enough to realize what might have happened that night and the next morning. Her first ever sighting of an owl coincides with what seems like an abduction event, but without any memories of a ship or beings. All she was left with were breadcrumbs.

Triangle in the desert

On a moonless night in the summer of 1999, Kristin saw something unusual while driving on a lonely road in Northern New Mexico. She was with her aunt, and they both clearly remember seeing a triangular-shaped craft moving low and slow heading towards them just off the highway. Then it was moving faster.

Kristin's aunt was behind the wheel and nearly panicked thinking it was going to crash into them. They swerved onto the shoulder just as it passed silently over them. They were both out of the car in seconds, but the triangle had vanished.

The craft was an evenly sided triangle with lights on each corner. It was dark and seemed fairly small, about twenty feet from the center point to the outer tips. She said, "It was so close I could have thrown a rock at it." This is nearly word for word what I've heard from other witnesses of triangle sightings.

Standing outside the car, they were shocked at its sudden disappearance. There were no lights in the sky, even off to the horizon. Everything was absolutely silent, and they were both terrified. Kristin said, "It was like a level of animal fear I had never before known existed."

The moment she got back in the car, Kristin began chanting out loud, "I don't want to remember. I don't want to remember. Don't let me remember." The fear was so profound that she couldn't sleep for days. She asked herself obsessively, "What the hell was that?"

In the weeks that followed, she was unable to think of anything else —it was as if the world no longer made any sense.

Upon reflection, her desperate pleas of "I don't want to remember" seem to imply something significant. She's very suspicious of what else might have happened during that sighting, and worries that something remains hidden.

Her feelings about the triangle sighting have changed over the years, "For reasons I can't explain, I have lost most of my fear of pursuing this." There seems to have been a change, and its abruptness has left her concerned.

When Kristin was in her early twenties, she had a serious boyfriend named Levi. They lived together for a year and a half in rural South Texas.

This was an intense time of odd experiences for both of them, things like constant bloody noses and waking with strange marks on their bodies. "I once found a three pronged scoop mark on my belly," Kristin said, "which healed completely in days." Looking back, she reluctantly admits that it all seemed to play out like abduction activity.

Kristin described an incident from that house, "During an intense night we both remember, I have a clear memory of trying to wake up because the sun was in my eyes but it was the middle of the night..." Levi remembers her being paralyzed and yelling to wake her, but she remained frozen. This really scared him.

That same night Levi looked out their living room window and saw oversized black dogs in the yard. He said they were dancing in a very odd manner, "They were about four feet tall and sort of prancing." Kristin remembers him making an eerie wave motion with his hands when recounting their movements. These dogs were well illuminated and easy to see, yet this seems impossible since it was the middle of the night and their yard was dark. He got the distinct feeling that this image was meant to distract him, but from what he can't remember.

The memories from that night are not linear, instead they are disjointed and choppy. It jumps from trying to wake Kristin in the bedroom to seeing the dancing dogs out the living room window. Presently, Levi is not sure of anything except that something happened. Both of them have considered using hypnotic regression in the hopes of understanding what happened that night, but neither has pursued it.

Kristin says, "I have known Levi since I was 19, and he is absolutely not prone to exaggeration or delusion. He is part of why I don't doubt my own sanity."

Levi and Kristin are still close friends. His mother and stepfather are Eladio and Gracia from the trailer in the desert where Kristin saw the owl, and they've had their own odd experiences. During her time in Big Bend, Gracia ended up being the go-to person whenever anyone in the park reported a UFO experience.

Once while Kristin was at their home, a frightened woman showed up on the doorstep. She'd had a close up sighting of something in the sky, and when she told the rangers what had happened, they sent her to see Gracia. The woman was a very level headed and thoughtful lawyer, yet was so scared she ended up staying in the trailer with Kristin for three days because she was afraid to be alone.

Kristin's connection to animals

Big Bend also presented Kristin with another profound experience during one of her camping trips. She described a morning when a small deer slowly approached her, close enough that she could gently pet the fur on its head.

She wrote, "The moment I touched the deer and looked into its eyes, I knew calmly what I had always known but somehow forgot—*there was a God*. It wasn't a discovery, but a gentle retrieval of a core part of myself."

She had been raised in an atheist home, so this realization came as quite a shock. It was as if some lost piece of herself had just walked on stage and said sweetly, "Here I am. I have been waiting."

The deer has a rich symbolic lore. It embodies gentleness and peace. Like the owl, it's a recurring screen memory in UFO abduction reports. Kristin was clear that this was very much a real deer. It walked up to her in a heavily used area with picnic tables and other witnesses—it was obviously habituated to tourists and looking for a handout. This would have been more of a storybook event if she had been deep in the wilderness all alone with the deer, standing by a trickling brook surrounded by wildflowers. But it played out as an animal begging alongside trash cans and parked cars, a mundane place for a revelation about God.

Kristin feels she's always had odd experiences with animals, like being swarmed by monarch butterflies as a child. She said, "Animals are attracted to me—deer, skunks, cats, dogs, bees, horses, and birds." Her husband calls her "Snow White" because of the way animals always seem to approach her.

Sometimes friends will explain how their dog or cat hates everyone, yet they'll become loving and attentive in her presence. They'll jump into her lap and offer their affection. She says, "This happens all the freaking time—so often I can't possibly be making too much out of it."

Kristin found a UFO meetup group near her home, but only attended one meeting. The gathering began with a group meditation outside in

Stigmata of St Francis by Bartolomeo Della Gatta, 1847

a remote wooded area. Kristin's eyes were closed for most of the time, yet there came a point where she felt she should open them. She was surprised to see a fox sitting facing her, no more than a few yards away. They simply sat and stared at each other for what seemed like a very long time. She had never seen a fox this close, and marveled at its beauty. She eventually closed her eyes again, and when the meditation was over it was gone.

St. Francis of Assisi, the patron saint of animals, is one of the most venerated figures in the Roman Catholic Church. The folklore is that animals would come to him as if they sensed something within his presence, and he is often portrayed in paintings surrounded by animals and birds. Some of these works feature owls. A particularly radiant canvas from 1847, *Stigmata of St Francis* by Bartolomeo Della Gatta, shows a beautiful barn owl looking away as St. Francis gets zapped by the floating apparition of Christ on the cross. There is something so bizarre about this image, I mean, there are thin little laser beams shooting off a glowing crucified Jesus hitting each point of stigmata on the saint. [2]

Variations of Kristin's name keep showing up in this research, too often to be dismissed as random. Christopher, Christian, Christina, Kristy, Chris, Kristin or Kristin, all seem to be stepping onto this stage to share their owl and UFO accounts. There may be no other word in Western culture that is more heavily loaded with mythic resonance than the first five letters of these names. The name Kristin traces back to Christine, the Latin translation would be, follower of Christ, and in Greek it means the anointed one. (3)

A circle burned into her vision

There is an unsettling set of events from 2013 that involved both Kristin and her then nine year old son. He came into her room and woke her in the middle of the night, saying he thought he was about to get sick. She got up and turned the light on in the bathroom, but when she returned he was asleep in the middle of the bed next to his dad. Kristen was wide awake and looked at the clock, it was 3:04 a.m.

She sat upright on the edge of the bed, briefly closed her eyes and suddenly saw a white image; it was circle shaped, and seemed burned into her vision. She described it, "...like when you are a kid and you stare at the sun and then close your eyes. It was very bright and kind of turning or pulsing in place. I opened and closed my eyes several times and it was still there. It was very bright." This wasn't a light in the room, it was some sort of persisting burn spot in her vision.

Worried she might be having a brain hemorrhage or a stroke, she stood up and muttered a few sentences but felt coordinated and lucid. She looked at herself in the mirror, and everything seemed normal. Right then she noticed light coming in from the windows. She said, "I was completely shocked when I realized that the sun was rising—it was dawn!"

She looked at the clock and it was now 6:15 a.m., even though it felt as if barely a few minutes had passed. She was standing up and fully awake the entire time, "I had missed about three hours of time with absolutely no sense of any loss... I am one hundred percent sure I had not been asleep."

Kristin feels certain this was an abduction experience—but she's quick to follow with "whatever that is." This caveat is something I understand and respect. Whatever is happening, it's terribly difficult to comprehend, let alone accept.

The next morning Kristin was sitting with her son as he happily ate his breakfast, and she told him that she was glad that he didn't end up getting sick the night before. He paused for a moment and then confessed that he had made it all up.

It wasn't at all like him to act this way, and when she asked him why he lied, he told an unsettling story. He said he was freaked out because he suddenly found himself standing next to his own bed not knowing how he got there. He described seeing a large orb floating through his room. It was about the size of a basketball, and bobbed around high up near the ceiling. He watched it for about two minutes and said it was glowing, but wasn't super bright.

He didn't understand why he was up and out of bed. Startled, he ran to Kristin's room and just made up the story about his stomach because he was afraid she wouldn't think the orb was important and would make him go back to his own bed. Kristin never would have done that, and she told him so. He replied, "I know, but I was too scared to think logically at that point."

Moments later while still sitting together at the breakfast table, their noses suddenly started bleeding. This wasn't just a slight dripping, it was a violent gushing that happened to both of them at the exact same time.

At present, her son is now thirteen years old. Despite his youth, he's the one person she feels most comfortable talking to about these things. She knows not to delve too deeply into what she shares. She'll wait for him to come to her with his own experiences, before volunteering some of her own.

Kristin feels strongly that her son is somehow involved as well, but for some reason he hasn't been traumatized by these experiences. She said, "If we are being taken, I think they are being careful not to break us psychologically. I have this sense that whatever is happening, they are aware that this is harrowing stuff and they take precautions to erase any memories."

The questionnaire

In the early months of 2014, Kristin spent an evening in front of her computer carefully filling out a detailed questionnaire. This was on a UFO site focused on experiencers. The long list of questions stirred up a lot of memories, and her mind was racing when she finally went to bed. She'd just written out a bunch of her experiences, yet still wasn't sure what to believe. She wondered if it was real, and if it was, would she have open contact soon? And would her husband witness it too? It was early springtime, and she had a gut feeling that open contact would take place that summer.

The next day, her husband left the house for an errand and forgot his smartphone. While he was gone, a message appeared as if he'd penned a response but hadn't yet sent it. He was angry when he saw it, thinking either Kristin or their son had used his phone, but he calmed down when he realized that nobody in the house could have typed the message. His phone locks down in seconds, and nobody had his passcode to unlock it. Here's the message:

> This is Kristen the letter was returned your story is indeed just it's all about moments don't know about this summer already

This message is odd in multiple ways. Kristin is misspelled using an "e" and there is no punctuation, something neither of them would do. And the reference to summer is precisely what she had been thinking about the night before, wondering if her husband would soon be a witness to Kristin having open UFO contact.

There is an eerily similar account on page 78 in *The Messengers*. A young woman named Ashlee told of a series of oddly worded text messages appearing on her boyfriend's phone. Here is one of the messages:

> It will identify all planes in the sky. Will detect unotherized flying objects and will warn them of aliens near by.

They appeared to be sent from Ashlee, but she has no memory of writing them. He had them in his inbox, she had copies in her outbox, but the time stamp was when she would have been asleep.

This happened a short time after she'd had both UFO and owl sightings. Neither messages make much sense, and both have an odd misspelling. The word unotherized doesn't actually mean anything, but in some absurd way, it sounds perfect. [4]

Why am I here?

A friend took Kristin aside and told her something that she wasn't expecting, that Kristin is a shaman. This announcement came from someone who has known her for over four decades.

Kristin said, "She had a whole rant about me and how I am. She is someone who has seen me work on people over the years and has been privy to more of the weirdness than most. I was taken aback and spent several days being weirded out. Finally I realized that it had made me upset that she would pull me out of my closet. She outed me!"

The term shaman can mean a lot of things, but in this case her friend was implying she had healing abilities. Her friend's accusation forced Kristin to admit that, outside a small sphere of family and friends, she's done very little with these talents and skills. "If I am indeed a shaman of some sort, I am not a very good one! The whole dilemma of what to do about all this is just a big headache I don't particularly want... But if I was given this stuff, shouldn't I do something good for the world? Why am I here? How can I help? When do I get to escape this meat puppet? These are the questions on an endless loop in my mind..."

These same questions get repeated by other experiencers. It's as if they are all reading from the same script, but the answers remain elusive. There is an emotional urgency to these unknowns, and they are left struggling.

Kristin said, "I never admit to being a healer for fear of ridicule, but I can often help people with my hands. I have known I could do this for twenty years, though I kept it tucked away in a space far away from my everyday thoughts. What happens is that I just do it when I have the opportunity. I don't explain anything." Then she said, "Even though I am the one doing it, I don't understand what is happening. I don't feel like I control it as much as I am some sort of conduit for it. Sometimes it comes on strong and sometimes nothing. I don't turn it off or on."

She shared an account of using her hands to relieve pain in a close friend who was suffering from the effects of chemotherapy. She said, "Sometimes my hands are so hot with energy that I feel like there's a fire coming out of them."

There is an unease with these abilities, yet not in the healing itself, but in trying to come to terms with her own potential, "…it is hard for me to admit. I really balk at the new agey-ness of this. But at the end of the day, I have to be honest about the patterns. My whole adult life I have had this energy in my hands and an aura about me." Then she said something I've heard many times, "I can break sensitive electronic equipment sometimes on command, but usually by accident."

The NDE and OBE

That Kristin has endured so many unusual events might raise a red flag in the eyes of some researchers. Instead, it seems their quantity and intensity tells an even deeper story. As a toddler, she nearly drowned in a swimming pool. "Even though I was only about two and a half years old, I remember it clearly. Looking upwards, the rising bubbles seemed so beautiful." There are no words to describe what she was feeling. There was no tunnel of white light and nobody spoke to her, yet she says, "It is hands down the nicest memory I possess." She feels a longing to return that place again, and has never had a fear of death.

Kristin has always felt that this near-death experience (NDE) changed her somehow. "I got to die at least once in childhood—that would open anyone's heart."

Something similar happened as an adult. She was stuck in bed for nine days with a high fever, and on the tenth day things took a turn for the worse. Her already shallow breathing became labored, and her husband was deeply concerned.

She said, "We were debating whether or not we should call an ambulance, when all of a sudden I realized that I couldn't lift my arms or legs—not even slightly move them. I was so exhausted and every breath was like lifting weights and barely giving me any air. I whispered to him that I thought my extremities were becoming paralyzed."

He insisted she take something to try to reduce the fever. The next step was calling an ambulance.

Her husband walked out of the bedroom and into the bathroom to get aspirin and "...as soon as he was out of my sight I floated up over myself. I didn't have a sensation of moving (my eyes were closed) but suddenly I felt wonderful, no pain, no labor to breathe, full of happiness and delightfully light and clear. I felt so terrifically awake and I opened my eyes and looked to my side and realized I was about six inches too far up and could see the bed below me and it was getting farther away! I was shocked and very confused and then I realized that I must be dying."

She felt unimaginably happy and shouted out to her husband, "Rey, REY! I am dying. Don't worry, it's so wonderful!" She was about to float off and was trying to reassure him before she left. He came bounding back into the bedroom in panic. "Instantly, I fell back down into myself."

It felt like a vacuum had quickly pulled her back into her body. Then suddenly she was trapped again by the struggle to breath. The sensation of pain everywhere. Kristin calls this as an out-of-body experience (OBE) and like her NDE as a child, it was profoundly beautiful.

The assumption to anyone peering into the lives of a UFO experiencer is that it should all play out as logical. Looking up at a mysterious craft in the sky should be a defining moment that impacts the rest of their lives. Fear, astonishment and wonder should be expected, but if there was an abduction event it would create overwhelming stresses. If that abduction event was forgotten, those stresses could still be simmering in their unconscious. If all this is truly happening, we should look for some affirmation in how they respond to these things.

Yet what is emerging goes beyond what we might assume if their interactions were with little beings on a metal spaceship. Instead, what seems to show up is entirely different. There is a depth and complexity that makes the easy answers crumble away, leaving a long list of much more difficult questions.

Listening to what people have experienced has become a full time job, and immersing myself in these stories leaves me both baffled and in awe. Why would Kristin's life have been invaded by an NDE as well as an OBE? Why, like so many others, does she have healing and psychic abilities? She is reporting things that are magical, a term that makes her wince—yet there may be no other word to describe it. What is the source of all these anomalous skills, and for what purpose? Whatever is happening, it's all playing out with a sort of transcendent power.

Glowing

What you are about to read next might be the most touching story of all the accounts I've ever heard.

Kristin was in Alpine, Texas waiting for the midnight train to Austin. This was in the early 1990s and she was in her mid 20s, a time when she had given herself over to wilderness travel. She'd just finished ten days of solo hiking in the Chihuahuan Desert about one hundred miles south of the train station. She stood alone in the dark on the platform, and as usual she was sobbing. It tore her heart out to leave the wilderness and return to her life in the city. When the train approached she collected herself, and wiped away her tears.

After boarding, the porter used his flashlight to escort her to the only available seat in the car. It was dark and everyone was sleeping.

The porter awoke a passenger who had been stretched out across two seats, and made him sit up so that she could take the empty seat he had been using. After sitting down she could only see the outline of a form of the person sitting next to her. Kristin wrote:

> The large observation window was behind him and the desertscape had enough moonshine to cast a silhouette of his shape. All I could tell is that he was a tall male and fairly slender. For a long time he was facing me and seemed to be pushing himself backwards against the train window silently. I could see no facial expression or make out any features. Too dark. I wasn't crying anymore or making any sniffling sounds so I was confused by what was causing his reaction. He was practically crawling up the wall!
> There were only two seats in our part of the row. He had the window and I had the aisle. It made me uncomfortable. It was as if he was trying to back away from me in a panic. It went on and on. Maybe twenty minutes! It was freezing in the cabin so I offered him half of my oversized thick blanket in a desperate attempt to strike up a conversation and break the tension. He accepted and we started to talk. It began a rolling conversation that grew into a hell of an all night discussion. He turned out to be a wonderful person and we talked til almost dawn.

He was only twenty-one years old, and spoke with utmost passion about a girl in his hometown. He was madly in love and on fire to get back home. She was his high school sweetheart, but she'd left him for his best friend. He was devastated and ran away to California for over a year.

When I met him on the train, she had called him asking him to come back. He was intent on returning and marrying her. He talked all night about her. I've always wondered if they made it.

Their conversation eventually gave way to sleep. They woke up the next morning to the announcement that the next stop was Austin. It was daylight and the first time they saw one another. He seemed shocked by Kristin's appearance and explained that because of her stories about hiking in the desert, he thought she would be darker skinned or native American. She was a very pale skinned brunette with hazel eyes. He looked very close to what she had imagined in the darkness, a young blond farm boy from the midwest.

As the train approached the station, most of the cabin occupants were moving about and dealing with their luggage.

I stood up and began pulling my own bags down from the overhead compartment. My new friend was traveling on to Chicago so he stayed sitting in his seat. The train came to a full stop and I shook his hand and we said goodbye. He seemed agitated but there was too much going on for me to worry much about it. I got out in the aisle and the line shuffled me about ten feet forward when the boy stood up and yelled my name across several rows of seats, "KRISTIN!"

Everyone in the car stopped what they were doing and turned to listen. I was embarrassed and had no idea what he was about to say. I am sure all the folks thought he was going to make some romantic proclamation but I knew he wasn't.

This is what he blurted out to me while sixty or so silent strangers watched intently, "What does it matter? I am never going to see you again in my whole life so I have something to tell you, I don't understand it but when you sat down next to me last night and I opened my eyes, *you were glowing*, listen, I don't mean light was shining off of you or anything like that, I mean literally glowing. Like a light—like a big light-bulb. All I could see was your moon necklace (I wear a simple bone carved crescent moon on a silver chain all the time) and bright light was coming from where your face should be, also from your body. I thought I was dying. I thought you were an angel coming for me. I have never seen anything like this in my whole life! I know I was awake. We talked and talked and it wouldn't go away. Finally I just decided to keep my eyes closed. I don't know exactly when if finally stopped. I don't understand what happened? But I had to tell you. You were glowing. You were glowing and I've

15: Kristin in the Desert

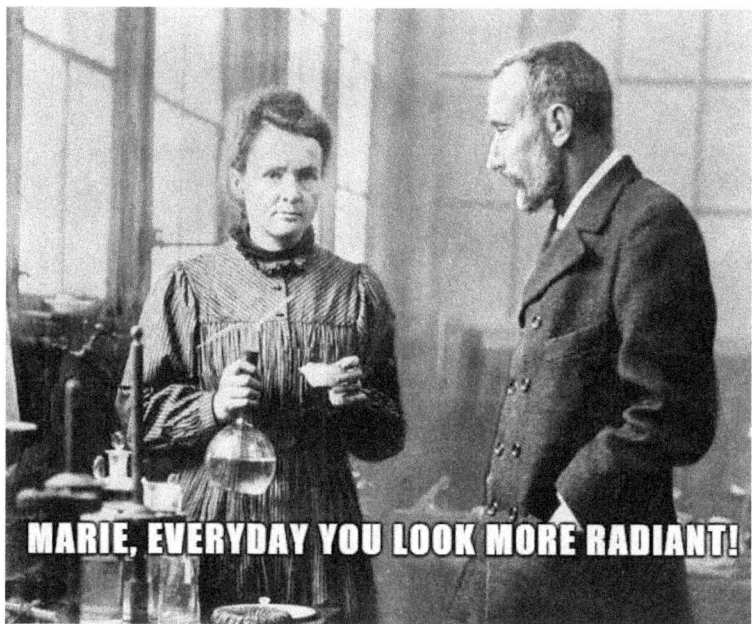

Marie Curie and her husband Pierre. Marie was a Nobel Prize winning physicist famous for her pioneering work on radioactivity. She was known to carry test tubes of radium around in the pocket of her lab coat, and she eventually died from prolonged exposure to radiation.

never seen anything like it and I will never forget last night as long as I live."

He stared plaintively at me. I was flabbergasted. Then all the people turned and looked at me, like I was going to have an answer to that! (which I did not) I shifted awkwardly as my cheeks burned up and before I could respond, the doors opened and the crowd started moving. I had to move too.

I never saw him again. I don't even remember his name.

People stared at me all the way off the train, into the train station and into the parking lot. I was mortified. I am not good in crowds. It never happened again (that I know of). I have always seen different kind of lights but never again was I the producer of light for someone else. I decided in the end that it had something to do with the desert, how I had somehow become imbued with the energy or essence of the land and the "shine" was still on me from so much hiking.

That hiking trip had been perilous and I had almost died of thirst during one leg of my trip. I decided that something about the drama of the trip had caused the glowing effect. These were all just guesses. I don't recall any UFO experiences associated with this particular trip but when you are hiking like that it would be so easy to lose time and not know it.

So, ever heard of anything like this before? The kid seemed very sane, intelligent and grounded to me.

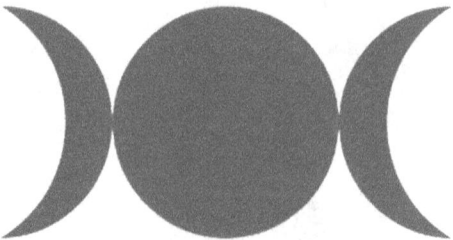

The Triple Goddess Moon

Five minutes after she sent this long account, I received another email from her with the subject: "hahaha holy synchronicity!"

She said, "This was the first image I saw on my Facebook feed seconds after sending you my last letter."

There was an attached image, it's an old black and white photo of a rather dour looking woman in a turn of the century laboratory, and the man next to her is saying, "Marie, everyday you look more and more radiant!"

I've never heard anything that matches Kristin's glowing account, yet it has an elusive mood that feels so consistent with other reports. That the young man on the train would focus on the crescent moon necklace is curious. He said, "All I could see was your moon necklace." The goddess Diana is often depicted in art with a crescent moon crown as well as a fawn. She was the Roman goddess of the forest, creatures of the wild, hunting, and the moon.

The moon shows up repeatedly in this account. First was the Cat Stevens' song *Moonshadow*, with a cartoon of the moon as a flying saucer. The next was her mistaken thought that the bright light shining in the window on that night in Texas was the moon. The way this account plays out, her memory of the moon might be a screen image for a UFO. Again, the moon and a UFO are transposed, and each are connected with owls.

Because of her relationship with creatures of the wild, with the hunt, and with the moon, Diana was known as "the triple goddess." This shows up symbolically as the waxing moon, full moon and waning moon. This image also represents the maiden, mother and crone. In *The Messengers*, there is an account of shamanic initiation where an owl appears and ushers a woman from mother to crone. [5]

Deer were sacred to the goddess Diana. When Kristin touched a deer she was struck with an instantaneous knowing that there was a god. This event took place while camping in the desert wilderness, the Texas version of the forest. Like Kristin, Jesus also went out into the desert alone.

Two flashes in the night sky

The "glowing" story was meant to be the last account in the chapter, but soon after this essay was finalized, I received an email from Kristin with a new experience to share. It felt as if the UFO occupants didn't think the story was finished, and they wanted to add a little bit more.

She told me that both she and her husband had seen a weird flash in the night sky while outside their country home. He seemed very concerned and tried to run through all the things that it may (or may not) be. Rey is the son of an astronomy professor, and very experienced with the night sky, yet he was stumped.

When they came in the house, Kristin told him, "Maybe the visitors were giving you a gentle wink? I see stuff like that all the time. Ask them to do it again, and tell them explicitly that you give permission to flash you again."

Though unlike him, he silently gave permission by thinking that he was "willing to see them again." When they'd finished eating they went back outside, and within a few minutes they both saw a second flash, this one much brighter than the first. He was rattled because both flashes appeared in the same area of the sky.

Kristin said that her husband talked about it incessantly for days after the event. He felt he could explain away the first flash as a meteor coming right at him, but to see the same thing twice within a half hour really freaked him out. She said, "It made me super happy for him to finally have something happen that he can't explain."

I've spoken to a lot of people who are relieved when their doubting spouse finally sees a UFO. I know a man whose wife didn't believe the stories he had told her about his contact experiences. The man prayed that she would see something so he wouldn't feel so alone. Soon after came a night that changed her beliefs. She opened the living room blinds and was face to face with a seven foot tall chalky white alien. It was standing right up close to the glass staring in at her. This promptly erased any skepticism.

Eleven days after the email detailing her husband's sightings, Kristin contacted me again. It felt like the UFO occupants were butting in once more. Seems they weren't satisfied with just some flashes in the night sky and wanted to end this story with something more conclusive. What follows is Kristin's confirmation event.

> I awoke yesterday in a normal enough way and had just pulled up into a sitting position to drink some coffee. Then the most dramatic thing happened. It was just one fleeting second of clear recall that hurled me away into a memory. It looked, tasted and seemed perfectly like a real memory and left me gasping literally. I remembered being walked down a hall by a little creature and because I was so much taller my view was from overhead looking down.

She was less than two feet away from the being. They were both facing forward moving down the hallway alongside each other, and she could only see the top and side of its head. There was something odd about her state of mind, as if her thoughts had been restrained by some source outside herself.

> I can think fairly normally but all the fight in me has been erased. I can't help but keep walking because it doesn't or it can't occur to me to do anything else. I think this distinction is important. I am not barred or paralyzed from movement but more like the violent choices I might choose have simply been removed from the menu. This doesn't seem like such an outstanding thing but it was fucking alarming.

There was no sense this was anything bad, yet the absolute strangeness was something beyond anything she could handle. What she saw was not human; it was somewhat like a stereotypical gray alien or mantis being. Seeing it so close and in such detail was profoundly distressing. It felt like she was being escorted by a giant spider.

> If this is a real memory then no fucking wonder we don't fucking remember our fucking abductions... the experience was of such out of bounds ontological shock. It was real and yet impossible... It seemed like an actual memory. Relating it to my husband left me crying and shaken. For several hours I could recall it viscerally and with great detail like it had just happened. [6]

To try to convey the impact of this short memory, Kristin used the term ontological shock. This implies the crisis point when one's entire worldview is forced into question.

15: Kristin in the Desert

> I have been asking for years to remember more of what I suspect has been hidden. Maybe this is beginning to happen? Maybe it is related to my husband seeing his first unexplainable lights in the sky recently? I don't know? Maybe it was just my mind giving me a show?
>
> It was just one second, but it was soul shaking. If this is what remembering is like I can see why they waited until I was about to semi-retire and live in the country before beginning a reveal—or perhaps my own mind is protecting me from the extreme stress of remembering until now? Or both? It's going to be hard work handling the trauma of remembering. I will need to be able to recover from it and since I find normal life so draining, perhaps the retreat from organized human life is necessary for me to be able to handle this unfurling? I dunno. I was shocked at how physical my reaction was. We are just scared wild animals mostly. I still want to work to get past the limitations of my primate shell. Maybe it has begun?

Kristin questioned her sanity. She repeatedly asked her very rational husband if he thought she was going mad, and he repeatedly assured her that she was very sane and functional.

> Maybe it was just a taste test? Do I really want to remember? Do I really want to be awake if it happens again? My answer is still 'yes' but I can see how hard it might be. I can believe that the stress could kill me. I was not exactly built to handle that kind of stress is what it taught me. One millisecond was absolutely overwhelming to recall. I will have to work enormously hard to conquer my instinctual fear. They will have to mete it out very carefully if I am to remember...
>
> I don't feel shattered in general but it was like a small earthquake for a little while.
>
> As disturbing as it was to sense the reality of it, I now feel oddly comforted by my memory (and my husband's light phenomena); having asked for these things and then getting a response of some kind denotes a relationship. Doesn't it? And if there is a relationship then I am not just a helpless victim? I am not just an animal getting tagged by a cosmic scientist. This is a step in the right direction. I have always had an allergy to fear and want to learn to overcome all fear including this kind. I think it is the right path for me.
>
> I long so much to be where you are. Out of the 'maybe' territory. I am tired of asking the same questions. Very very tired. More tired than afraid.

Kristin was addressing me when she said she longed to be where I am. That was hard to hear, because it isn't that simple; these experiences are a mess to try to untangle. She's right, I'm no longer in the "maybe" category with this stuff, but I'm still completely overwhelmed by the questions. I'm no longer asking, "Is this real?"

Instead I'm asking, "Why is this happening, and what does it mean?"

I am at a loss for answers, but Kristen has been extremely cautious and thoughtful on how she frames her own experiences, perhaps more so than anyone I've met.

She told me that she's spent most of her life caring for children, working in daycare centers and raising her own kids. She emphasized one thing she's learned: that all toys should be open-ended. She wrote:

> Never give children materials that limit their imaginations—do not present conclusions or answers. At my daycare I would do things like leave a giant pile of nothing but PVC pipe and some tools in the backyard and give them zero instructions. The amazing things they would invent! Beyond anything I would be expecting of them. Sometimes I think the visitor experience is like this for us. Like we are never supposed to get to an explanation of it. The wet edge is always moving because there is no other way to have ourselves expanded. Maybe it is for our own good? I like to think so anyway. I like to think they care about us as much as I have cared about so many many children.

This was sent to me on the day she gave a big bin of legos to a single mom in her neighborhood. For Kristen, these legos represent literally thousands of hours of imaginative play.

> Maybe the visitors see their ships, orbs, crop-circles, four foot owls, Sasquatch, giant dogs, poltergeists, implants etc. as nothing more than psychological legos inspiring us to imagine more deeply, and to keep reaching a bit further.

What does it mean to imagine more deeply and reach further? We are here in this place with day to day challenges, but there has to be something more. I would love nothing more than to reach into some other realm and pull out the perfect answers to all my questions, but I don't expect this will happen. It might not be answers that await us, but something so entirely different that we can't recognize it. I've met and become friends with a lot of people who've had these experiences, and they are all trying to reach out beyond what is right here around us, hoping to grab onto something more vital.

Chapter 16
Owls and the Road at Night

"About four days before the UFO, by a weird coincidence, I bought a little brass owl."

Seeing the words UFO and owl together in one sentence means something—it's a tiny clue in a mystery that yearns to be solved. This line was in the first of many emails from a woman in Scotland named Maggie (a pseudonym). From the tone of her letters, she was clearly in the midst of something difficult, and what she shared over the next few months was complex and jumbled. The story that emerged didn't seem to have a clear progression, but played out with a kind of shaky urgency.

Buying a little brass owl might seem insignificant, but it was the first in a series of four odd owl events leading up to a powerful UFO sighting. As an aside, my partner Andrea had a nearly identical tiny brass owl figurine on the mantle in our home, and it's now on my desk.

Maggie felt the need to have the little owl when she first saw it, and despite being low on cash, she bought it. The next day, she took her dog for a walk in a nearby field, a place she visits often. For the first time ever, her husband Peter decided to come along, and he brought his camera. There was another dog walker in that field whom she spoke with often, and he mentioned to Peter that he might like taking pictures of owls. He said the huge tree above them had an owl and three babies. Maggie and Peter looked for a long time but never saw them.

The following day, Maggie found a big owl feather in front of their house. The UFO event happened the next night, Tuesday July 14, 2015.

Maggie and Peter had offered to play the role of driver for a friend named William, who had a dinner date but no car. They picked up William first, followed by his friend Laura. After dropping them off at a somewhat fancy restaurant, Maggie and Peter grabbed a bite at a more modest eatery, then went to the seashore. They walked along the beach together to pass the time. Peter brought his camera and was happily taking photographs. Maggie chatted with the locals who were hanging about with their boats or walking dogs.

A complete stranger came up to Maggie and started talking about owls. "With all my owl coincidences over the last few days it gave me that special feeling of being in the right place at the right time! He told me that further up the beach there was a huge snowy owl who fed her three chicks every night at 8:20 p.m. He went on and on talking about them like he was obsessed."

This was the second time in two days that someone told her about an owl with three babies, and both times she was with her husband. Maggie checked the time and it was 9:15, too late for her to see them.

They returned to the restaurant and met up with their friends at about 10 p.m., then began driving. They dropped Laura off at her home and spent about 15 minutes saying goodbye. It was while driving toward William's home that they saw the UFO.

At this point Maggie forewarned me that things become unclear, "Now bear with me because it's slightly confusing as I've ended up with three different memories of the encounter. I actually forgot that this was my original memory, if that makes sense."

Here's how it initially played out in her mind, "Peter is driving, I'm in the front next to him and William is in the back. There are trees to the left of the road, and it's dark, but I see a large dark craft in the trees. It's very close to the ground and hovering silently. It looks huge."

She remembers thinking, it's not possible to be there, to be still, to be so close to the trees. Then it turns on its side and shoots off at incredible speed. The whole thing happened in all of three seconds. Peter exclaimed, "Oh my God! Did you see it?"

Maggie barely reacts, all she can say is, "Yeah, that's weird." She had no emotions, no thoughts or feelings. Nothing.

Peter talked about what they'd just seen as he drove, yet the moment he'd pause, Maggie would forget that anything had happened. "I may as well had seen a leaf fall off a tree. That's how it seemed."

They got home that night at exactly 12:30 a.m. Maggie is certain of this because her daughter called and the time was noted on her phone. That night Peter tried to talk about what had happened, but she barely had any reaction. All she could do was respond with an unemotional mutter.

Peter later told Maggie that he knew something was wrong. She was acting so distant, and he was worried he would upset her. He didn't mention it again.

Seven weeks later, Maggie and Peter were sitting together on the sofa, when she was suddenly hit with the memory of that night, "I jumped up and started freaking out. What the hell was that we saw? That was a UFO, it had to be! How had I forgotten? It made no sense, how do you forget something like that?"

Her mind was flooded with vivid images. She was frantic, but Peter remained calm. He told Maggie he thought she didn't want to talk about it, so he'd remained silent since that night. Her mind was racing, "What? I didn't know what freaked me out the most, seeing it or forgetting it."

Maggie now had a new memory, "We are driving, we go over a little bump in the road and then the road curves slightly. Straight in front of us, in the road there's a craft. Hovering silently, totally still. We're driving towards it. It then rises up about 30 feet off the road, then it turns on its side, then it shoots off through the trees at tremendous speed."

She was too shocked to tell any of this to Peter, it just seemed too strange. This second memory played out over and over in her mind for the rest of that night, but she didn't speak a word of it.

The next morning she was laughing to herself, everything from the previous night just seemed funny. What they had seen was impossible, and she figured it was nothing more than an airplane of some type. "What was I thinking? I was pretty sure UFOs didn't want to be seen. An alien craft would have been hidden in the trees, not in a road! And not near a town at 11 p.m.!"

When she told Peter that it was obviously just some kind of plane, the look he gave made her blood run cold. He replied that there was no way that what they saw was of this earth.

She now had two distinct memories of what happened that night, and the stress of this discrepancy was too much to bear. Things were unraveling. She told me, "As mad as it seems, it took weeks to separate these memories."

Eventually, a third memory emerged. This one begins in the car with Peter when they see the UFO. "I'm getting closer and closer. I'm really close, I see that it's a charcoal grey color. There are no obvious joints but there are deep ridges like maze patterns. I can't see windows but there's an amber light on the top and one on the bottom. The nose of it is in the trees but I'm sure there's another light."

This new memory seemed to be about ten seconds long. What she saw was bright and glowing. It wasn't the typical saucer shape, it seemed more arrow shaped, like something out of Star Wars.

At this point she felt she was close to the craft, perhaps just twenty feet away. She said, "I studied it looking for windows or doors. All in a slow motion, calm, accepting way. I don't remember thinking anything was strange, or questioning anything. Oh my God, another thought popped up that's blown me away... I wasn't looking through the car windows. I wasn't, I wasn't in the car. There was nothing to block my view. I was not in the car. I'm stunned. I have this memory the whole time and I never questioned it. Nothing blocked my view. There was no wind screen. Peter wasn't beside me. There was no noise. How could I just realize this now?"

This was the moment she could no longer deny that something had happened. Her memory was of seeing it from the outside, but she was now overwhelmed by the feeling that she'd actually been on that craft. "I still can't accept I was on it. My mind can't process it, I'm sure I was, I must have been, I just can't fully get my mind to agree with me."

When she told Peter these details, he said he hadn't seen anything like that. It was at that moment when Peter knew his wife had been aboard the craft. Initially he told her nothing, knowing it would have frightened her.

Peter remembers being conscious during the initial sighting, and unlike Maggie he was composed for the entire event, as well as the follow up experiences. The only time he was shocked about anything was when they rounded the corner and saw the craft so close. These kind of experiences should create an emotional panic, but he said, "That's just not me."

The timeline was confusing, and they tried to piece together what had happened. They both remembered William and Laura chatting away in the back of the car at the moment of the sighting, but that was impossible because they'd already dropped Laura off. So if William had been alone in the back seat, he might not have witnessed anything, but

16: Owls and the Road at Night

he certainly would have heard Maggie and Peter talking about what they'd seen. Peter eventually asked William, and he roared with laughter. He had no memory of any such thing. Had they already dropped him off? Or, was he in the back seat the entire time, but without any memory of anything unusual?

Maggie checked the time of the sunset for July 14, which was around 9:30 p.m. This matches up with when they left the beach to pick up William and Laura at the restaurant. She had a phone call at exactly 12:30 a.m., just as they arrived home. Taking into account the time to drive and drop off their friends, they should have been home much earlier. The math doesn't add up. They are left with at least an hour of unaccountable time, and perhaps as much as an hour and a half.

Here's one more curious detail. About a month before the UFO encounter, Maggie's daughter became obsessed with aliens. She was sketching, painting, and even making collages of beings with oversized bald heads and big black eyes. One drawing had a series of grays shown from different angles, along with a flying saucer, and the words ALIENS DO EXIST printed large across the bottom. Maggie asked why she was so preoccupied with creating these images. She didn't know. After the UFO sighting in July, her obsession went away.

Maggie found a feather the day before their sighting. This was mentioned earlier, but there's more to this story. She was walking their dog and saw a big feather in their front garden. When she picked it up, she literally got the tingles, feeling certain it was an owl feather. She went into the house and showed it to Peter, and he confirmed that it was indeed from an owl. He had spent twenty years as a student of Native Medicine people in North America, and understood this kind of animal totem.

Maggie told me, "He knows feathers and their importance. He knew something special was happening between me and owls so he presented me with a huge owl feather from his collection. That's kind of a big deal."

When I read this in her email, I was struck with an instantaneous knowing—Peter is a shaman. I asked about it, and she cautiously confirmed what I knew on a gut level. Yes, he's a shaman. I understood her reticence, this is something to be addressed discreetly.

That Maggie would share these experiences and her life with a shaman is astounding. His spiritual role seems so appropriate given the torrent of memories and experiences that were welling up around her. Trying to come to terms with these experiences means navigating the deepest waters, and who better to help confront and untangle these grand mysteries than a shaman.

Maggie's story came to me in a series of emails just as she began reading my book *The Messengers*, so she was telling me her story at the same time I was telling her mine. It was a bit unsettling for me, because I recognized a similar sort of release in both of us. She was using me to help make sense of her confusing memories, just as I had used the writing of that book to make sense of my own confusion.

There is a chapter in the book on shamanism. I put forth the idea that an initiate might be required to have a near-death experience (NDE) in order to actually take on the role of shaman. This wasn't my idea—I'd heard the late Anne Strieber talk about it in one of her audio interviews. There was something about this concept that resonated strongly with me, that passing over into the province of death, and returning, would be a prerequisite. That is the role of the shaman, to journey to those other realms and come back with a message. This is also at the core of almost all the world's owl mythologies—to fly into the darkness is a metaphor for crossing those boundaries.

When Maggie reached that point in the book, she told her husband about my rather bold notion straight away. She'd never thought about this connection, but she realized Peter was a shaman who'd also had his own near-death experience. The event happened as a young man during his shamanic apprenticeship. He died in a car accident, experienced leaving his body, then returned. Peter calmly pointed out that she'd asked him about the NDE on the anniversary of his own death.

I can't help but marvel that Maggie had a shaman sitting in the driver's seat next to her when she saw that craft above the road. These things are connected—the owls, the UFO and the shaman. I don't understand how or why, but I am certain they are linked. It just feels important that these three aspects are all part of this story.

Maggie was aware that there had been something ominous about all of the owl experiences in the days leading up to the UFO sighting. These coincidences felt important, especially the dog walker on the beach telling her about the snowy owl and its babies. Nothing seemed random; she felt a deep knowing that it had all been planned by whomever was on that craft.

Peter eventually told Maggie what he was feeling, that she'd been aboard the craft they had seen that night. Hearing this left her in a state of shock, and there was no way to rationalize what might have happened. She was desperate to know if any of this was real, especially if she'd truly been aboard the craft. She needed confirmation, so she asked for another owl sign.

She spoke out loud, demanding a response, "I meant it. I wanted one before the day was out or else!"

She walked the dog that afternoon and couldn't help but search for any sign of an owl, like a feather on the ground, or the sound of hooting off in the distance. She realized she was obsessing, and had to force herself not to look for signs. Instead, it had to come to her.

She fell asleep on the couch that evening. The TV was on when she began to wake up, and in that dreamy state she saw a program with kids in the woods at night. They hear a hooting sound, and one kid says, "It's okay, it's only an owl."

What brought her out of her sleep state wasn't the television, but the overpowering smell of vanilla, "...and I mean overpowering!" She asked Peter, who was in the room, or if anyone was eating ice cream. He didn't have a clue what she meant, neither did her kids. No one else smelled anything.

A half hour later she was standing by the back door having a cigarette with Peter, and there was an owl in a nearby tree. She said it was "hooting like crazy!" She'd lived in that house for over a decade and in all that time she couldn't recall ever hearing an owl nearby.

About four weeks after the event, Maggie and Peter returned to the site where they'd seen the UFO. They stopped their car at a good vantage point in hopes of better understanding what might have happened. Maggie's initial impression was that the road was much busier than she'd remembered. Within seconds of parking, they watched two cars nearly collide. One car swerved to avoid an accident, ending up off the road and on the grass—exactly where they had been looking the night of the sighting. She said, "The timing of it was just too spooky. I honestly didn't know what to think and it freaked me out."

They left and went to a McDonald's drive-through just up the road.

They pulled up to the little ordering signpost with the speaker and microphone, when suddenly there was a raven standing on it. Neither of them saw it land. It seemed to appear out of nowhere and it startled them. "I felt like it was a sign in my gut... but what? Again, was I reading too much into this?"

I pay attention when something like this shows up—it's a clue that needs to be examined. The raven is steeped in symbolic power, a sign of magic and introspection. Like the owl, ravens are seen as messengers between heaven and earth. Where it stood is also a clue. There's nothing metaphoric about a speaker and microphone, these are tools of communication.

Maggie would set aside time to meditate in the weeks after the sighting, a time before any of the memories had emerged. At one point during her meditation, she had a momentary vision of floating down a bright white curved corridor. She said, "There were no visible lights, but it was lit up. I was in an upright position. It only lasted for about four seconds, but it was really clear, like HD. It was a bizarre thing to pop in my head from nowhere but I didn't think much of it."

It was after all these follow-up events that she had to admit to herself that she did see a UFO, but any memory of what happened was out of reach. She said of the craft, "It was like a rectangle, and then on its side it was more like a triangle." Peter tells a different story; he remembers it as three cylinders that moved together and morphed into one. Their accounts should match, but they don't. It seems impossible to try to untangle which memory emerged when, and what happened next. It's not just that these memories are mixed up—they are too mixed up. It feels like this chaotic uncertainty was intentional, that it had been orchestrated for a reason.

It was about five days before Christmas when Peter awoke to see a small grey being in their bedroom, leaning over Maggie as she slept. He was torn the next morning, unsure if he should tell his wife or not. When he finally did confess to what he had seen, her reaction was a bland, "Oh, okay." She later found painful bruises on her arm and leg.

He saw what seemed to be the same being again the next night, yet it had more of a blue tone.

Maggie struggled to describe her odd reactions:

I'm confused by all this because I'm just not bothered. I'm forcing myself to write this... it was like I just switched off. I'm not scared. Peter is way more concerned than I am. I don't have the energy. But saying this I know I have to get help and get to the bottom of this. Before I was amazed and excited, like I was being chosen to be part of a great universal secret. If they can make me forget, they can make me think anything, what if it's not what it seems?

That's the question isn't it—*what if it's not what it seems?* This isn't theoretical speculation, these are terribly challenging experiences without any answers. Some people have been destroyed by the weight of what has invaded their lives, yet others have come through with a renewed sense of purpose and compassion. Something is happening, and there must be a reason why these things are unfolding. Whatever the reason, it feels important.

Maggie eventually had to accept that something more had happened than just a sighting. She said:

I had flashbacks of such powerful feelings of love, followed by sadness because I missed them.... After I remembered the UFO my brain went a bit mushy! It was like I was having downloads of information. I would sometimes be awake all night filling notebooks. And then one night I got it, everything came together and I had the most amazing vision of a group of light beings throwing their arms up in celebration, I could feel it. Just amazing. I was struggling trying to find answers outside of myself, and my lesson was to look inside.... It was weird and frustrating, but it was only because they were teaching me not to absorb or listen to other people's truths. They were twiddling their thumbs waiting for me to remember that I needed to trust myself and them, and my connection to the source.

I had heard this before from other experiencers, but she said it beautifully.

A funny thing happened while I was working on this chapter. The challenge in trying to tell Maggie's story is that events overlap and circle back in on themselves with a kind of frenetic urgency. I take this role of storytelling very seriously, and it was difficult trying to rein it all in.

I was trying to work on this chapter on a calm afternoon in September. The document was open on my desk, and I was overwhelmed at just how much I was juggling. All of it felt so important, and I wanted to capture that power, but it was daunting. Right in that moment, at the height of my own apprehension, a grasshopper landed on the desk next to me with a little click sound. I wanted to shoo it out the door and slowly eased my hand towards it. Then it hopped onto me. It jumped about five times, each time landing somewhere else—my arm, my shoulder, my shirt. Eventually it landed right on top of my bald head. I just sat still, not sure what to do. After about 30 seconds, it leapt off my head and landed on my glasses, which were on the desk just inches from my keyboard. It sat there for the next ten minutes, staring at me as I worked.

This was all taking place as I was searching info about dragonflies. Maggie had just told me about an encounter with a dragonfly, and I was curious about its totem lore.

So, as I was searching the mystical meaning of one insect, another was sitting on my head. I was already on a website about animal symbology, so I looked up the spirit message for the grasshopper. It represented (among other things) the leap of faith and leaping over obstacles, so it seems I was being told to just jump forward and write.

Maggie's dragonfly experience happened in 2003 while visiting the medieval Chirk Castle with her family. Everyone was out by a pond, and the air was full of dragonflies. Maggie said, "As we were all admiring them, a huge one appeared and within seconds it was nose to nose with me, I mean an inch or less. And there it stayed.... I was mesmerised, I could have stayed there all day... This dragonfly was eight inches long or more, it was like a blue cigar with wings. HUGE!!"

After what seemed like ages, it flew off. The communion with the dragonfly left her "on a high" for a long time afterwards. She said something about else this experience, "I didn't know it at the time (only in the last year actually) but this was the start of my huge Spiritual Awakening."

The dragonfly, in almost nearly all the world's traditions, symbolizes change and self realization. That grasshopper sat on my head in September of 2016, and I'm writing these words almost exactly a year later in September of 2017.

With all its contradictions, much of Maggie's story could be easily dismissed by a cynical investigator. Yet if these events played out in the way they are described, then I should expect exactly what she's shared—a desperate storm of emotions. That it's all so confusing points to it being real, at least to me.

16: Owls and the Road at Night

There may never be an answer to what happened that night on the road. We are hungry for a conclusion, yet the phenomenon doesn't seem to behave in a way that offers up tidy answers. Whatever is unfolding, it seems to have its own agenda, and it seems to be smarter than us.

During the writing and our correspondence, Maggie was planning to visit a medieval church near her home, a site with healing wells. She said, "My mum kept joking 'Oh, we're going on a pilgrimage!'"

She added, "I'm not religious in that sense and know I don't have to go anywhere to talk to God, but I do love old churches with their history and atmosphere!"

Before heading off, she asked if I needed any healing and offered to light a candle for me. I replied, "I could use a bit of healing so please pray! I just feel sort of frazzled these days. Hard to write and to concentrate."

This was true, I felt shaky and hopeless. It's unlike me to ask for help, and re-reading my own email was a surprise. I was pressing forward, but I wanted it to be easier.

She later sent me a few photos from her visit. One was of the candle she had lit for me. The stone wall behind the candle looked bleak and old, the little flame stood out warm and yellow. Another picture was a handheld selfie of Maggie between her daughter and mother—three generations all smiling from within this dark ancient church. The maiden, the mother and the crone. The three chapters of the divine feminine.

This work can be overwhelming. There is more than just the research and writing, I'm pursuing something mysterious. The elusive thread begins with owls, then leads off into the darkness. It can feel like a burden, but there are moments of such heartfelt grace. Seeing the photo of that little candle was one of those moments. I pull on these threads because it somehow feels vital, like I need to do it to truly be alive.

Maggie said one thing that rang so true, it was like someone had rung my head like a gong. (As an aside, while writing this Andrea has struck a large Tibetan gong downstairs below my office. I typed the word "gong" just as I heard the low vibrations coming up through the floor.)

Here's what Maggie told me, and it's something I understand in my heart. She said, "Oh how I love a hair tingling synchronicity, I could probably write a book… even if they don't have reference to UFO's… I just HAVE to tell someone! They are proof that our lives are guided by a mysterious force, that we are being spoken to if we decide to listen. I used to think that it was just now and again we are being guided and listened too… now I know it's all the time, down to the smallest detail of our lives."

Chapter 17
Owls and Gratitude:
Don's Owl Experience

> "Oddly enough, I had never thought of the following experience as an 'owl story,' although it definitely is, albeit the owl played only a seemingly minor part."

This was the first line of an incredible account. It arrived in a rather long email from a fellow named Don, and I was deeply moved while first reading it. My initial thought was that it could be an excellent chapter for this book—there wouldn't be much to do, just plop the text of the email into the manuscript and call it done. What I didn't realize was there would soon be a follow up owl account from another fellow, and his story eerily mirrored Don's. Shortly after that, I received a third very similar owl account from a woman in Massachusetts.

On some level, all three people were telling the same story. There was a depth and subtlety that left me awestruck, and I felt each account needed to be thoroughly explored. These final three chapters reveal something more about the role of the owl, an aspect that's both elusive and vital. Don's initial email is the centerpiece of this chapter, shared below in its near complete form. It's a simple story, but at the same time, it speaks to the deepest of mysteries.

Don was raised on a Missouri farm and spent his childhood outdoors. He began his letter describing a sense of connection to his home, "I grew up hunting, farming and raising cattle and, like most 'hillbillies,' I knew every inch of the land around our farms. I knew every rock, every tree, and I knew the habits of the animals in the forest as well as I know my own."

He left Missouri as a young man, and returned in 2001 when he was 35 after living in Florida for five years. Now back in his hometown, he ran into his brother who was all geared up for deer hunting. What follows is a wonderful story in Don's own words.

> He was dressed in camouflage, had a bottle of 'doe scent' (which supposedly gives off the smell of a doe in heat and is supposed to attract

the bucks), and told me he had a place on our farm where he had been spreading corn all summer to attract the deer. I laughed at him, saying something like, 'You don't need all that. Just go out in the woods, climb a tree along the right deer trail and wait. It's easy.'

He told me hunting wasn't as easy as it used to be, and pointed out that I had not deer hunted in over ten years. So I made a bet with him. I told him I could go out in the woods and have a deer within 30 minutes. I knew where the deer were at any given time of day at any time of year because I spent my entire childhood playing in those woods. I borrowed my dad's 30-30 rifle, and that afternoon around 4:30 p.m., I drove to my great-grandparents' farm and walked into the woods, intent on winning that bet. I should note that—as I was raised to do—I never, ever hunted for a trophy. I always hunted only for the table, for meat.

At this point in his letter he states, "I've always been rather psychic." In his family, there seems to be one in every generation with what his Scottish great-grandmother calls "the sight." Among his siblings, it turned out to be Don.

He described a lifelong fascination with all things paranormal, "Everything from Bigfoot to ghosts, to UFOs to prophecy." A few years earlier he'd read a book about remote viewing, then began to train and practice these skills. He put in a lot of hard work, and had some remarkable results. This aspect seem to play into what unfolded on the afternoon he was hunting. There will be more on this later in the chapter.

> When I set out into the woods, I said a quick, quiet prayer, thanking God and the universe for this opportunity and asking for a quick, clean kill—knowing that my wife and I would be eating that deer over the coming winter. I found the tree I was looking for, a huge white oak, on top of a ridge at the edge of a wide, flat field. I climbed up and stood on a large limb about twelve feet off the ground. I leaned against the tree trunk and watched the old trail that leads up onto the ridge from the deep hollow nearby. I knew from childhood days that the deer always come up that old trail—or near it—and feed on the grass in that ridge-top field every night. I knew their habits as well as I know my own.
>
> After only about ten minutes, as I stood there, leaning against the trunk, I began to get a strange feeling. The hair on the back of my neck stood up and everything in the forest went totally silent. It was extremely strange. It almost seemed like time itself stopped. It was as if myself and the area around me was in a bubble where everything had just stopped, as if the world was still going on around me but only outside that bubble that I was in.
>
> It felt like I was in a sort of limbo, somehow outside of normal time

17: Owls and Gratitude: Don's Owl Experience

and space. And I felt a sense of being watched. It felt like I was in a bucket with entities peering down in at me, watching me as if I was a science experiment or something—now, I don't mean that exactly, I mean that was the sense I had, the sense of being watched by a group of invisible beings that were somehow looking down and in to where I was at.

I began to feel something behind me. It was the feeling of a "presence" of an energy building. I turned around.

Across that brushy field, among the small trees and saplings here and there and at about level with my height in the tree, I could see a small white dot—about 150 yards away. This small white ball was gently moving up and down and slowly getting bigger and bigger. I realized it wasn't getting bigger. It was getting closer.

As the white orb got larger and larger (actually closer and closer), at about fifty feet away, it resolved into what it actually was—a pure white snowy owl. The owl was gently and slowly beating its wings, causing it to sway gently up and down, and coming straight toward me. As it neared me, it glided right past, only around ten feet away and exactly at my eye level. As it passed me, the owl turned its head and stared directly into my eyes.

I was in awe. Snowy owls, while not completely unknown in south Missouri, are very rare. I spent my entire childhood in the woods—as I have described—and I've only seen a snowy owl twice in my lifetime prior to this. I've seen hundreds of barn owls, screech owls, great horned owls, etc. but only two snowy owls.

As the owl glided by, I turned my head and followed it with my eyes. The owl, after looking me directly in the eyes, turned its head forward again. It flew straight down the trail I had been watching previously and disappeared into the trees. At that exact instant, a huge doe stepped out onto the trail right below the spot where the owl disappeared, and stood there.

She turned her head and looked directly at me, as if saying, "Here I am, shoot." I slowly raised the rifle and shot. The sound of the rifle was odd, sort of muffled sounding. The doe jumped and ran. I knew it was a good kill and I knew she wouldn't run far. But anyone with any hunting experience will tell you—you don't immediately run to the deer you have just shot. Instead, you wait and give them time to die. A deer will usually lay down close by somewhere and die. But if you scare them up before they expire, you'll be tracking that deer all day. A deer that has been shot through the heart can still run over a mile before dying. So I waited for what seemed like about ten minutes and think I might have even drifted off to sleep for a second or two. I gradually but steadily 'came to' and looked around. It was still deathly quiet.

I climbed down from the tree and started looking for the doe. I couldn't find her anywhere. I noticed that the crunching of the dead leaves under my feet seemed muffled and dead-sounding. The woods were very quiet. Even the breeze was completely still.

I could not believe that I couldn't find my deer. I knew it was a good shot and had to be through the heart and probably at least one lung. She couldn't have gone far. But I could not find her anywhere among the trees. I said another prayer, asking God and the universe to help me. I did not want to waste this deer's life—although I knew that even if I never found it, the coyotes would eat well that night.

Just then, another very strange thing happened. A red squirrel began chattering and scolding in a tree nearby. I stopped and looked at it. He was sitting on a small branch about seven feet off the ground, around 30 feet away from me, and was staring directly at me. I stopped in my tracks and, my mind blank, just stared back, not knowing what to think or feel. Suddenly, the squirrel ran down the tree and took off running through the dead and dry leaves. After moving around 30 more feet away, he stopped, turned and looked at me and began chattering away again.

I took this as a sign, a sort of omen. So in my mind, I communicated with the squirrel, asking him to help me find the doe so she wouldn't go to waste. I realize now how ridiculous this sounds. But at the time, in that strange, timeless limbo-like state the squirrel and I both seemed to be in, it seemed completely normal and reasonable.

As if in response to my request, the squirrel wheeled around and took off leaping and running through the woods, jumping over dead branches, racing through the leaves, and every now and then stopping and turning to watch me as I struggled to keep up. After following him in his twisting and turning path for what was probably only about fifty feet, I lost sight of him when he raced around behind a big red oak tree.

I approached the tree and stepped around it. I was shocked at what I saw. The squirrel was hanging on the trunk of a huge white oak tree, about three feet off the ground, staring at me and chattering away again. In front of him in a shallow depression lay the dead doe. It was that depression that had caused me to miss finding the doe when I had repeatedly searched for her earlier, she could not be seen until I was almost right on top of her. But what really shocked me was the glimpse of something that pulled my eyes upward. On a branch around 30 feet above the ground sat the snowy owl, also staring at me. The instant that I saw the owl, the squirrel fell completely silent.

Despite the huge number of paranormal events that have occurred over my lifetime, I was in total, complete shock. Despite the close, soul-deep connection with nature that I have always had, and despite my easy communication with animals of all kinds, I was teetering on the edge of plain disbelief. I was having a very difficult time assimilating everything that had just occurred over the last twenty minutes or so.

Moving slowly, I began easing my way toward the doe. But the instant I moved, the squirrel ran away to a nearby tree about 30 feet away and ran up it, stopping and sitting on a limb, seemingly now oblivious to me. At the same instant the owl flew away, disappearing into the forest. The

17: Owls and Gratitude: Don's Owl Experience

oddly silent, in-a-time-warp atmosphere went away gradually.

It didn't change all at once. First, I began to notice the slight breeze. Then I began to hear birds singing and chirping and, in the distance, I heard some crows cawing. A sense of normalcy sort of trickled back in. I took out my hunting knife and cut the scent glands from the doe's legs and dragged her out into the edge of the pasture. After gutting and field dressing her, I left the doe there and walked out of the woods to get my pick up truck so I wouldn't have to drag this huge doe all the way out of the woods. She was very old. Her teeth were worn down and she was very large—at the butcher shop, she weighed out at 165 pounds! Most large whitetail does never exceed 140 pounds after field dressing. It was obvious she was reaching the end of her lifespan. I was grateful that I was able to give her quick, relatively painless death and, in the process, she provided food for me and my wife. By the way, I was in and out of the woods in 27 minutes—I won the bet with my little brother.

To this day, some fifteen years later, I still think about that whole experience. From beginning to end, it was exceedingly strange. It was as if the snowy owl was helping by causing me to look exactly where the doe stepped out onto the trail.

Then the doe stood there, broadside to me, watching me raise the rifle and shoot—and this was several days into hunting season; she should have been spooked and jumpy by that time. Then the squirrel literally led me to where the dead doe was lying—and the owl was there waiting for me, perched above the doe! All of that, coupled with the odd, silent, timeless feeling of it all... It became an event I will never forget and probably never totally understand.

In many ways, Don's story reads like a UFO report without a UFO. Certain details sound like they were lifted from an abduction account, he was aware of this, and said this was one of the reasons he contacted me. He wrote me later:

> I hope I was able to communicate the sheer strangeness of my experience. The eerie silence and sense that time itself had stopped was so strange.... I've read where people who investigate UFO abductions refer to that as 'The Oz Factor.' [1]

Beyond the strange silence, there was something more. He presented it all as something heartfelt, as if the physical act of hunting was something deeper—an act of divine grace.

> One thing I know I failed to relate is what a spiritual experience the whole thing was. I mean, I prayed beforehand for a quick, clean kill, thanking God for the deer ahead of time, and through it all I felt so in tune with the universe, with life, with the Creator.... The whole thing felt like a gift from God. I said a prayer of thanks afterward and I thanked the doe

herself for giving her life so my wife and I could eat.

I suspect hunters throughout the ages have told similar stories around the village campfire, and our mythologies have arisen from the seeds of their experiences. Perhaps Don had confronted something universal in the human experience—the mystical elements of the hunt. His connection with nature and gratitude are at the heart of this story. I am certain our hairy ancestors confronted the same thing, albeit with a pointed stick instead of their father's 30-30.

Hunting has been passed down from father to son since the dawn of man. I recognized something very powerful in Don's account, an awareness of the sanctity of his actions, and his relationship to the wild. The Greek goddess Diana is referenced a lot in this book, and in my research. The goddess of the forest and the hunt, she is often depicted with a fawn and bow. Hunting seems like it should be something bold and masculine, but the myths of our ancestors have been entrusted to a maiden.

Don said, "I was raised to hunt for the table." He went on to explain, "Oddly enough, neither I nor my brother hunt at all anymore. I just dislike killing an animal. I remember my father got to be the same way when he got older."

Don saw not just an owl, but a white snowy owl. Its color and rarity makes me pay closer attention. Within many of the world's shamanic traditions, especially the Native American lore, the white owl has a deeper spiritual role than other owls. If one sees a white owl, it's thought to be delivering an inward message. The communication isn't meant for anything worldly; it's a message for the soul. [2]

Abductees will often report unusual animal sightings in the context of their UFO experiences. The witness sees one thing, but it might not be what it appears to be. There seems to be a form of psychic projection in the mind of the observer, and this illusion hides something, like a skinny gray alien.

There are commonalities in what gets reported as a screen memory, and first on the list is owls, followed by deer. After that, within the short list of less common animals are squirrels, which might be reported as absurdly large. An owl, deer and squirrels were all key players in Don's account, as well as the UFO abduction lore. [3]

Two UFO sightings

Given the power of Don's owl experience, I wasn't surprised that he's also had two UFO sightings. The first took place while playing outside with his older brother when he was around 10 or 11 years old. He heard a crackling noise from overhead, "I looked up and saw a reddish-orange fireball traveling across the sky, directly above us. I watched it as it traveled to the horizon and disappeared. I kept expecting an explosion from over the horizon, but none ever came."

This sighting might have been nothing more than some kind of rare daylight meteorite, but similar reports are taken seriously by UFO investigators.

Don's second sighting seems more significant. It happened as an adult in 1997 while driving alone in south Florida. He saw three cars parked alongside the highway with people standing on the shoulder, pointing to the sky. Looking up through his windshield he saw a huge black triangle. Like the others, he pulled over and got out of his car.

It was perfectly silent and moved very slow, and even more strange was that it seemed to disappear when he focused on it. He said, "You could only see it if you looked at a place in the sky beside it. When you looked directly at it, all you could see was a kind of hazy, shimmering place in the blueness of the sky—like heat rising off a highway. But when you looked off to the side of where it was, then it popped into view. We all stood there and watched it as it slowly made its way out over the Everglades."

Within Don's deer hunting story there is one detail that seems significant—his commitment to remote viewing. Don was 30 years old when he read his first book on the subject, and the text described training techniques to test and practice the procedure. He said, "I nailed my first target and I was hooked."

After his initial success, Don devoured every book he could find on the subject. He began a daily practice of remote viewing exercises to hone his skills, and this involved up to five double-blind training targets every day. He said, "It took a lot of hard work but, after six months or so, I was very, very good."

For the next several years, he dedicated up to five hours each day on remote viewing sessions. It was during the height of his obsession that the white owl appeared to him while deer hunting.

Remote viewing and high strangeness

Remote viewing is a controlled process that uses psychic abilities to acquire information across time and space. Typically, a remote viewer is expected to describe an object, event, or location hidden from physical view or separated by distance. These procedures were originally developed by the United States military and intelligence services for espionage purposes. The program began in the mid-70s, and was allegedly terminated in 1995.

The viewer would work with a partner (referred to as the handler or monitor), and would be asked to give a mental impression of something hidden from view. The monitor might ask, "What is in this envelope?" or "Describe what you see at the coordinates written on this paper." During the Cold War, targets might have included a Soviet missile base in Siberia, or the contents of a locked drawer in The Kremlin. Many of their descriptions were eventually verified, indicating these psychic techniques were a viable intelligence gathering tool. They apparently had similar success with accessing people, entering their minds the same way they could enter a Russian airplane hangar. They also found they could view forward and backward in time.

To insure that the viewer wasn't being influenced by any subtle clues or impressions from the monitor, a series of strict safeguards were put into place. The target would be decided by a third person beforehand, and any description or coordinate would be assigned a series of random numbers. These would be typed onto a single page, sealed in a envelope, and handed to the monitor. Neither the monitor nor the viewer would have any clue as to what they were going to view. These double-blind measures were created to ensure there was nothing to influence what the viewer would see.

Investigative journalist and author Jim Marrs wrote what is considered the first comprehensive book on remote viewing. He interviewed most of the key people involved with the initial military program. Marrs said something interesting about these men, "Every single one of the military trained remote viewers had experiences with UFOs… they all had these experiences." [4][5]

17: Owls and Gratitude: Don's Owl Experience

Author and scientist Dr. Jacques Vallee was connected with the remote viewing program in its early stages, and he said one of the reasons he was brought into the research was his knowledge of the UFO phenomenon. Vallee said, "They noticed many of their subjects related their becoming aware of their talent through a light in the sky, or what you would call a UFO incident." [6]

It seems like you need "UFO abductee" on your résumé to get a job as a remote viewer. Does that mean they are all abductees? Maybe. Some of the viewers involved have come forward with compelling accounts of their own abduction.

I asked Don the same question I've asked everyone who's had both an odd owl experience and a UFO sighting—if he thought he might be a UFO abductee. He said no, but then went on to share two stories, both that sound a lot like what an abductee might tell. The first was a missing time event that coincided with an odd light in the sky. The other was a night when he and his wife were both surprised to wake up with their pajamas on backwards, inside out, and buttoned up wrong.

Lyn Buchanan views evil and peace

Lyn Buchanan was one of the most acclaimed of the first generation military remote viewers. He also speaks openly about his UFO contact experience, and states plainly that it was an abduction. [7]

Lyn's abilities proved especially useful when accessing the mind of a human target. The intention of these mental access sessions was to dig deeper than what would be possible in a standard psychological profile. These were military assignments, so he was tasked with viewing drug lords, terrorists, and brutal dictators. Yet entering the mind of the target meant feeling their feelings and thinking their thoughts. His days were spent inside the minds of murderers and tyrants, and it was tearing him apart. "In a very real way, you actually become that person, at least partially, for the span of the session."

While driving home on a sunny spring day after a long stretch of these dark assignments, he casually began making plans to kill his wife.

Lyn wrote:

> I almost laughed that such a stray thought had come into my mind. Yet, as I rode on toward home, I realized that I actually did have plans to kill

my wife. The realization of it sent a shock of electricity through me which is impossible to describe.

He pulled over, got out of his car and stayed there on the side of the highway until those horrific ideas had been cleared away. After that, he worked to create a set of strict protocols to detoxify these mental access sessions. From that point forward, this detox process became a standard part of every such session. [8]

There came a day when he had a very different viewing experience. His monitor held a sealed envelope, and said it was going to be a personality profile. As soon as the session began, Lyn felt compelled to say, "Whatever evil you think this guy did, he didn't do it." His monitor simply motioned that he continue.

Soon Lyn was experiencing sensations, "I felt as though I were glowing inside." Then something very rare happened—Lyn found himself standing beside the man.

> He did not seem to take notice of my presence. I started to put my hand on his shoulder, to get him to think something, so I could gain better mental access. As my hand touched him, I felt a sudden rush of the most peacefully energetic power I have ever known.... As I tried again to gain better contact, I felt something I remember vividly to this day, but which I will never be able to adequately describe to anyone.

The two soldiers, Lyn and his monitor, had both been working double-blind. Neither one had any way of knowing who the target was. When the session was over, the monitor opened the envelope and unfolded a single sheet of typing paper with one word written in the middle: *Jesus*.

Lyn wrote, "This was the most moving and soul-stirring session I have ever done.... A quiet glow filled my entire being for months afterward, a glow that returns every time I remember that session." [9][10]

As part of this research, I spoke with Dr. John Alexander. He enlisted in the Army in 1956, retiring as a Colonel in 1988. He was one of the initial team members that developed and studied remote viewing, and he's also written and lectured on the reality of UFOs.

John listened patiently as I described the otherworldly aspects of Don's deer hunting experience; the eerie silence, and how an owl and squirrel seemed to play roles in a staged drama. At the time of this event, Don had been deeply immersed in his own practice of remote viewing, and it was this connection that intrigued me. I asked John, "When someone is involved with remote viewing, do these things happen?"

John paused and slowly asked the question again, "Do these things happen? Yeah, they do happen—sometimes."

He went onto explain that as the military got more deeply involved in remote viewing, many of the people working in the program began to have these kinds of mystical experiences. He was clear that it was certainly not all of them, but it happened often enough that it was recognized as an aftereffect. John then said, "The question arose, what are the ethical concerns with using the mystical in a military application?" He didn't follow up on that.

Nathan, owls and thoughts made real

I have a close friend I'm calling Nathan (a pseudonym) who's had a long list of unsettling experiences with both UFOs and owls. Like Don, he's also taken on remote viewing as something more than just a hobby. I asked him the same question I asked Colonel Alexander, but I pressed him for more information, wanting to better understand the why of it. Could the repercussions of the focused psychic process of remote viewing actually influence reality? Could thoughts manifest into the physical realm?

Nathan understood my question, and reflected on the protocols created by Lyn to fully close a session. He sensed that if a session isn't ended properly, there might be interactions and overlays between two worlds. He told me, "It's as if the window to the subconscious mind and the non-physical universe is open."

Then he described something that had happened just four days earlier while driving at night. He hit and killed a deer, and at the exact moment of impact a huge owl flew in front of his windshield. He wrote, "thus symbolically linking the two worlds in my mind yet again."

Deer and owls show up together repeatedly in this book, and in many of the accounts privately shared with me. These are archetypes made real in the lives of experiencers.

I was spinning my wheels trying to write about these issues. It had morphed into something that left me struggling, and I needed Nathan's help. I sent him a work-in-progress document, and we began a long correspondence to make some sense of all these tangled threads.

Nathan sent me an email on February 5, 2017 with the opening line, "You aren't going to believe this."

He described something that had happened earlier that day before dawn. While driving 50 miles an hour on a lonely road with a coworker, there was a sudden loud thud. He wasn't sure what had happened, then his co-worker said, "Well he's dead. A big owl just hit the windshield!"

Nathan had endured a lot of experiences like this, and said, "I started looking around for anything else strange and it dawns on me that this was the same town where an owl had hit my windshield back on Super Bowl Sunday, 2015."

He was writing me two years later, on Super Bowl Sunday 2017. He said, "Then it hits me. Super Bowl, *Superb Owl*. I can't believe it! The trickster strikes again? What does any of it mean?"

He was unnerved, and I understood why. We both felt the same thing, that helping me with this chapter had somehow generated a weird set of owl synchronicities. I need to add that Nathan has had a lifetime of odd experiences that certainly seem to imply ongoing UFO contact. Something very odd is at play. It seems that the act of remote viewing can open a door into our physical reality, allowing in all kinds of strange experiences—both good and bad.

Remote Viewer No. 1

After his initial success with his first attempt at remote viewing, Don reached out to Joseph McMoneagle, perhaps the most highly acclaimed remote viewer in the world. They began a correspondence in the late 1990s, and Joseph suggested he avoid any remote viewing courses and train himself. They were in touch with each other via email several times a week for the next few years.

Fitting the pattern of other remote viewers, Joseph has also seen a UFO. It happened in 1966, two years after enlisting in the Army while stationed in the Bahamas. It was a calm moonless night when he walked towards the sleeping quarters with a comrade named Steve, when suddenly:

...the whole area lit up like daylight. We found ourselves enveloped within a very bright cone of light, which was coming from the undercarriage of something hovering directly over us.... It was making no noise. In fact, it was like standing inside a vacuum bottle.

The object was elliptical in shape, and seemed to be quite large. After a few seconds, the light winked off, the object accelerated away, and disappeared from sight. Joseph said, "The following morning we both were suffering from what appeared to be a severe sunburn. In fact, Steve's burns were serious enough to put him in a hospital back in Homestead, Florida, for a short period." [11]

Joseph feels he's been psychic since birth, but had always been wary of these abilities. All that changed in the aftermath of a near-death experience. It was this powerful event that enabled him to truly accept his talents.

In 1970, Joseph was a young Army officer now stationed in Germany. He was in a restaurant with comrades, when he suddenly felt strange. He excused himself, and walked out the door. He wrote, "I found myself standing on the cobblestone road out front, watching with curiosity as the rain passed through my hands... I drifted over to see what the commotion by the door was all about and found myself staring down at my own body, lying half in and half out of the gutter."

His friends loaded his lifeless body in their car and raced to the nearest hospital. After being declared dead upon arrival, he found himself floating within an intense white light. He describes, "...being totally whole, totally complete, totally loved.... I knew this must be what God is. And I didn't want to leave. I just wanted to be there in that light forever."

He heard a voice telling him he could not stay—it was not time for him to die. "You have to go back. You have things to do." He tried to argue, but to no avail. There was a sudden popping noise, and he sat up on the hospital gurney and looked around. Joseph wrote, "Once you have had an NDE, it is almost impossible to act normal again. It alters the very color of the light in which you see things.... It was as though my inner sight had suddenly become crystal clear."

Eight years later, this man would be referred to as Remote Viewer No. 1 by the Army's psychic intelligence unit at Fort Meade, Maryland. [12][13]

In the flow

Don is grateful for Joseph's role as mentor during this journey, "Joseph was kind enough to offer a lot of advice and tips along the way... I was obsessed with remote viewing for the first four or five years after I discovered it. Even though Joseph advised doing one to two sessions daily, I did three to five sessions daily. That meant three to five hours every day spent in a floating, dream-like, almost OBE-like altered state."

Don was consistently operating at a level that Joseph considered, "world-class remote viewing." Of that time he said, "I was also meditating daily. I felt very much in close connection with the universe during those days. Synchronicities happened all the time. I was 'in the flow' and felt constantly close to God and the universe. This was my state of mind when I went deer hunting that day."

It seems significant that Don was deeply immersed in remote viewing leading up to his experience with the snowy owl. He was "in the flow", and felt "close to God" when something magical happened. It's as if some part of him was halfway through a door, interacting with that other world.

Don undertook a simple remote viewing session around 2003. As always, it was done double blind, and his wife helped with the process. She wrote a set of words on a single piece of paper and sealed it in an envelope.

> After meditating, when I opened to the target, my first perception was a sense of incredible peace and love emanating strongly from seemingly everywhere. It was unbelievably powerful. I just sort of floated there, bathing in that feeling for a long time. Then I got an image. It was a vision of the earth, rolling slowly, turning over and over. Across the earth was a huge brown cross that was bent so that it seemed to be stuck to the surface of the globe. As it turned, the feeling of love and happiness kept increasing until it was unbearable. At some point, I passed out. When I woke up, an hour and a half had passed. I sat up. My eyes were red and swollen and I realized I'd been crying—but I don't recall crying at all. It must have happened while I was passed out.

Don opened the envelope and read the words: "The impact of Jesus Christ on the world and humanity."

For the next week, I felt like I was floating on air. That sense of joy and peace stayed with me for many days after that. I wish I could have hung on to it... It really reaffirmed my spirituality. I know this probably doesn't sound like much to someone else. It's very hard to put these spiritual experiences into words. But they meant a lot to me and always will.

His experience is remarkably similar to how Lyn Buchanan described meeting Jesus, as well as how Joseph McMoneagle described crossing over into death.

Don shared a beautiful story from his childhood. As a very young boy, he would walk from his home through the woods to his great-grandparents' farm. He loved spending time with them, and would often sleep there.

There was a night at their house when he woke with the feeling of being watched. It was deathly quiet, and without raising his head from the pillow he could look out the window. He was astonished at what he saw:

> I was looking at a huge green man. He was very big, maybe eight feet tall and very muscular. Vines and branches were tangled all around his muscular arms, and he had very dark, curly hair almost down to his shoulders. As terror began to course through me and I started to rise up from the pillow, he grinned at me. I had the strange sense that he knew what I was feeling, and that he was laughing at me.

Don started screaming. His great-grandparents both woke up and asked what had happened. All he could say was that there had been something out the window. His great-grandfather took this seriously and went outside with a rifle. He never saw anything. The next morning his great-grandmother waited until she was alone with Don at the breakfast table, then asked what he'd seen.

> I remember describing the man as looking like the guy on the old Jolly Green Giant vegetable commercials. She didn't say much for a long time. She just kept asking me details about it. Finally, she asked me "Well, what do you think that green man was?"
>
> My answer still strikes me as being incredibly sophisticated for the age. I must have been about four. I told her it was like he was the forest and everything that grows in it. I didn't know the word "represented" but that's what I was thinking, that it was like he represented the spirit of the forest, the grass, the hills, the land, the water, the wildlife, everything in nature.
>
> My great-grandma got real serious and said, "That's right. That's what he is. And you don't need to be afraid. He won't hurt you, he can't hurt

you. Are you afraid of the woods?" And I said no. "Then you don't need to be afraid of him either."

I asked her if she had ever seen him. She said yes, when she was a little girl that she saw him several times and that he never hurt her or hurt anything. I asked her why we saw him. "Some can and some can't. That's all." she said, "You'll see lots of things others can't see. That doesn't mean they'll hurt you or that you need to be afraid."

I asked her what did she call him. She just smiled and said "The Green Man" and then she got up and started clearing the table. That was it. The conversation was over and she wouldn't speak of it anymore.

This was the Scottish great-grandmother who told Don that he had "the sight." Throughout our correspondence, Don has been passionate about his deep connection to nature. It seems fitting that one of his earliest memories is of an ancient Celtic archetype of the forest, smiling at him.

Chapter 18
Owls and Gratitude
Joe's Owl Experience

Three months after reading Don's deer hunting experience, another story arrived by email. Like so many other letters, it began with the opening line, "I would like to share my own owl experience." What followed was a familiar sort of checklist: UFO sightings, paranormal experiences, synchronicities, psychic insights, and heartfelt ideas about reality. The man's name is Joe, and he said, "I've always been a believer in this hazier realm of our existence, though I'll admit that there has often been a part of me that tries to rationally chip away at these matters and discount them."

Part of Joe's letter was his grudging acceptance that "rationally chipping away" wasn't working anymore.

> It was early on the morning of Nov 29, 2014 as I was walking out to my deer hunting stand when this sighting happened. About halfway out to my stand, I stopped at the corner of a field to cool down and enjoy the surroundings. It was early, and still very dark. I happened to notice what I thought was a very bright star. As I was watching, the light began moving in an odd way. It would slowly move in one direction across a small portion of the sky, only to stop abruptly and make sharp angle cuts and then zip in another direction. This light would slow down and then speed up and all the while zigging and zagging. I sat and watched this light for probably five minutes or so as it made all of these interesting maneuvers, but one thing that seemed to stand out was that I had a feeling that it was almost trying to entertain me. I say that and realize it may seem a little silly, but that's how it felt.

As this was happening, he pulled out his cell phone and tried to capture what he was seeing on video. It was too dark for anything to show up, but his spoken comments were recorded, along with the digital time and date. After a while, the light moved away and he lost sight of it.

> Now I was pretty excited by this little encounter, but as I continued to walk toward my deer stand, I did begin to feel a little uneasy about it. This feeling wasn't anything too profound, but mostly just a product of my

imagination running to stories of abduction and such things. It took me about ten to fifteen minutes to get to my stand after I lost sight of the light. I climbed up the ladder to the stand's platform, pulled the safety bar over my head, and the minute I sat on the seat I felt/heard a whoosh right by my face.

Now, it was still dark at this point and I do mean that I had literally just sat down when this whoosh occurred and considering my mindset from the incident in the field, I was pretty startled. I quickly grabbed my flashlight and started scanning the area around me, only to find a barred owl perched in a tree about ten yards from where I was sitting. The owl watched me for a time, but eventually flew off. Aside from the interesting timing and the fact that it came so close to my face when it flew, nothing else seemed unnatural about this owl.

At the time when this experience took place, I didn't give the owl a whole lot of thought other than that it punctuated the strange morning. About a month ago, the memory of that morning came back to me and for some reason it occurred to me that I should go online to see if anyone else has had similar experiences. I was vaguely aware of some connection between UFOs and owls, but I really didn't know much about it. As I did a little searching online, I came across your site and your book.

People are reaching out to me, mostly through email, with their owl and UFO experiences. These are usually part of a larger web of troubling stories, and I don't need to read between the lines to sense their unease. It usually shows up in the first few sentences. Joe adds:

> After reading your book, I do find it a little more difficult to just write off my owl as a coincidence. Actually, since that morning in the field, I've had some interesting synchronicities involving owls. I didn't recognize these moments as significant as they were happening, but now that I've read your book and I'm reflecting on them, they do seem to stand out.
>
> So—I've tried to spare you some of my deeper thoughts, feelings and conjecture on all of this to keep is short. Honestly, there may be a perfectly rational explanation for the light that I saw which would make the owl component just another beautiful brush with nature and nothing more. That said, I feel there is more to this which is why I've taken the time to share. To further that point, outside of a few friends and family, I've never shared any of my stories broadly but for whatever reason, I feel oddly compelled to share this one with you.
>
> Well, that's it, nothing too spectacular but perhaps worth filing away as another thread in the tapestry.

Joe's story is one more thread in what has become a very dense tapestry, but there's more to it. His experience is so similar to Don's that I am forced to pay even closer attention—not only to the details, but the mood of the stories themselves.

I ask pretty much every witness the same two questions; what was going on in their lives in the moments leading up to the sighting, and what changed after the sighting.

Joe said this about the zigzagging light in the predawn sky, "Directly leading up to the sighting I can't tell you exactly what I was thinking, but I can tell you I was probably just taking in the beauty of the walk. Part of why I enjoy hunting is just the connection with nature."

Joe had two highly charged things happen that morning—the appearance of a UFO, followed by an owl sighting. He said, "Before the owl event, I was definitely thinking about the light in the sky as well as the previous UFO sighting I had back when I was younger."

Joe was careful in his answer to the second question about what had changed in his life after the sighting. He said, "I would say that my thinking, specifically when it comes to things like theology, the paranormal, just general metaphysics etc. seems to have taken a different course. I'm not sure I could easily define this yet, but the notion that there is some grand unified theory keeps showing up.... For me it's more about the feeling of making progress in my thinking and that's exciting, and also kind of comforting. I feel I've made strides in this way of thinking over the last couple of years."

The black triangle

Joe saw a UFO when he was 17 years old. It happened on a summer evening in 1995 on a rural Wisconsin road near the Mississippi River. He had just recently received his driver's licence, and was alone in his truck. Driving over a slight hill, something off to his left side caught his eye. He said, "This object was a very low, slow flying black triangle. My initial thought was that this was a military plane of some kind."

At first he slowed down to watch the craft, then drove faster to keep up with it. He said, "I got to the point where I had entered a hallway of trees, and this craft came right over the top of my truck." It was totally silent, flying very low just above the trees. He looked up at the strange lights on the underside as it passed directly over him.

He said, "This is where my memory is a bit hazy, but from what I recall, the lights weren't individual points but were almost like illuminated lines. The best way I can describe it is that they looked sort of like a diagram of the vascular system with thin lines that branched off in multiple directions. These lines weren't very bright either, that combined with the matte black look gave the whole thing a sort of muted appearance."

He lost sight of the craft as it moved beyond the wall of trees alongside the road. There were no feelings of any strange perceptual distortions or lost time connected with this sighting.

Joe said something that has been echoed by others. After listening to so many people share their experiences, what he told me next seems normal. He wrote:

> We get our share of wildlife in our yard and around our home, but I can't remember ever hearing or seeing an owl in the time that we've been here. That changed shortly after my [UFO and owl] encounter in Wisconsin. It's hard to know the exact date, but sometime in early 2015, I started hearing the monkey-like screech of a couple owls coming from the valley. This screeching got to the point where almost every night my wife and I would go out on our patio and listen to these owls. Sometimes they sounded like they were right in the trees in our yard, but I never caught a glimpse of one. This went on for about a year and has now mostly trailed off.... As we were hearing these owls, I didn't think much of it and definitely didn't make any mystical connection to the owl I saw in the woods during my hunting trip. That said, as I've read your book and as I've looked back on that, the timing seems mighty suspicious.

That owls would show up around the home of a UFO witness in the days and weeks after a sighting is very common. Those monkey-like calls belong to the barred owl, one of the loudest owls in North America. This is a common, albeit noisy, bird.

Here's another bit of synchro-weirdness from Joe. The morning of his UFO and owl sightings he used his phone to try to capture the light in the predawn sky, but all he got was a black screen. When checking his digital picture library to get the exact date of the UFO sighting, he saw he had only one other video with an all black screen. The other was an attempt to record the owls from his patio at night. Joe said, "I couldn't actually see the owl, so the video I took was strictly just to get the audio of the owl call, but I was also chattering away and explaining what was happening. So out of hundreds of videos, only two have black screens and my commentary—and both have something to do with owls."

He's describing a UFO in one, and a hooting owl in the other. These two all black clips mirror each other in a way that shows up over and over in this research. This has been my challenge, to find the meaning of UFOs and owls. It's as if that black void is a metaphor for something deeper; an elusive secret in the dark.

Finding God

Beyond seeing an owl, Joe had another important experience in his tree stand while deer hunting. He had spent his young adult years struggling with his own spirituality; questioning, rebelling, and arguing over the meaning of God. With time, this hostility faded, "...and it evolved to a more earnest search for spiritual truth."

It was during this searching when something happened that changed his life. He was thinking about these spiritual issues while sitting alone in his tree stand. It was a peaceful moment with snow gently falling when he felt something, "A peace came over me. There was an understanding that I gained. Not just an acceptance, but an understanding that the unanswered questions I had were part of the mystery that draws us back to the source."

I spoke with Joe at length about this, and he was very clear what happened—at that moment, he found God. It happened while sitting in a tree stand, very close to where would later see the owl. He felt a distinct knowing that, "There is something to all this, stop fighting it."

It was right after we first connected that Joe told me something I understood completely. He wrote, "I've been rapidly encountering new ideas and more clarity of thinking. After I sent you the email and we started to exchange, I feel like that process has intensified where I'm seeing connections almost everywhere I look."

This kind of thinking can be both exciting and frightening—I know all too well from my own experiences. Real events unfold with symbolic power, and it's easy to ascribe mystical significance to things that might be meaningless. There is a danger of getting lost. Seeing connections everywhere can become a sort of mania. His thoughts were evolving, and he was questioning everything. He also sensed something dark within these experiences, where deception can arise and lead one astray.

Synchronicities seemed to ramp up right after we began our email correspondence. He described a day with a tightly knit web of meaningful moments, all tying back to a quote from Whitley Strieber he'd read that morning, "...the enigmatic presence of the human mind winks back from the dark." Seconds later, he heard a woman on the radio describe seeing a red cardinal, she said it was "grandma winking back from the beyond." When Joe told his wife about this little coincidence, a red cardinal landed on a branch just outside the closest window. [1]

It was during this intensified time of soul-searching that he felt the need to pray. He'd been alone all day at his mother's house, and stepped out onto her back deck to smoke a cigarette. It was calm and snowing softly. He used this quiet moment to ask for help in prayer.

At first, he questioned what he was supposed to be learning from all of this, "...actually, I was sort of struggling in my prayer to get to what was really on my heart."

After about five minutes into the prayer, it suddenly occurred to him what he was looking for—confirmation that he is on the right path. At that instant, five red cardinals landed right in front of him, dropping onto the snow one at a time. He wrote:

> Everything was covered in snow and there was almost a haze beyond my circle of vision, so to have those five bright red cardinals land in front of me and see how starkly they contrasted with the rest of the world, it was just too powerful to ignore, especially considering the timing of their appearance. I know it's not unusual to see a cardinal in the winter, but I'd been outside on and off all day and hadn't seen one and then to suddenly have five of them land in succession and then leave in succession after a minute or two...is beyond normal in my experience.

The word cardinal is an adjective, it means, of the greatest importance, crucial, paramount, essential. It's also a noun meaning the bird itself, as well as a dignitary of the Roman Catholic Church.

Joe had three powerful events that all seem somehow tied together. The owl and UFO experience, the five red cardinals, and the transformational moment of finding God. All three events happened either on, or very close to his family property. He said, "I feel a deep connection to that land, and have since I was a kid. Still to this day, it's my spiritual touchpoint."

Chapter 19
Owls and Gratitude
Kelly's Owl Experience

Barred owl on an autumn day. Photo by Kelly.

On October 19, 2016 I saw a post on Facebook titled: "Sappy nature story alert!" It had been written by a friend named Kelly, and her UFO sighting was featured on page 132 in *The Messengers*.

> Just about every time I am out hiking I crane my neck skyward, peering high up into the pines trying my darndest to spot an owl. I oftentimes hear them, but have never seen one other than a few fleeting moments. Never just posing for me to photograph. In fact, just yesterday while out in the woods I repeatedly said to my friend, "I just want to see an owl!" We even heard a great horned one during our hike, turned and walked in the direction of the call, but caught no sight of it.

Kelly had the day off from work, something she'd requested weeks earlier. It was a glorious fall day in New England, and she was hoping to do a long ambitious hike with a friend, but events conspired in ways that forced her to change those plans. She ended up hiking a shorter trail alone in a nearby wooded area, and here's what happened:

> I strolled the golden woods, yellow leaves and pine needles raining all around me. I went off the beaten path on a trail just wide enough for one. All the while, looking up in the boughs for a you-know-what. Suddenly, the chickadees, titmice and warblers were making quite a racket all around me. Flitting from branch to branch, close enough for me to reach out and touch them as if trying to tell me something. I stopped to listen to their chatter. I thought "I'm just going to sit down, be still and quiet and center myself in appreciation of all of this." I barely got the thought out as I plopped myself down and a large, swooping bird flew past me, landing on a branch DIRECTLY in front of me. My heart started racing, as it startled me, and I immediately stood up, thinking "Could it be?! Noooo, it's probably a hawk..." Nope. A stunningly gorgeous barred owl and I hung out for a HALF HOUR today. Staring at each other, watching him preen himself, trying to take a nap, and then eventually flying away in the most majestic manner. I'm feeling SO BLESSED! Beyond grateful. Ask, and eventually ye shall receive. [a little heart emogi was tagged on at the end.]

The day before she had been repeatedly saying, "I just want to see an owl!" But she wasn't getting her wish. The next day her thoughts were much more peaceful, "I'm just going to sit down, be still and quiet and center myself in appreciation of all of this." No demands, just gratitude—and that's when the owl appeared.

I pointed this out to her by saying, "Now that's as good a manifestation cue as there ever was."

> You are sooooo right!! That was exactly what it took. And I was SO hoping you'd see this post. Mike, I cried. We STARED at each other. Like, it would not even look away from me. INTENSE! AND LOVING! And oh so wise. I was not even originally supposed to be there, but an actual physical "detour" and other roadblocks to where I was headed had me traipsing just five minutes from my home instead. And it was a random day off that I'd requested two weeks ago. And I was pleading to see an owl yesterday. Gahhhhh. I am so grateful tonight!

This all plays out so similar to what Don and Joe experienced when they saw those owls, especially their reactions. Both described the same emotional awareness and appreciation.

Kelly told me, "Some may say I'm crazy, but I think the more time you spend in nature the more you pick up and resonate with earth's frequencies, it induces a calming vibe." Again, both Don and Joe told me essentially the same thing.

Kelly was alone in the forest seated near the edge of a little cliff

19: Owls and Gratitude: Kelly's Owl Experience

when the owl landed in a tree. She was up off the forest floor and the tree was lower, so the owl was perched right at her eye level.

She said, "The timing, the exact right place at the exact right time, when I had been pleading to see one the day before, and I wasn't even planning on going there today. Synchronicities!"

Don stated that his owl sighting while in the tree was "exactly at my eye level." Joe's owl sighting in the tree across from him was also at eye level. All three of these sightings seemed to be staged for maximum impact, each owl flying very close to the witnesses, and each owl making direct eye contact.

Kelly and I have been friends online for a few years, and we spoke at length while writing about her UFO sighting. During those phone conversations she said she loved owls, yet had never really gotten a good view of one. She remembers a fleeting glimpse from decades earlier, but she barely saw anything. That changed on the beautiful autumn day when she locked eyes with that barred owl. Then a few weeks later she saw another owl, and people around her began seeing them too. One was the friend she had been hiking with the day before her emotional close up owl sighting, she was the first to see an owl just four days after.

She told me, "The fact that two of my very best friends saw owls in a week's time, when they have never seen owls before is just too hard to dismiss! AND the fact that the owls that they saw were all eye level with them, as mine was." Kelly's next note, a month later, told of more owls:

> A few weeks ago another one of my very close friends saw an owl. In his driveway. Got a very blurry pic. But he was so stoked to tell me! A snowy owl. And also, a co-worker has heard an owl outside of my work at dusk some nights, and I actually saw it one night recently while leaving, swooping really low across the railroad tracks about 10:30 p.m. It is unreal how many owl incidents have taken place in my life since that owl encounter.

It was around this same time I received a blurry picture from a friend named Rachel, one of only two people in a nearby town who had a copy of *The Messengers*. She took the picture with her phone while in the driver's seat of her car. The photo shows a white owl standing in the center of a dark road lined up with a mailbox. She was there to pick up

Owl and a mailbox: both represent message delivery.

her son from that house, but the owl was standing in the one spot that blocked her from turning onto the driveway. Curiously, the person with the other copy of the book lives in this house, and both were signed by me.

Rachel ended up getting quite close to the owl, closer than the photo shows, and she described feeling a deep connection. Also, she was surprised that the owl was so small. She only remembers ever seeing an owl once before, and it was also standing in the middle of the road at night. She described that one as being three and a half feet tall to four feet tall.

The Chinese girl

As a child, Kelly lived directly across from her elementary school. She said, "I could literally walk out of my apartment door, cross the street, and up the four concrete stairs into the entrance of the schoolyard."

Each morning, Kelly's mother would accompany her outside to watch her walk safely across the quiet street to the school. And each afternoon, she would be waiting in the same spot to watch her walk back home. "This was our ritual from kindergarten until the time we moved to the countryside, in the middle of third grade."

One afternoon when Kelly was in second grade, around seven years old, her mother waited across from the school as usual, "All the other kids came running out and into their mom's arms, but much to my own mother's concern, I did not come across the schoolyard, nor down the steps to the street. This was SO not like me. My mom began to panic…"

Her mother got all the other parents to scour the neighborhood, yet nobody found her or had any idea where she could have gone. Kelly has only a hazy memory of that afternoon:

> I am at a Chinese girl's house. She is very friendly and her mom is making us delicious buttered toast with cinnamon and sugar on it and I am loving it and keep asking for more. I can even recall the strong smell of cinnamon when I look back upon it. The atmosphere was very warm and inviting. Her mom did not speak English, and in fact, I don't recall much of any kind of verbal conversation going on between any of us. The little Chinese girl, about my height, had these eyes that were so full of love and compassion and yet so deep and dark. She could connect with me and convey her emotions so well, just by looking me in the eyes. I recall staring at one another at one point, and even though she didn't have tears in her eyes, I could sense that she was crying inside. A very deep sadness filled her for a time. I could feel it.

After a while, the mother of the Chinese girl "said" something, although Kelly doesn't remember her speaking words, just that the little girl somehow conveyed that it was now time for Kelly to go home because her mom was very worried.

> After that, I don't have a single memory of anything that happened. Not how I got home. Not the time of day. Not arriving at home. Not my mom yelling at me for making her so worried. Not even how I was feeling. Zero recollection of any of it.

Kelly's first memory is an uneasy feeling of "coming to" in the kitchen with her mother after it had gotten dark outside. It's difficult to know, but there seems to have been over two hours where she couldn't be found. She doesn't have any negative impressions around this strange experience, it feels positive.

> My most intense memories are of the toast and the Chinese girl's eyes. It certainly is odd, but all my life I honestly just thought I went over to this friendly girl's house after school without telling my mother. Which is actually quite uncharacteristic of me. What is even more odd, is the fact that my mom never called the police or anything like that. For her, it was like this numbness took over, and there's a hazy weirdness about it for her, as well… It was like a kind of amnesia was put over us.

A couple of things stand out in Kelly's memory. One is the preoccupation with the deep dark eyes of the Chinese girl, and how they could convey emotion. I can't help but see this empathic little girl as a screen memory of a gray alien with big almond shaped black eyes. The other is "the strong smell of cinnamon."

Whitley Strieber wrote about his desperate emotions in the presence of strange humanoids in his book *Communion*. One of the beings asked, "What can we do to help you stop screaming?" He replied, "You could let me smell you."

He described a being holding its hand near his face, and how the odor anchored him in reality. "It was not a human smell, but it was unmistakably the smell of something alive. There was a subtle overtone that seemed a little like cinnamon." [1] Cinnamon is one of the more common smells associated with the contact experience, second in reports after sulfur. British author and researcher Jenny Randles says that the smell of cinnamon is often linked with the UFO occupants, having documented many examples over the decades. [2]

Author Joshua Cutchin has written two books on the UFO contact experience; one about food, and the other about smells. His work examines the reports of people who've had direct contact with alien beings, and these are compared to medieval faerie lore. Both modern and ancient reports tell of food served and eaten in the presence of other-worldly beings, as well as smells. Joshua explores the similar aspects of these phenomena, and contends that UFO reports and faerie mythology are essentially the same thing. He's noted a clear pattern; the sweetness of the treats is very consistent with the more pleasant encounters, and conversely, those having bad experiences will often tell of eating bitter food. [3]

Kelly had an extraordinary experience that was detailed in chapter nine of *The Messengers*, titled "Back to Back Reports." Her story is told alongside the story of Susan Kornacki, also noted briefly in Laura Bruno's chapter earlier in this book. Kelly and Susan had curiously similar accounts that both took place while lying in their backyard hammocks. Susan saw two owls, one in each of the two trees that held her hammock. Kelly saw a cone-shaped UFO while lying in her hammock, shining like a diamond with a million facets reflecting every color imaginable. These are two of my favorite accounts in the book.

What's interesting is that up until recently, Kelly had only ever caught a fleeting glimpse of an owl, but her UFO sighting had so clearly mirrored Susan's two owls. When I spoke to Kelly for that chapter back in 2014, she went on and on about her frustrations of wanting to see an owl.

Both women lived just 43 miles apart in Massachusetts at the time of this experience, and didn't know each other. They had been acquaintances on Facebook, but had never communicated. I sent them a formal introduction while working on their conjoined accounts from the previous book. At that point Susan was living in Hawaii, so their long distance hellos were shared online. [4]

They finally met in person while writing this chapter. Susan was back in Massachusetts visiting family, so they picked a restaurant to meet halfway. The booth where they sat had graffiti scratched into the wood which included a prominent gray alien head. But what really caught them by surprise were two owl statues alongside the fireplace right next to where they were sitting. These identical owls were posed standing side-by-side, as if mirroring their first hello in person. Kelly said that meeting Susan was, "Like meeting myself." I have to agree—they aren't quite twins, but they certainly look like sisters. And, they also share a set of powerful experiences with both UFOs and owls.

Healing Lulu

I asked Kelly if she had any healing abilities, and she shared something that had happened a few years earlier. Her mother-in-law Lulu was hospitalized after having an aneurysm. Emergency surgery was performed to stop the internal bleeding in her brain, and after the procedure she laid motionless in her hospital bed. This was devastating for both Kelly and her family.

It was on the day that Prince William and Kate Middleton were getting married when Kelly went alone for the first time to visit Lulu in the hospital. The wedding ceremony was on the television above her bed when she entered the room, and before her aneurysm Lulu had told everyone that she was excited to watch it. Kelly told me:

> A quietness seemed to fill the room, and I don't even recall hearing the television in the background during what happened next... Something compelled me to lay my hands on my mother in law. One on her shoulder and the other on her back. These words suddenly filled my mind, and I

spoke them with great intention: 'Please surround her with the white light of healing.' At that same moment I visualized her entire body being bathed in this beautiful, bright, glowing, white light.

Kelly said her behavior was completely unplanned, "I had never done anything like this before. I envisioned this white light energy coming through my palms and into her. My eyes were filled with tears of love and compassion and the desire to heal her was so so very strong."

This lasted about five minutes. When she felt she was finished, the sound of the Royal Wedding slowly came back into her awareness. Afterwards, several family members entered the room to visit Lulu, and they all spent the next few hours together. Lulu hadn't moved the entire time, and was motionless when Kelly left.

The next morning, Kelly returned to the hospital with her husband and son. She said, "As soon as the electric doors of the ICU swung open, this beautiful sound filled the halls. It was Lulu—and she was singing! We all looked at each other in total shock and astonishment." One of the nurses walked past Kelly and whispered, "It's a miracle."

Like so many others who have told me their stories, Kelly's home is crammed with owl knickknacks. This didn't surprise me, but I was curious to know when she started collecting these owls. She thought for a moment before answering, and said it began about the time her son was born; this would have been years before pondering her own experiences. My home is crammed with owl stuff too, but this is a direct result of writing a big fat book about owls.

Here is one more experience, yet without owls or UFOs. Kelly joined a global meditation event that took place on 11/11/11 at 11:11 a.m. Her intention was of hope, love and the betterment of mankind. She sat alone in a square of sunlight that was beaming in through her bedroom window. At first nothing was happening, and she felt frustrated. This was unusual because she would normally quickly enter into the meditative state. She said, "I wasn't giving up so easily. I began really concentrating on my third eye, focusing inward, breathing deeper… then suddenly I was there!"

For Kelly, the feeling of going into meditation is like that moment of transition on a roller coaster—after slowly reaching the peak, everything drops. At that point nothing exists outside of her mind, yet this session it was more intense. "Within my mind was an overwhelming emotion of love and being connected to everything. The earth, the universe, all living things… I was immediately surrounded by a warm, red, glowing light of what I can only sense was pure love." She sat with these feelings for a long time, and eventually started crying.

> I was aware of being a grand part of the whole. The sensation of pure elation filled my heart and soul… all at once I started to get images flooding into my mind's eye. The first of whom I translated as Jesus. The image was of him from the shoulders up surrounded by a colorful halo, like the ones he is depicted with in stained glass or paintings. I was taken aback by this! I gazed in wonderment at his face in my mind, and he looked back at me very lovingly.

Kelly doesn't go to church and has never read the Bible, so this was odd for her, but also very comforting. Soon after, another image flooded her mind and she felt it was Mary, again with a glorious halo.

> I was surprisingly filled with gratitude and wonder at seeing her face. To me, seeing Jesus and Mary was symbolic in a reassuring way…. After a few minutes the faces turned into swirls of colors that changed and pulsed with feelings of emotion and compassion. I came out of the meditation with an overwhelming sense of awe and feeling so so loved.

Kelly was weeping as she slowly opened her eyes to the bright sunshine. She said, "I was still in a hazy, awestruck state, and wiping my eyes. What a fantastic, magical, unreal experience. One I will never forget. And one certainly not easy to translate into words."

After hearing all these stories, I asked Kelly if she thinks she may be an abductee. She replied, "Honestly, I don't know."

Kelly contacted me while finalizing this chapter, and she described what had happened the night before. It was summertime, and she'd slept out in her yard. There had been a meteor shower, and she was hoping to see some shooting stars. She pitched her tent without the rain fly so she could look up through the bug netting at the sky. She was all set up with a sleeping bag, pad and pillow. She even had a stuffed owl in the tent.

At first she didn't see anything but a few fireflies, then after about an hour she noticed something in the top of an ash tree near her tent. It looked like nothing more than a clump of leaves, but it didn't seem like it was there before. She paid close attention to that spot, "…and just then a bluish-white meteor came streaking across the sky from south to north right above me. It was awesome! So bright!"

Moments later there was loud hooting directly above her. "Just then, the owl soared ever so slowly right across my field of vision through the small window at the top of the tent." That suspicious clump of leaves in the darkness was an owl, and after passing over Kelly, it remained nearby and continued hooting loudly for the next twenty minutes.

Kelly wrote, "I started crying... I was so blown away I wanted to go wake everyone up and tell them... but I just lay there in my euphoric state of gratitude."

After that, Kelly couldn't get any sleep. She was restless, uncomfortable, and eventually the sky got cloudy. "I retreated inside to my own bed where I was shocked to discover it was somehow four in the morning!" It was a little after 1 a.m. when she saw the owl and listened to its calls, and it seemed impossible that it could be that late when she entered her house. She was describing missing time and she knew it. I pressed her on this, but all she could say was, "I truthfully don't know what to make of those three hours."

The three experiences

Don, Joe and Kelly each shared a heartfelt story of seeing an owl. These three accounts blurred together, so much so that it was hard for me to keep them straight. Beyond the core owl experiences, there were other similarities worth listing. First and foremost, all three are UFO witnesses. Both Don and Joe have seen an unknown triangle shaped craft, and Kelly has seen a rotating crystalline cone-shaped craft.

Both Don and Joe sent their initial emails to me with just two words in the subject: Owl Story. At one point in the midst of the writing process, they both sent me an email at the exact same moment. Seeing their nearly identical messages side-by-side in my inbox was a simple visual that highlighted the strangeness of this stuff.

At the time of their deer hunting events, Don was 35 and Joe was 36. Kelly was a few years older.

Kelly told a story of using her hands to heal her mother in law Lulu, and Don told me about reducing pain with his hands. He does it by clearing his mind and relaxing, "then by concentrating on focusing energy into my palms, I could generate a kind of heat." Though he doesn't call himself a healer, he has helped loved ones suffering from rheumatoid arthritis and headaches. Both describe healing skills using the palms of their hands. Joe said he's never physically healed anyone, "But apparently I'm helpful for psychological healing... I have heard from many people that I'm a good listener and a lot of people come to me with their problems looking for thoughts, advice or to just vent. I've had that with people I hardly know as well."

Don and Joe are both practicing Christians. When I asked Kelly about her religion, she simply replied, "Nature." Both Don and Joe were hunting on their family land, an area that had been a part of their lineage. Kelly's first close-up owl sighting was five minutes from her home. All three described an emotional and spiritual bond with nature. Each was clear that the natural world is their way to connect with the divine, and seeing an owl at eye level seemed to personify that connection.

Don fell unconscious while remote viewing the impact of Jesus, Joe found God while sitting in a tree, and Kelly had a powerful vision of Jesus and Mary during meditation. These are three UFO witnesses, each with life changing experiences confronting the divine. I am cautious to read too much into this, but to me, the similarities are crystal clear.

It's difficult to grasp the true meaning of these stories—I am feeling them more than knowing them. For me, there is one consistency that truly stands out. All three of them clearly expressed their gratitude in advance. This is a powerful life lesson, and I will try to take it to heart.

Something unseen is trying to express itself, and the clues are showing up symbolically. These experiences are outside any fixed understanding of what we perceive as real, and attempting to analyze them will ultimately fail. The fable told around the campfire isn't something literal, it's meant to seep into that core part of us that makes us human. Yes—people are seeing owls at highly charged moments, and lives are punctuated with a flying metaphor. These are real experiences, with real owls, all pointing to a deeper reality.

Conclusion

This book, along with *The Messengers*, have both addressed the same mystery. That's over 650 pages trying to answer one question—why owls?

The bigger question might be, what does it all mean? After years of exploration, all I've gained is a fleeting sense of something. It's been a struggle to find meaning in these stories, yet to move forward means letting go of the literal, and trusting your intuition. Simply put, you won't understand these stories using your brain, but a deeper truth might emerge if you listen with your heart.

A photograph in an old newspaper is just a bunch of little dots. Looking closely, they all seem separate, yet each is a tiny detail in a bigger narrative. At times, I've been so focused that my nose is literally pressed against the paper. These two books have been a way for me to step back and see the overall picture. The emerging image isn't an owl, but a deeper aspect of reality. Although the picture is unclear, I'm now keenly aware something significant is at play, but we have a hard time seeing it. And if we do see it, we doubt it.

What is a synchronicity, and what is a UFO? Both seem to have the same transformative power, and both seem to be using the owl as a symbolic tool. Part of that source might be aliens in their spaceships, but that seems too simplistic given the strangeness of these stories.

Something has been happening with a consistency I don't understand. I've been playing a role in some of these stories, as if the act of researching and writing about these events allows my entry into someone else's experience. It happens often enough that I should be at peace with it, but it still affects me. The ultimate example is in chapter thirteen, where Mike C saw an owl and then a UFO—all while listening to my voice on his car stereo talking about owls and UFOs.

The only way I can interpret this is that the owl and UFO connection is real, and I'm directly tied into it. I am not just writing books—I'm on the stage in someone else's drama.

Here's another example. During the final editing of this book, Kristin (from chapter fifteen) contacted me with a story of walking in the woods alone at dusk. She was in a quiet mood, and delighted to be out in nature. She'd set an alarm on her phone to know when to turn around and walk back before it got too dark. As she walked, she talked aloud to them—them meaning the UFO occupants. She asked, "... I have been meditating with such dedication, and now I am out here in this beautiful isolated piece of nature, and this would be such an ideal time to give me a little nod or some encouragement." At that exact moment, she'd walked into the center of a perfectly round flattened patch of grass about twenty feet across.

It didn't seem natural, and she paced around trying to figure out how this could have formed. The precision of the edges left her baffled, and her only thought was that she'd found a mini crop circle.

Her next thought was, "Maybe I should tell Mike about this?" She suddenly felt an electric zapping on the back of her neck. It was distinct and powerful, but not painful, "It felt like I was hit with a Barbie sized taser! I've never had this kind of sensation before."

The alarm went off. She turned around, left the circle and started walking back. This oddness left her confounded, but happy. She spoke aloud, "Thank you, now if anything else happens you'll just be showing off." Eight steps later, a big great horned owl flew across her path. Seems like they were showing off, not just to her, but to me too.

My friend Suzanne Chancellor was the editor of this book. This has meant scrutinizing every single word, so she knows all the details of every story here. She's also been my therapist, and has listened patiently during my struggles to make sense of the experiences within these pages. Suzanne is also an experiencer, and some of her stories show up in *The Messengers*, as well as in the book in your hands. So it should be no surprise that she's been hearing owls, almost nightly, all throughout the process of this work.

Yet sometimes it just gets a bit more overt than owls.

Suzanne and I have talked a lot on the phone for this book. There was a night when we reviewed some of the text, and our call started breaking up. I could barely hear her, so we tried hanging up and calling again, but the disturbance continued.

It was a warm summer night, and she was sitting outside with her computer. We were editing a shared document, when she suddenly gasped, "Oh my God! Oh my God! Oh my God!"

Her voice was fraught with emotion as she described a strange light in the sky above the trees in her yard. She spent the next ten minutes giving me the play by play over the phone.

Suzanne said, "It was moving very slowly, sometimes coming to a complete stop. It flashed very brightly, then dimmed and remained dimmed, then flashed bright again in an irregular sequence. It would 'power up', then dim again. I thought that was quite strange, as lights on an airplane wouldn't flash erratically."

Two experiencers were working on a book about UFOs, and one of them is presented with a UFO. Who is orchestrating these events, and why?

This book took a long time to complete. I could have worked harder and finished it sooner, but there was another aspect to this process. These stories are emotional, challenging and complex—each with their own deeper message. I've had so many similar experiences that I can't help but feel a connection with the people who've shared so much with me. I have a responsibility to tell these stories.

During the two years of putting this book together, many of the people involved went through major life changes. There were divorces and marriages, parents died and grandchildren were born. Some found religion, and others were diagnosed with serious ailments. I saw so much unfolding within their lives, and was humbled to do this work. Many saw UFOs (and owls), and they felt this was directly connected to the process of my writing their stories.

One consistency is crystal clear; this book is full of people who tell of healing abilities. I've come to expect this pattern, but it's still remarkable. The experiencers in these stories are using their hands to heal, many using skills like reiki. If it isn't hands on healing, then it's some other work to help people—they are nurses, psychic intuitives, mediums, shamans, life coaches, and tarot readers. This describes nearly every person in this book.

The near-death experience (NDE) shows up in several chapters. This is part of the ancient lore of the owl, to travel to the land of the dead and then return. I pay close attention to NDE accounts, especially when the person has also had UFO experiences.

From my limited research, it seems that anyone who's had both an NDE and UFO contact is a powerful psychic. In this book, all the

Conclusion

people who've had an NDE are outright shamans, or playing a shamanic role.

Something that surprised me was the amount of Christian imagery showing up in some of the stories. I am not at all churchy, so I feel I can remain somewhat detached. I am cautious not to make too much of this, but it needs to be addressed. Some people spoke openly about their Christian faith, but there was more to it than that. There was symbolism that I didn't expect. These examples might seem subtle, but to me they stood out.

I've seen a pattern, albeit anecdotal, of people with some variation of the name Chris showing up in this research, and I wrote about it in *The Messengers*. Christopher, Christina, and Christian are common enough names, but they appear with a heightened frequency within these owl experiences. There may be no other word in Western culture more loaded with mythic resonance than the first five letters of these names. That someone with the name Kristin would walk out into the desert alone wasn't lost on me.

Another example is the NDE, which is quite literally death and resurrection, and this is at the core of Christian faith. It might be nothing more than mythological symbolism welling up, demanding to be seen. These are powerful stories, so we should expect powerful symbolism.

Some people agreed to be a part of this book while still having strong doubts about the reality of their experiences. The writing process required a lot of back and forth correspondence and long phone calls, and my goal was to tell their stories accurately.

Along the way there was a need for them to review documents in progress, and the act of carefully examining their own experiences provoked a change. Their doubting ended, and they accepted something had happened in their lives that directly involved UFOs. Reading their own stories was a transformational event.

This book has been an exploration of elusive ideas, and I've looked for patterns in the smallest details. Some of the jigsaw puzzle pieces are fitting together, and I can see parts of the overall image. But pieces are missing, leaving an empty space in the center. Within that void is the source, and I want to know what's hidden there. I have a sense of something transcendent, something important. I am cautious to call it

"God," but it feels okay saying "the gods," and by this I mean the spirits and magicians of our folklore. I sense this is somehow our home—an ancient home, a deeper home, the place that holds the vital aspects of what makes us human. It is the source of our myths.

The owl can fly into that empty space, and then return.

Endnotes

Chapter 1: The White Owl and the Hound of Hell
(1) *The Messengers*, p. 144.
(2) This chapter relies heavily on an article written by Heather from 2011. http://www.inkavisions.com/articles/article02.htm.
(3) Gwenhwyfar is the Welsh version of the Guinevere. She was the wife of King Arthur in the Arthurian Legends. She also had an affair with Lancelot, her husband's chief knight.
(4) Dragon line information from Maria Wheatley, http://www.theaveburyexperience.co.uk/power_centres_and_hidden_energies.html.
(5) Images and map showing the West Kennet circle from May 2011. http://cropcirclesdatabase.com/20110517UKww Note: I cannot find any references to this circle on the CropCircleConnector site.
(6) Glenn Broughton's blog, Sacred Britain - http://sacredbritain.blogspot.com/2011/05/first-crop-circle-in-beautiful-barley.html

Chapter 2: The Awakening of Susan MacLeod
(1) Audio interview with Susan MacLeod, Sept 18, 2012, http://hiddenexperience.blogspot.com/2012/09/audio-conversation-with-susan-macleod.html.
(2) Her website on the "about me" page, http://www.healingquest.ca/healingquest-aboutsusan.htm.
(3) *The Messengers*, page 216.

Chapter 3: Owls and the Lakehouse
(1) *The Messengers*, page 94.

Chapter 4: Gypsy Woman and a White Owl
(1) Story by Gypsy woman titled "White Owl as Messenger," on the Synchro Secrets site. Excerpt edited slightly. http://blog.synchrosecrets.com/?p=18063.
(2) "UFO seen from the bus and a visit from the men in black." From Gypsy Woman's blog, The Gypsy's travel Journal. Excerpt edited slightly. http://thegypsytraveljournal.blogspot.com/2009/09/dish-ran-away-with-spoon-or-bus-tried.html.
(3) "Seeing flying cigars with her family and her father's mysterious work." From Gypsy Woman's blog, The Gypsy's travel Journal. Excerpt edited slightly. http://thegypsytraveljournal.blogspot.com/2012/07/ufos-in-desert-aand-guns-at-area-51my.html.
(4) "NDE in the hospital." From Gypsy Woman's blog, The Gypsy's travel Journal. Excerpt edited slightly. http://thegypsytraveljournal.blogspot.com/2009/07/out-of-body-back-to-here.html.
(5) Gypsy woman comments with a story in the post titled: "The Owl and the Money Clip," on the Syncro Secrets site. Excerpt edited slightly. http://blog.synchrosecrets.com/?p=269.

Chapter 5: Stacey, Owls and the Psychic
(1) "Owl and the Money Clip," Sept 30 2019, http://blog.synchrosecrets.com/?p=269
(2) Stacey's blog post on owls: http://staceyjwarner.blogspot.com/2009/10/owls.html.
(3) "More Owl Weirdness," posted Oct. 4 2009, http://hiddenexperience.blogspot.com/2009/10/more-owl-weirdness.html.
(4) Stacey's blog, Chop Wood, Carry Water, posted Oct. 4 2009: https://staceyjwarner.blogspot.com/2009/10/chop-wood-carry-water.html
(5) *The Messengers,* page 114.
(6) Hidden Experience Podcast, Title: "October 2009" (audio), Saturday, September 18, 2010 http://hiddenexperience.blogspot.com/2010/09/october-2009-audio.html.
(7) The present online version no longer matches to the second. Someone I interviewed requested I remove a short comment. It wasn't much, but it was something they wished they hadn't said. I snipped out the single sentence with my audio editor, and it was just enough to throw off the exactitude of the synchro-time count.
(8) Two quotes from *American Psychic,* an unpublished autobiographical manuscript by Marla Frees. Marla Frees, American Psychic: A Spiritual Journey from the Heartland to Hollywood, Heaven, and Beyond, Post Hill Press (June 5, 2018). "I prayed to be rescued by someone or something, even aliens in a spaceship. Since that didn't happen, I had to intuit ways to survive." "Nothing could have prepared me for what I saw when I lifted up my little telescope. Behind the puff of a cloud the object sat motionless. It appeared to be a dome top with a saucer-like bottom. It looked exactly like objects I had heard so many people describe. There it was and I was witness to it."

Chapter 6: Kenneth Arnold and the Dawn of the UFO Era
(1) Audio interview by Race Hobbs with daughter Kim Arnold, speaking about what her father had said, "as solid as a chevrolet." http://hiddenexperience.blogspot.com/2012/02/kenneth-arnolds-daughter-talks-about.html. Kim Arnold said: (timecount 31:45) "I would say that his first sighting, the one on June 24th 1947 was his most powerful sighting. There is no doubt about that. His second sighting was not too much later and he saw a cluster of about 25 of them, and they looked like ducks and they were very small. This sighting was very, very short and didn't last very long. But the most interesting sighting he had was in 1952. It was sighting two flying saucers over Susanville California. He described that one was as solid as a chevrolet car, and the other one that flew under his plane he could see the pine trees through the center of this other craft. That's when he concluded, that whatever these thing were, they had the ability to change their density. And that was very thought provoking for him. The only way he could describe that was very physical… He referred to them that they were possibly like jellyfish in the ocean. You know how jellyfish can look perfectly solid one minute yet they can be invisible.
(2) Gregory L. Little, Introduction to Andrew Collins, *Lightquest: Your Guide*

to Seeing and Interacting with UFOs, Mystery Lights and Plasma Intelligences (Memphis: Eagle Wing Books, 2012), 15. (Kindle location 24% location 1588 0f 6661).

(3) *The Mammoth Encyclopedia of Extraterrestrial Encounters*, by Ronald Story, Dolphin Books; 1st edition (1980), ISBN-13: 978-0385136778 No page number available.

(4) Interview excerpts from Bob Pratt's 1978 interviews with Kenneth Arnold: "...some intelligence somewhere that was able to read my mind." http://www.ufoevidence.org/documents/doc1998.htm.

(5) Bob Pratt's 1978 interview with Kenneth Arnold about the crashed plane on Mt. Rainier, http://www.ufoevidence.org/documents/doc1998.htm.

(6) Arnold was disturbed by the deaths of the two officers that died in the On August 1, 1947 crash of the B-25 in Washington. *The Coming of the Saucers*, by Kenneth Arnold and Ray Palmer (first published in 1952) Legend Press; (1996), ISBN-10: 0964499711 (no page number).

(7) *The Coming of the Saucers*, by Kenneth Arnold and Ray Palmer (first published in 1952) Legend Press; (1996), ISBN-10: 0964499711 Electronic text (no page number) found at http://www.saturdaynightuforia.com/html/articles/articlehtml/positivelytruestoryofkennetharnold10.html.

(8) Gulyas, Aaron John. "Paranoid and Paranormal Precursors from the 1960s to the 1990s." *The Paranormal and the Paranoid: Conspiratorial Science Fiction Television*. Rowman & Littlefield (2015). pp. 30–31. ISBN 9781442251144.

(9) *JFK & UFO: Military-Industrial Conspiracy and Cover-Up from Maury Island to Dallas*, by Kenn Thomas. Feral House; Revised Edition edition (May 31, 2011) ISBN-10: 193623906X, p. 13. Excerpt: "Garrison had Crisman pegged as one of the trigger men on the grassy knoll."

(10) "He felt that he had these experiences for a divine purpose." Audio interview by Race Hobbs with daughter Kim Arnold. http://hiddenexperience.blogspot.com/2012/02/kenneth-arnolds-daughter-talks-about.html.

(11) Race Hobbs interview, (timecount 41:31) audio interview by Race Hobbs with daughter Kim Arnold. http://hiddenexperience.blogspot.com/2012/02/kenneth-arnolds-daughter-talks-about.html.

(12) Long., Gregory, "Kenneth Arnold: UFO Pioneer," *MUFON UFO Journal*, (ed. Richard Hall) Seguin, Texas. #165, Nov. 1981, page 7, https://issuu.com/disclosureproject/docs/mufon_ufo_journal_-_1981_11._novemb.

(13) Audio interview by Race Hobbs with daughter Kim Arnold. http://hiddenexperience.blogspot.com/2012/02/kenneth-arnolds-daughter-talks-about.html. Kim said: "Near the end of his life... he believed it was possible that the flying saucers were the connection between the living and the dead. That's what he believed." (timecount 16:35).

(14) Long, Gregory, "Kenneth Arnold: UFO Pioneer," *MUFON UFO Journal*, (ed. Richard Hall) Seguin, Texas. #165, Nov. 1981. http://www.slideshare.net/mufonnexus/mufon-ufo-journal-1981-11-November. Arnold points to the work

of Charles Fort as similar to his own conclusions.

(15) Long., Gregory, "Kenneth Arnold: UFO Pioneer," *MUFON UFO Journal*, (ed. Richard Hall) Seguin, Texas. #165, Nov. 1981. http://www.slideshare.net/mufonnexus/mufon-ufo-journal-1981-11-November. Arnold talks about the government's fear of religious fervor.

(16) James Fox interview Kim Arnold. Youtube VIDEO - (timecount 1:20) Kim speaks about the government being scared. https://youtu.be/zDX02ba5MSE.

(17) Audio interview by Race Hobbs with daughter Kim Arnold - http://hiddenexperience.blogspot.com/2012/02/kenneth-arnolds-daughter-talks-about.html. Kim told Race Hobbs: (Time count 5:15) "He felt like this was a spiritual experience. He felt like this had happened to him for a reason. He thought that perhaps he was supposed to do speeches about the experience. I mean, he felt like this had happened to him for a reason... and explain to people about what he saw. Or to talk about it openly and honestly with many people. So he did do some speeches here in boise Idaho... And actually, the government men came in and stopped him from doing speeches. It was very frightening." (Time count 6:40) "There was a gentleman in town that was a friend of my father's and he took my father in a car. He took him out to the desert here in the Boise Idaho area In confidence he said, 'Ken, these government men are nothing to mess with.' My brother works for the government and he's seen them eliminate their own men. That is the kind of story that we, as small children, had to grow up and live with. We had to live in fear that the government would eliminate our parents, or do something to harm our parents. So it was not a light threat... It was a serious threat."

(18) Tim Beckley interview. Arnold's granddaughter Shanelle Schanz. https://www.youtube.com/watch?v=qRoFPBp0_w8. Reference to Arnold's distrust of the government: Kenneth Arnold died when Shanelle was just seven years old. At present, she is a paranormal journalist and investigator. "When I was younger before he died he sat me down and told me not to trust the government, to think for yourself." (timecount 59:00).

(19) Paola Leopizzi Harris, *UFOs: How Does One Speak to a Ball of Light?* (San Antonio, Anomalist Books, 2011), Kim Arnold interview, p. 1-32.

(20) Tim Beckley interview. Arnold's granddaughter Shanelle Schanz. https://www.youtube.com/watch?v=qRoFPBp0_w8. Psychic family experiences: "My grandmother was from Norwegian descent, and she was somewhat of a psychic medium and Telepathic and they both believed in reincarnation." (direct quote by Shanelle Schanz, (timecount 11:11:45).

Chapter 7: The Alan Caviness Report

(1) *The Messengers*, p. 46 (the shorter version of this account).

(2) "The Owl and the Deer Incident," by Alan Caviness; http://www.cavinessreport.com/CD1.html.

(3) "The Allen Jay Incident," by Alan Caviness; http://www.cavinessreport.com/ED4.html.

(4) *The Messengers*, p. 28 (full chapter on screen memories).

Endnotes

Chapter 8: Owls and Drones
(1) Cindy's YouTube channel link - https://www.youtube.com/user/cindymd51/videos?sort=da&flow=grid&view=0.
(2) "Owl inspire drones," https://www.wired.com/2012/07/owl/
Note: Cindy's radio show "The Drone Report" is no longer archived on the KGRA site.

Chapter 9: Denise Linn and Three White Feathers
(1) This chapter makes extensive use of the book, *If I Can Forgive, So Can You: My Autobiography of How I Overcame My Past and Healed My Life* by Denise Linn, Publisher: Hay House (December 15, 2005) ISBN-13: 978-1401908881.
(2) Open Minds, "The possible unsettling implications of UFO sightings," Mike Clelland, July 30, 2014. http://www.openminds.tv/possible-unsettling-implications-ufo-sightings/29256.
(3) Strieber, Whitley, *Communion. A True Story*. p. 21. Avon Books, paperback edition. Copyright © 1987 Wilson & Neff, Inc.
(4) Personal email correspondence with David Carson, August 25, 2103
(5) Linn, Denise, *The Secret Language of Signs*, page 209. Wellspring/Ballantine (October 1, 1996) ISBN-13: 978-0345406934.
(6) Linn, Denise, *Kindling the Native Spirit: Sacred Practices for Everyday Life*, Hay House, Inc. (November 3, 2015), ISBN-13: 978-1401945923.
(7) Mack, John. *Passport to the Cosmos*, p. 215.
(8) article http://www.metatech.org/wp/aliens/reptilians-africa-zulu-shaman-elder-credo-mutwa-alien-abduction-reptilians-1/
(9) "downloading of some kind of special energy" from a personal email with Linn from Feb 2016.
(10) Cutchin, Joshua. *A Trojan Feast: The Food and Drink Offerings of Aliens, Faeries, and Sasquatch*, Anomalist Books (May 1, 2015), ISBN-13: 978-1938398353.

Chapter 10: Adrienne and Owls
(1) *The Messengers*. p. 261

Chapter 11: Blipping off the Map
(1) An Interview with Stanislav Grof, M.D., on Transpersonal Psychology and the Meaning of Psychedelic Experience. Interview conducted by David Van Nuys, Ph.D. http://gracepointwellness.org/7-schizophrenia/article/41802-an-interview-with-stanislav-grof-md-on-transpersonal-psychology-and-the-meaning-of-psychedelic-experience Relevant text: "... in his essay on synchronicity, [Jung] actually distinguishes these extraordinary coincidences from synchronicity. What's characteristic for synchronicity is that it seems that the psyche is entering into a kind of a playful interaction with the material world, where something happens in your dream or in your visions, and then the material world kind of plays it out. Let's say you have a powerful shamanic experience involving an owl, and you walk out after the session and there is an

owl or a wounded owl and so on."

(2) The Stormy Search for the Self by Christina Grof & Stanislav Grof. http://www.creativespirit.net/learners/counseling/docu35.htm

(3) Joseph Campbell Rising, Interview with Stephen Gerringer, PlanetShifter.com Magazine - Community Relations, Joseph Campbell Foundation, by Willi Paul. http://www.planetshifter.com/node/1660 - Relevant text: "Christina Grof, a student of Joseph Campbell at Sarah Lawrence, turned to him for support years later when she found herself overwhelmed with visions and psychic experiences, suffering from an apparent mental breakdown that almost led to her institutionalization; Campbell identified her experience as a "kundalini awakening" common to Eastern cultures and placed her in touch with a colleague, psychiatrist Stanislav Grof, who not only helped but eventually married Christina. Together the Grofs were able to persuade the editors of the DSM-IV - the diagnostic bible of modern psychiatry - to include a distinction between mental illness and spiritual awakening. Change comes slowly and the shamanic crisis is still regularly misidentified, but the field of psychology is at least beginning to recognize it as a valid experience."

(4) Campbell, Joseph and Moyers, Bill. *The Power of Myth* (Anchor, 1991) p. 107.

Chapter 12: Owls and Healing

(1): Laura Bruno, page 19, *If I Only Had a Brain Injury: A TBI Survivor and Life Coach's Guide to Chronic Fatigue, Concussion, Lyme Disease, Migraine or Other "Medical Mystery"* (Xlibris; First edition 2008) ISBN-13: 978-1436322461

(2) "Synchronous Owls," Blog post, January 27, 2010 by Laura Bruno. https://laurabruno.wordpress.com/2010/01/27/synchronous-owls/ - >

(3) Devil Inside (1988) written by Andrew Farriss and Michael Hutchence. Single by INXS from the album *Kick*.

(4) https://taniamarieartist.wordpress.com/2014/12/23/soaring-through-a-new-shade-of-white/.

(5) The Integratron is a domed structure in the Mojave Desert designed by one of the earliest American UFO Contactees, George Van Tassel. He claimed the building was capable of rejuvenation, anti-gravity and time travel. Tassel said the design of the building came telepathically, the source was aliens from Venus.

The 35 foot high, 16-sided dome was built of wood and fiberglass without nails or screws. Construction began in 1957, the structure erected in 1959. It was financed by donations, including funds from none other than Howard Hughes.

A plaque at the site reads: "...The purpose of the Integratron is the rejuvenation of the human body, similar to recharging a battery, and basic research in time travel. According to Van Tassell, The Integratron is located on an intersection of powerful geomagnetic forces that, when focused by the unique geometry of the building, will concentrate and amplify the energy required for cell rejuvenation."

Endnotes

For over two decades, Van Tassel organized a series of conventions for UFO enthusiasts. These were held at nearby Giant Rock, purported to be the largest freestanding boulder in the world. These conventions were held out in the desert and had up to 11,000 attendees. Van Tassel wrote six books about his experiences, including I Rode On a Flying Saucer (1952). This short book is mostly of channeled statements from the Ashtar Command.

Presently the Integratron is used as a space for sound baths. The acoustics of the domed interior enhance the vibrational sounds from quartz crystal bowls. These meditation-like sessions are thought to be therapeutic, both physically and spiritually.

(6) Laura's 2010 painting of an owl. This image is a copyrighted image, used with permission from Laura Bruno, 2018 >
(7) *The Messengers*, page 265.
(8) *The Messengers*, page 133.
(9) *The Messengers*, page 45.
(10) *The Messengers*, page 338.

Chapter 13: Between Two Bridges
(1) *The Messengers*, p. 271.
(2) *The Messengers*, p. 338. Smith is quoted as saying "announce initiation." This came from a channeled communication, supposedly from the spirit of a barred owl.
(3) *The Messengers*, p. 348.
(4) *The Messengers*, p. 293.
(5) *The Messengers*, p. 228.
(6) *The Messengers*, p. 41.

Chapter 14: The Owl and the White Buffalo
(1) Brenda used the term gypsy. This was not meant literally as the ethnic Roma population, more the traveling troupe. They made their living by traveling from festival to festival all over the country. Most of them lived on the road and had no real home. They were artists, musicians, psychics and tarot readers; much like what the gypsies were known for.
(2) The UFO sightings and subsequent calls came in a frenzy on March 8, 1994 (Near Grand Rapids Michigan) as mysterious objects in the sky were described as flickering Christmas lights moving in frenetic fashion. http://www.mlive.com/news/us-world/index.ssf/2017/03/ufo_1994.html.

Chapter 15: Kristin in the Desert
(1) The song Moonshadow by Cat Stevens (now known as Yusuf Islam) was the 4th track on side two of his 1971 album Teaser and the Firecat. This animated short was part of the feature film Fantastic Animation Festival released in 1977. https://www.youtube.com/watch?v=x0awe6OJB0o&app=desktop
(2) Painting from 1847, Stigmata of St Francis by Bartolomeo Della, Gattahttps://commons.wikimedia.org/wiki/File:Bartolomeo_Della_Gatta_-_Stigmata_of_St_Francis_-_WGA01336.jpg.

(3) *The Messengers*, p. 115.
(4) *The Messengers*, p. 78.
(5) *The Messengers*, p. 127.
(6) Kristin's brief memory of being escorted down a hall sounds very much like what Maggie described during meditation earlier in this book, although Kristin remembers being accompanied by a bald being. Unlike Kristin, Maggie's momentary glimpse of moving down a hall happened without emotion.

Chapter 16: Owls and the Road at Night (None)

Chapter 17: Owls and Gratitude. Don's Owl Experience
(1) Oz Factor, *The Messengers*, page 60.
(2) *The Messengers*, p. 244, (quoted text, "the white owl has a deeper spiritual role than other owls… it's a message for the soul").
(3) *The Messengers*, p. 28.
(4) "What I found really fascinating in my research was … Every single one of the military trained remote viewers had experiences with UFOs. Not all of them would talk about it at the time. Some talked very openly about it then, and now. Others talked very guardedly, they would simply admit they'd had some anomalous experiences, and others wouldn't talk about it at all. But it became clear to me though my interviews with the various remote viewers who were trained and operated under the intelligence and security command of the U.S. Army— that they all had these experiences… They all had experiences with UFOs although technically and officially they were never ever tasked to go look for UFOs… As [remote viewer] Mel Riley once told me, he kind of lost interest in Soviet submarines when he realized he could see UFOs." (Jim Marrs from 2013, Hidden Experience audio, time-count 6:40) http://hiddenexperience.blogspot.com/2013/04/audio-conversation-with-jim-marrs.html.)
(5) Jim Marrs wrote, "Although not all of them will speak openly about it, every single one of the remote viewers experienced firsthand knowledge of unidentified objects. Some were tasked to seek out UFOs, but most ran across them in their psychic searches. They reported a variety of types as well as a variety of beings crewing them." (*Psi Spies*, Kindle 93%).
(6) The Daily Grail - http://www.dailygrail.com/Alien-Nation/2015/7/Jacques-Vallee-UFOs-Remote-Viewing-and-the-COMETA-Report. Youtube video, Jacques Vallée Talks About The UFO Phenomenon, Remote Viewing & Alien Abduction, https://www.youtube.com/watch?v=Ib2h0sElUro
(7) Lyn Buchanan's abduction experience. Link: http://ufotrail.blogspot.com/2011/11/lyn-buchanan-military-intel-and-alien.html
(8) Buchanan, Lyn (2009-11-20). *The Seventh Sense: The Secrets of Remote Viewing as Told by a Psychic*, (pp. 130-132). Pocket Books. Kindle Edition.
(9) Buchanan, Lyn (2009-11-20). *The Seventh Sense: The Secrets of Remote Viewing as Told by a Psychic*, p. 152-154. Pocket Books.
(10) Online interview, Lyn Buchanan and Remote Viewing: http://www.superconsciousness.com/topics/knowledge/lyn-buchanan-and-remote-viewing

(11) McMoneagle, Joseph. *The Stargate Chronicles: Memoirs of a Psychic Spy: The Remarkable Life of U.S. Government Remote Viewer 001* (Kindle Locations 932-945). Crossroad Press. Kindle Edition.

(12) "Psychic Spy Joe McMoneagle Tells How His Near-Death Experience Led to Remote Viewing," *Skeptiko,* episode 166 by Alex Tsakiris. http://skeptiko.com/psychic-spy-joe-mcmoneagle-near-death-experience-led-to-remote-viewing/

(13) McMoneagle, Joseph (2014-02-27). *The Stargate Chronicles: Memoirs of a Psychic Spy* (Kindle Location 1065-1120). Crossroad Press. Kindle Edition.

Chapter 18: Owls and Gratitude. Joe's Owl Experience

(1) Strieber, Whitley; Kripal, Jeffrey J. (2016-02-02). *The Super Natural: A New Vision of the Unexplained* (p. vii). Penguin Publishing Group.

Joe read the quote from Whitley Strieber in *The Super Natural*, (2016) although it was originally published in *Communion* (1987). "Instead of shunning the darkness, we can face straight into it with an open mind. When we do that, the unknown changes. Fearful things become understandable, and a truth is suggested: the enigmatic presence of the human mind winks back from the dark."

Chapter 19: Owls and Gratitude. Kelly's Experience

(1) Strieber, Whitley, *Communion: A True Story*, Beech Tree Books, New York; First Edition edition (1987), page 19.

(2) Bryan, C.D.B., *Close Encounters Of The Fourth Kind: Alien Abduction, UFOs, and the Conference at M.I.T.*, Knopf; 1st edition (May 30, 1995); Kindle 5% Location 449 of 10405.

(3) Personal correspondence with Joshua Cutchin about the smell of cinnamon in UFO contact reports. Cutchin, Joshua. *The Brimstone Deceit: An In-Depth Examination of Supernatural Scents, Otherworldly Odors, and Monstrous Miasmas*, Anomalist Books (September 26, 2016), Kindle 18% Location 1606 of 9433.

(4) *The Messengers*, page 132.

Index

abductee, 11, 29, 39, 51, 71, 72, 88, 106, 107, 111, 214, 237
abduction, 45, 48, 51, 60, 63, 72, 78, 93, 94, 97, 98, 100, 115, 150, 153, 170, 173, 175, 177, 178, 180, 184, 208, 209, 212, 221
Alexander, John, 215-216
aliens, 52, 72, 79, 83, 88, 97-99, 103, 106, 109, 132, 133, 139, 171, 181, 190, 197, 210, 232, 233, 238
Allison (first name only), 111-120
Andrea (first name only) 149, 194, 204
Arnold, Kenneth, 54-61
Arnold, Kim, 58
Ashlee (first name only), 182
Athena (goddess), 99, 144
Audrey (first name only), 29-30
ayahuasca, 99-100
Bacchanalia, 99
Bible, 108, 109, 119, 125, 235
Bosley, Walter, 81
Brenda (first name only), 153-171
Briggs, Anya, 23, 50-51
Bruno, Laura, 121-140
Buchanan, Lyn, 213-215, 219
Campbell, Joseph, 118-119
Carol (first name only), 33-35
Carson, David, 95
Caviness, Alan, 62-74
Chancellor, Suzanne, 30, 31, 148-150, 239, 240
Christianity, 107-109
cinnamon, 231-232
Communion (the book), 83, 84, 94, 95, 232
consciousness, 1, 11, 41, 49, 54, 56, 64,
Credo Mutwa, 97-100
crop circle, 5-8, 14-16, 239
Cutchin, Joshua, 50, 232
David (first name only), 91-93, 98
death, 1, 19, 23-25, 35-37, 40-42, 59, 87, 93, 98-100, 108, 127, 137, 138, 183, 198, 208, 216, 218, 240, 241
depression, 107, 116, 137, 138, 170, 208
Diana (goddess), 188, 190, 211
Don (first name only), 205-220, 228, 229, 234, 235
Dove, Cindy, 75-89
dreams, 1, 24, 25, 52, 104, 106, 118, 122, 123, 126, 133, 143, 151, 167, 169
drones, 75, 78-82, 89
Dumas, Adrienne, 102-110
Easter, 133-135
eating the God, 99
experiencer, 29, 73, 78, 82, 88, 89, 134, 143, 171, 184, 239
flying saucer, 29, 54, 55, 80, 156, 172, 188, 197
folklore, 4, 12, 37, 39, 41, 133, 178, 242
Fort, Charles, 59
Frees, Marla, 43, 47
ghost, 46, 124, 125, 135
God, 21, 24, 58, 90, 99, 107-110, 130, 160, 164, 177, 190, 203, 205, 206, 208, 209, 217, 218, 225, 226, 237, 242
Green, Alan 111-112
Grof, Christina 119
Grof, Stanislav, 118
Guiley, Rosemary Ellen, 143
Gypsy Woman, 36-42
Halloween, 133, 156, 165, 171
healing, 23, 25, 109, 121, 123, 125-127, 129, 135-137, 139, 183-184, 203, 233, 234, 237, 240
Heather (first name only), 6-12, 15, 16
intuition, 25, 52, 126, 238
Jack (first name only), 31, 34, 35, 148-151

Janssen, Bert, 5-16
Jesus, 24, 109, 110, 180, 189, 214, 218, 219, 235, 237
Joe (first name only), 221-228, 236, 237
Jung, Carl 13
Kelly (first name only) 227-237
Kornacki, Susan, 134, 232
Kripal, Jeffrey, 3
Kristin (first name only), 172-191, 239, 241
kundalini, 118, 133, 134, 159, 164, 170
ley lines, 7
Linn, Denise, 90-101
Linn, Meadow, 94, 98, 113
MacGregor, Rob, 37
MacGregor, Trish, 37
Mack, John, 97
MacLeod, Susan, 17-28,
Maggie (first name only), 193-204
Marler, David, 93
Marrs, Jim, 212,
McMoneagle, Joseph, 216, 219
meditation, 18, 93, 132, 177, 178, 200, 234, 235, 237
Mike C (first name only) 141-146, 148-152, 154-156, 238
missing time, 34, 35, 63, 115-117, 167, 212, 236
Moniz, Matt, 30
mothman, 76
MUFON, 77
Nathan (first name only), 215-216
near-death experience (NDE), 37, 55, 183, 184, 198, 217, 240-241
Numbers
  11:11, 31, 131, 133, 142, 234
  1234, 51
  333, 142, 144, 152
orb, 5, 6, 32, 58, 60, 75, 77-80, 83, 85, 145, 146, 148, 151, 180, 192, 207
out-of-body experience (OBE), 183, 184, 217
Owl (types)
  barn owl, 62, 94, 179
  barred owl, 17, 26, 27, 30, 35, 141, 142, 223, 225, 229-231, 251
  great horned owl, 54, 79, 94, 96, 111, 115, 122, 136, 239
  little owl, 144, 193
  white owl, 5, 6, 8, 9, 12, 25, 28, 36, 37, 41, 100, 129, 174, 210, 212, 229
  wounded owl, 109, 110, 118
oz factor, 96, 209
Palmer, Ray, 57
Pamela, (first name only) 33, 34
paradox syndrome, 3, 135
paranormal, 23, 44, 59, 63, 65, 66, 75, 76, 78, 109, 133, 143, 148, 205, 207, 220, 222
Peter (first name only) 193-201
psychedelic, 1, 98, 99, 113, 115, 118, 173
psychic, 6, 17, 23-25, 31, 32, 37, 42, 43, 47-52, 56, 61, 88, 101, 107, 115, 125-127, 130, 139, 165, 183, 204, 208, 209, 212, 214, 218, 238
reiki, 35, 93, 108, 127, 129, 136, 140, 238
remote viewing, 207, 211-217, 237
Roswell, 80
sasquatch, 19-22, 193
Schanz, Shanelle, 60
screen image, 189
screen memory, 64, 72, 104, 178, 210, 232
sense of mission, 65, 87, 100, 106, 107, 127
shaman, 6, 11, 12, 73, 92, 97, 101, 117-119, 183, 198, 199
shamanic initiation, 1, 97, 189
Smith, Jacquelin 139
spiritual awakening/transformation, 1, 2, 113, 117, 119, 202
Stacey (first name only), 43-53, 138
Strieber, Anne, 3, 199
Strieber, Whitley, 3, 43, 47, 50, 83, 94, 225, 232
suicide, 137
symbol, 1, 13-15, 45, 95, 99, 100,

123
symbolism, 6, 12, 48, 241
Synchro Secrets, 37
synchronicity, 29, 37, 41, 43, 44, 47, 51, 102, 111, 118, 129, 141, 188, 203, 238
Tania (first name only), 129, 131, 132
telepathy, 56, 61, 97
The Messengers (book), 1, 2, 5, 12, 37, 43, 62, 95, 102, 111, 133, 134, 139, 150, 153, 181, 188, 198, 227, 229, 232, 238, 239, 241
totem, 2, 17, 26, 30, 73, 118, 197, 201
transformation, 1, 2, 61, 95-97, 100, 118, 136, 225, 241
triangular UFO, 176
unconscious, 13, 41, 51, 119, 184, 237
windshield, 76, 102, 141, 144, 173, 210, 214, 215

About the author

Mike Clelland has been writing about owls, UFOs and synchronicities since 2009. It was his first-hand experiences with these elusive phenomena that have been the foundation for his research.

His website (www.hiddenexperince.blogspot.com) explores these events and their connection to the alien contact. This site includes the podcast series *Hidden Experience*, featuring extended audio interviews with visionaries and experts examining the complexities of the overall UFO experience.

He also hosts The *Unseen* for author Whitley Strieber on his website *Unknowncountry*. All these shows are archived and easily searched online.

Mike has worked for over twenty-five years as an outdoor educator and guide, spending up to thirty days backpacking in remote mountain wilderness. He has taught and travelled in Alaska, Canada, the Pacific Northwest, the desert Southwest, and all throughout the rockies. He is also considered an expert in the skills of ultralight backpacking, and is been a professional illustrator since he was in high school..

Other books by Mike Clelland

The Messengers

A classic by one of the most exciting new authors in the UFO field. This is a collection of firsthand accounts in which owls manifest in the highly charged moments that surround alien contact. There is a strangeness to these stories that defy simple explanations. This is also a deeply personal story, and an odyssey of self-discovery as the author grapples with his own owl and UFO encounters.

Hidden Experience

This is a collection of the most vital posts from the popular blog Hidden Experience. It's a roller coaster journey of doubts and fears as I wrestle with UFOs, missing time, synchronicities and owls. The story that unfolds is scary, mysterious, disturbing—and at times funny. It's an insight into the strange challenges of otherworldly contact. Confronting the darkest unknowns ultimately lead to an awakening of consciousness.

Ultralight Backpackin' Tips

A backpacking instructional with cartoons! This humorous book carefully explains advanced techniques to reduce your pack weight, without sacrificing safety or comfort. This is the ultimate guide for traveling ultralight in the wilderness.

www.ingramcontent.com/pod-product-compliance
Lightning Source LLC
Chambersburg PA
CBHW071704160426
43195CB00012B/1567